The
Complete Prophecies
of
NOSTRADAMUS

The
Complete Prophecies
of
NOSTRADAMUS

Translated, Edited and Interpreted by
HENRY C. ROBERTS

NEW REVISED EDITION

Re-edited by
Lee Roberts Amsterdam and Harvey Amsterdam

Published by
NOSTRADAMUS CO.
OYSTER BAY, NEW YORK

"Up! Flee! Out into broad and open land!
And this book full of mystery,
From **NOSTRADAMUS'** own very hand,
Is it not sufficient company?
The stars' course then you'll understand
And Nature, teaching you, will then expand
The power of your soul, as when
One **SPIRIT** to another **SPEAKS.**"

Faust, act 1, scene 1.

TABLE OF CONTENTS

INTRODUCTION TO THIRD EDITION

In the forty-five years that have passed since my father, Henry C. Roberts, wrote this book, there has been a renewed interest in the writings and prophecies of Nostradamus. Since my father's death several years ago, I have tried to carry on his work and interest in Nostradamus and with my husband, Harvey Amsterdam, have continued my father's research into Nostradamus's writings and the effect of his prophecies on the present generation.

Through the years many people from all over the world have written to me to express interest and offer suggestions for a new edition. It is for this reason that we have re-edited this book in the light of events that have transpired in recent years, and we have made every attempt to incorporate ideas from our readers and answers to their questions. We have updated some of the interpretations and included an index to facilitate ready reference to all material. In every instance, we have endeavored to maintain the continuity and format of my father's writing and we add our "blessing" to that of my father's to all readers who wish to make their own interpretations and analyses.

Will mankind heed the warnings that Michael Nostradamus gave to the world more than 400 years ago or will we continue to make his most dire prophecies come true? That depends, of course, upon the actions of our world leaders and whether each of us is willing to follow them blindly in the path of destruction that seems to lie before us.

LEE ROBERTS AMSTERDAM

Oyster Bay, N.Y.
July 28, 1982

INTRODUCTION

Nearly everyone, at one time or another, has heard or read something about Nostradamus and his prophecies. Yet, the astonishing fact is that not since 1672 has there been printed an English edition of his complete quatrains. As a bookseller, I was struck by this lack because of the great number of people, interested in predictions and other phenomena of this nature, who had come to me over a period of years, inquiring for the complete works of Nostradamus in English. As a student of the occult, always seeking materials on the subject, I too was anxious to procure the unabridged work of the man who is acknowledged as one of the greatest seers in the history of occult science.

Spurred on by these incentives, I began to search the field for all books, old and new, pertaining to Nostradamus. The reward was scanty. The current available books on Nostradamus dealt with but a few of his more noted quatrains, discussing them at length, but making no attempt to bring to light more than a few hundred out of the thousand he had purportedly written.

At long last I obtained, at an almost prohibitive price, a copy of the afore-mentioned 1672 edition: *The True Prophecies or Prognostications of Michael Nostradamus*, translated and annotated by Theophilus de Garencieres. I had perused but a few pages when I was struck by the sense of familiarity that these verses seemed to hold for me. Words that the author claimed held no significance for him, took on for me a definite meaning, became clearly focused into patterns of events—past, present and future. Here, I felt, was my book.

Such being the case, I determined to start the long and arduous task of making available, a new complete edition of Nostradamus, using all the materials at hand, bringing to them new interpretations in the light of recent events, taking as much as possible the same position as if Nostradamus were alive today—speaking with both our voices.

Avoiding the hitherto lengthy explanations that, I felt, bewildered rather than enlightened the reader, I have tried to make the interpretations concise and simple; I have also, as much as was feasible, tried to preserve the spirit and cadence of the original quatrains. The present text is the result, and I believe it to be clean and true. At all times, where there were discrepancies or ambiguities in the French text, I have accepted the oldest versions, especially considering Garencieres' book as the most authoritative.

From the time of the Delphic Sibyl it has been the characteristic of occult prophecies and utterances, often to seem unintelligible and garbled to the uninitiate. The strange, broken, and often incoherent nature of the quatrains, both in French and English, is the hallmark of prophetic media.

Nevertheless, at this point, I feel that a few words of explanation are necessary with regard to certain questions that may arise in the reader's mind. Primarily, we must clear up the fact that the word "prophecy" does not, in its literal sense, apply to every one of these quatrains. A good number of the verses have reference to events of the days before and during the time of Nostradamus—events that distressed, pleased, or shocked him, and which he considered important enough to record for posterity. But the bulk of his work was based upon his awesome gift of prognostication, and it is this that we are mainly concerned with. Even after deep study and wide consultation of occult materials, it was not always possible to assign these predictions to definite places or people. It would have been an easy matter to lightly attribute certain doings to certain people, but that would have taken on the nature of "guessing," and we say, in closing, that we prefer to leave that to the reader; for he will inevitably attempt to do so, and we urge him so to do—with "our" blessing.

HENRY C. ROBERTS

New York, N. Y.
November, 1946

INTRODUCTION TO SECOND EDITION

Beyond a shadow of doubt, the methods employed and results obtained by Nostradamus in looking into the future were outside of the physical framework.

What to the contemporary critics of his day, for want of a better term they chose to call magic or occult, we today now recognize as the operation of certain tenuous and imponderable laws that permeate the entire Cosmos. These intangible but all pervading forces we group today under the general title of "Extra Sensory Perception."

Such startling and apparently miraculous phenomena as mediumism, telepathy, telekinesis, etc., are today the serious subject of study by such accredited scientists as Dr. Rhine of Duke University and Prof. Gardner Murphy of New York University. An entirely new line of investigation is in progress in this new science of "Para-psychology" which promises rich rewards for mankind.

Who knows? Perhaps some day this new line of scientific activity may be developed to a point where it will have a practical application to our every day life and make possible a revolutionary concept of nature's forces.

HENRY C. ROBERTS

New York, N. Y.
March 2, 1949

ONLY KNOWN AUTHENTIC PORTRAIT OF NOSTRADAMUS
PAINTED FROM LIFE BY HIS SON CAESAR

A rare item from the Henry C. Roberts Collection.

WHO WAS NOSTRADAMUS?

Much of the information known about Nostradamus is apocryphal but there are certain facts that have been documented. It is known that he was a French physician of Jewish descent who was born in Provence on December 14, 1503. Michael was born within the sphere of the Catholic Church and spent his childhood under the guidance of his grandfathers, who instructed him in the rudiments of the classic languages and in Hebrew and astrology. When he was an adolescent he was sent to Avignon, where he studied philosophy, and then to the University of Montpelier in 1522 to begin his study of medicine. After spending three years at this institution renowned for its training of doctors, he graduated with a bachelor's degree.

Shortly after receiving his license to practice medicine in 1525, he interrupted his studies to concentrate on the practical applications of his knowledge. An outbreak of the plague at Montpelier, and later at Narbonne, first earned him a reputation as a "healer of the afflicted ones," and his courage, combined with his unorthodox and successful treatments, led to his initial recognition and following. Using his own formulas and psychological guidance, he was able to cure many patients who had been regarded as incurable.

Did an insight into human needs, motives, and failings, and where they could lead, begin at this time, or was it later, during his studies at the library at Avignon, when he began to read books on alchemy, magic, and the occult? It is impossible to say, but he had been regarded as a bright child with a penchant for learning, and it is said that he "soaked up knowledge of all kinds like a sponge."

After further treatment of victims of the ever-present plague, he returned to Montpelier where he obtained his doctoral degree in medicine. Despite what many doctors regarded as his unorthodox treatments, his refusal to "bleed" patients in accord with the customs of the time, and his "home-made remedies," he was asked to join the faculty, a position that he kept for only a year; he soon found it confining and decided to leave Montpelier in order to travel. While he was traveling through Bordeaux, La Rochelle, and Toulouse, he received a summons to visit with the learned Jules-Cesar Scaliger. Nostradamus enjoyed sharing confidences and knowledge with this eminent physician and philosopher and decided to settle in Agen, where he married a beautiful young woman of "high estate" and proceeded to raise a family.

Did forebodings of coming disaster trouble the prophet at this time of bucolic domesticity? The plague struck once again, this time in Nostradamus's own family. What a paradox! The esteemed physician who had saved the lives of so many "afflicted ones" was unable to prevent the death of his own young wife and children. To compound his misfortune, this tragedy was followed by a quarrel with his friend Scaliger and by a lawsuit from his wife's family to regain her dowry. The old adage "troubles come in threes" proved true; at this same time Nostradamus was summoned before the Inquisitor at Toulouse. This was the result of a chance remark made to an artisan, regarding a bronze model he was making of the Virgin, which the artisan mistakenly claimed to be heretical. Rather than appear before the Inquisitor, Nostradamus resumed his travels and spent the next six years wandering and practicing medicine until he decided to settle in Salon, a town situated in the south. This became his home until his death in 1566.

In Salon in 1550 he published his first almanac containing prophecies for the coming year. This proved so successful that he continued to publish a new almanac containing predictions every subsequent year.

It was about this time, too, that Nostradamus conceived the grandiose plan that occupied him for the next two years: writing the *Centuries*. This was a complete series of prophecies dealing with events from his time to the end of the world in the year 3797. It is these prophecies, translated into English, which are reprinted in this book. They were written in "quatrains," or verses of four lines, with their meaning purposely obscured in order to prevent his being labeled a magician. The *Centuries* referred not to calendar years but to the fact that they were a series of 100 quatrains to each section; thus, a century of quatrains means 100 verses.

The fame of Nostradamus spread to the royal court, and no less a person than the queen, Catherine de Medici, summoned him to the court to plot the horoscopes of the king and the royal children. The queen held Nostradamus in high esteem throughout her life and in 1564 visited him in Salon.

Nostradamus spent his remaining years in Salon with his second wife, who had been a well-to-do widow. His fame as a prophet led to much controversy. His detractors claimed that he represented the devil, but his followers visited him from all parts of France.

Several famous anecdotes about the seer help to account for the reputation as a prophet that he enjoyed during his lifetime.

While traveling through Italy, he is said to have bowed before a passing young Franciscan monk, addressing him as "His Holiness." The astounded onlookers could not understand this strange behavior, but years later that Franciscan monk, the former swineherd Felice Peretti, became Cardinal Peretti and in 1585 was elected by the College of Cardinals to become Pope Sixtus V. This occurred years after Nostradamus's death.

Another famous legend concerns the tale of the black pig and the white pig. While walking in the courtyard of the château of a certain Monsieur de Florenville, Nostradamus came upon two suckling pigs, a black one and a white one. He was asked by Monsieur de Florenville what would become of the two pigs. Nostradamus replied with alacrity, "We will eat the black one, and the wolf will eat the white one." To prove Nostradamus a liar and to discredit him, the lord ordered the chef to roast the white one on the spit and to serve it for their dinner. At dinner, Florenville again asked Nostradamus about the fate of the white and black pigs and Nostradamus maintained that what he had said earlier was true: They ate the black pig and the wolf had eaten the white one. The chef was called in to refute Nostradamus's statement. All were astounded when the chef admitted that a tame wolf cub had nibbled at the white pig while it was roasting on the spit and that he had served them the black one instead.

Nostradamus's fame lives on today despite villifiers and detractors during his lifetime and in the centuries that have followed. Some have claimed that his "prophecies" were no more than "ambiguous guesswork," but many of the prophecies that are included in this book seem too precise and accurate to be dismissed as mere guesswork. Four centuries after they were written, we can judge for ourselves whether they have proved true and whether they will continue to anticipate events yet to occur.

The
Complete Prophecies
of
NOSTRADAMUS

PREFACE TO FIRST EDITION

A Letter of Dedication to his son, Caesar Nostradamus

Thy late coming, Caesar Nostradamus, my son, hath caused me to bestow much time in continual and nocturnal watchings, that I might leave a memorial of me after my death, to the common benefit of mankind, concerning the things which the Divine Essence hath revealed to me by astronomical revolutions. Since it hath pleased the immortal God that thou art come late into this world, and canst say that thy years are but few, and thy months incapable to receive into thy weak understanding what I am forced to define of futurity; since it is not possible to leave thee in writing what might be obliterated by the injury of time, for the hereditary gift of occult prediction shall be locked up in my breast; considering also that events are definitely uncertain, and that all is governed by the power of God who inspired us not by a Bacchic fury nor yet by Lymphatic motion, but by astronomical effects—"*Soli numine divino afflati praesagiunt et spirito prophetico particularia.*" *

Although I have often foretold long before what hath afterwards come to pass, and in particular regions, acknowledging all to have been done by divine virtue and inspiration, I was willing to hold my peace by reason of the injury—not only of the present time, but also of the future—because to put them in writing, the Kingdoms, Sects, and Regions shall be so diametrically opposed, that if I should relate what shall happen hereafter, those of the present Reign, Sect, Religion and Faith, would find it so disagreeing with their fancies, that they would condemn that which future ages shall find and know to be true. Consider also the saying of our Saviour, "*Nolite sanctum dare canibus neque mittatis margaritas vestras ante porcos, ne forte conculcent eas pedibus suis, et conversi dirumpant vos.*" (Matt. vii. 6)

For this reason I have withheld my tongue from the vulgar, and my pen from paper. But, afterwards, I was willing for the common good to enlarge myself in dark and abstruse sentences, declaring the future events, chiefly the most urgent and those which I foresaw (whatever human mutation happened) would not offend the hearers, all under dark figures

---

* "Such alone as are inspired by the divine power can predict particular events in a spirit of prophecy."

3

more than prophetical. Although "*Abscondidisti hoec à sapientibus, et prudentibus, id est, potentibus et regibus, et enucleasti ea exiguis et tenuibus.*" * The prophets, by means only of the immortal God and good Angels, have received the spirit of vaticination, by which they foresee things, and foretell future events. For nothing is perfect without Him, whose power and goodness are so great to His creatures, that though they are but men, nevertheless by the likeness of their good genius to the Angels, this heat and prophetical power draws near us, as do the rays of the sun, which cast their influence alike upon bodies that are elementary and non-elementary. As for us, who are but men, we cannot attain anything by our natural knowledge, of the secrets of God our Creator. "*Quia non est nostrum noscere tempora, nec momenta,*" etc. (Acts i. 7)

There are, or may come some persons, to whom God Almighty will reveal by impressions made on their understanding some secrets of the future, according to judicial astrology, as it hath happened in former times, when a certain power and voluntary faculty possessed them as a flame of fire. So by His inspiration, they were able to judge of divine and human things, for the divine works that are absolutely necessary, God will complete.

But, my son, I speak to thee a little too obscurely. There are secrets that are received by the subtle spirit of fire, by which the understanding is moved to contemplate the highest celestial bodies, being active and vigilant to the very pronunciation without fear or any shameful loquacity; all of which proceeded from the divine power of the Eternal God, from whom all goodness flows.

Now, my son, although I have inserted the name of prophet here, I will not attribute to myself so sublime a title, for "*Propheta dicitur hodie, olim vocabatur videns,*" ** and prophets are those properly, my son, that see things remote from the natural knowledge of mankind. Or, to put the case, the prophets, by the means of the perfect light of prophecy, may see divine things as well as human (which cannot but be seeing the effects of future predictions) and do extend a great distance, for the secrets of God are incomprehensible, and their efficient power is far remote from the natural knowledge, taking their origin in the free will, causing those things to appear which otherwise could not be known, neither by human auguries nor by any hidden knowledge or secret virtue under Heaven. Only by the means of some indivisible eternal being, and by Herculean agitation the causes come to be known by the celestial motion.

I say, therefore, my son, that you may not understand me well, because

---

* Thou hast hidden these things from the wise and prudent and hast revealed them to the small and weak."

** "He who is called prophet now, once was called seer."

the knowledge of this matter cannot yet be imprinted in thy weak brain. Future causes afar off are subject to the knowledge of human creatures, if (notwithstanding the Creator) things present and future were neither obscure nor hidden from the intellectual seal; but the perfect knowledge of the cause of things cannot be acquired without the divine inspiration, seeing that all prophetical inspiration received hath its original principle from God the Creator, next, from good luck, and afterwards from nature. Therefore, causes, independently produced or not produced, the prophecy partly happens where it hath been foretold, for the understanding being intellectually created cannot see occult things, unless it be by the voice coming from the limbo, by the means of the thin flame, to which the knowledge of future causes is inclined. And, also, my son, I entreat thee not to bestow thy understanding on such fopperies which dry up the body and damn the soul, and bring vexation to the senses. Chiefly abhor the vanity of the execrable magic forbidden by the Sacred Scriptures and by the Canons of the Church; except from this judicial astrology by which, and by the means of divine inspiration, with continual calculations, we have put in writing, our prophecies.

Although this occult philosophy was not forbidden, I could never be persuaded to meddle with it, although many volumes concerning that art, which hath been concealed a great while, were presented to me. But fearing what might happen, after I had read them, I presented them to Vulcan and, while he was devouring them, the flame mixed with the air, there was an unwonted light more bright than the usual flame and it was, as if there were lightning, shining all the house over, as if it had been all in a flame. Therefore, that henceforth you might not be abused in the search of the perfect transformation, as much lunar as solar, and to seek in the waters uncorruptible metal, I have burnt them all to ashes. But as to the judgment which cometh to be perfected by the help of the celestial judgment, that I will manifest to you that you may have knowledge of future things; rejecting the fantastic imaginations that may arise, and limiting the particularity of places which were arrived at by divine and supernatural inspiration, according to the celestial figures, by an occult property, and by a divine virtue, power and faculty—in the presence of which the three aspects of time are comprehended by eternity, an evolution that ties into one the cause that is past, present, and future; "quia omnia sunt nuda et aperta. . ." *

Therefore, my son, thou mayst, notwithstanding thy tender brain, comprehend things that shall happen hereafter, and may be foretold by celestial natural lights, and by the spirit of prophecy, not that I will attribute to myself the name of a prophet, but as a mortal man, being no

---

* "For all things are naked and open."

farther from Heaven by my sense than I am from Earth by my feet. *"Possum non errare, falli, decipi,"* * (albeit) I am the greatest sinner of the world subject to all human afflictions. But being surprised sometimes by a prophetical mood, and by a long calculation, pleasing myself in my study, I have made Books of Prophecies, each one containing a hundred Astronomical Stanzas, which I have joined obscurely, and are perpetual prophecies from this year to the year 3797, at which some perhaps will frown, seeing so large an extension of time, and that I treat of everything under the Moon. If thou livest the natural age of a man thou shalt see in thy climate, and under the Heaven of thy nativity, the future things that have been foretold.

God only knoweth the eternity of the light proceeding from Himself, and I say freely to those to whom His incomprehensible greatness hath by a long melancholic inspiration revealed, that by the means of this occult cause, divinely manifested, chiefly by two principal causes, there is comprehension and understanding in him that is inspired and prophetic. One is that which cleareth the supernatural light and foretelleth by the doctrine of the planets, and the other forecasts by inspired revelation, which is a kind of participation in the divine eternity, by means of Him, of God the Creator. And by these means he knows that what is predicted is true, and hath taken its original from above, and such light and small flame is of all efficacy and sublimity, no less than the natural light makes the philosophers so secure, that by the means of the principles of the first cause, they have attained the greatest depth of the profoundest sciences.

But I must not wander too far, my son, from the capacity of thy sense. I find that learning shall be at a great loss, and that before the universal conflagration shall happen so many great inundations, that there shall scarce be any land that shall not be covered with water, and this shall last so long, that except for Ethnographies and Topographies all shall perish. Before and after these inundations in many countries there shall be such scarcity of rain and such a great deal of fire, and burning stones shall fall from Heaven, that nothing unconsumed shall be left. All this shall happen a little while before the great conflagration.

Although the planet Mars makes an end of his course, and is come to the end of his last period, nevertheless he shall begin it again. Some shall be gathered in Aquarius for many years, others in Cancer also for many years. Now we are governed by the Moon, under the power of Almighty God; which Moon before she hath finished her circuit, the Sun shall come, and then Saturn. According to the celestial signs, the reign of Saturn shall come again, so that all being calculated, the world draws near to its anaragonic revolution (death-dealing).

---

* "I am able not to err, be deceived nor fail."

From this present time that I write this, before 177 years, three months, eleven days, through pestilence, famine, war, and for the most part, inundations, the world between this and that prefixed time, before and after, for several times shall be so diminished, and the people shall be so few, that they shall not find enough to till the ground, so that they shall remain fallow as long as they had once been tilled. We are now in the seventh millenary, which ends all and brings us near the eighth, where the firmament of the eighth sphere is, which, in a latitudinary dimension, is the place where the Great God shall make an end of this revolution, where the celestial bodies shall move again, and the superior motion that maketh the Earth firm and stable, "*non inclinabitur in seculum seculorum,*" * unless His will be accomplished and not otherwise.

Although by ambiguous opinions exceeding all natural reasons by Mahometical dreams, also sometimes God the Creator by the ministers of His messengers of fire and flame, shows to our external senses, and chiefly to our eyes, the causes of future predictions, signifying the future event, that will manifest to him that prophesies. For the prophecy that is made by the internal light, comes to judge of the thing partly with and by the means of external light, although the part which seemeth to come by the eye of understanding, comes only from the lesion of its imaginative sense. The reason is evident why what he foretelleth comes by divine inspiration, or by the means of an angelical spirit, inspired into the prophetic person, anointing him with vaticinations, moving the fore part of his fancy, by divers nocturnal apparitions, so that by astronomical administrations, he prophesies with a divine certitude, joined to the holy prediction of the future, having no other regard than to the freedom of his mind.

Come now, my son, and understand that I find by my revelations (astrological), which agree with the divine inspiration, that the swords draw near to us now, and the plague and the war more horrid than hath been seen in the life of three men before, and also famine, which shall return often, for the stars agree with the revolution, "*Visitabo in virga ferrea iniquitates eorum, et in verberibus percutiam eos.*" ** For the mercies of God shall not be spread for a while, my son, before most of my prophecies shall come to pass, thus oftentimes shall happen sinister storms. "*Conteram ego, et confringam,*" (said the Lord) "*et non miserebor.*" † And a thousand other accidents shall happen by waters and continual rains, as I have more fully at large declared in my other Prophecies, written *in soluta oratione*, limiting the places, times and prefixed terms, that men coming after, may

---

* "Whence it shall not deviate from age to age."
** "I will visit their iniquities with a rod of iron, and with blows will strike them."
† "I will trample them and break them, and not show pity."

see and know that those accidents are certainly come to pass, as we have marked in other places, speaking more clearly, although the explication be involved in obscurity: "*Sed quando submoventa erit ignorantia*"; * the case shall be made more clear. Making an end here, my son, accept this gift of thy father, Michael Nostradamus, hoping to expound to thee every prophecy of these quatrains, praying to the Immortal God that he will grant thee a long life in felicity.

---

* "When the time arrives for the removal of ignorance."

From Salon, this 1st of March, 1555.

1

Estant assis, de nuit secrette estude,　　Seated at night in my secret study,
Seul, repose sur la selle d'airain,　　Alone, reposing over the brass
Flambe exigue, sortant de solitude,　　　　tripod,
Fait proferer qui n'est a croire vain.　　A slender flame leaps out of the
　　　　　　　　　　　　　　　　　　　　solitude,
　　　　　　　　　　　　　　　　　Making me pronounce that which
　　　　　　　　　　　　　　　　　　　　is not in vain.

Nostradamus clearly shows his method of preparing for a nocturnal visitation from divine sources, from which he shall gain the knowledge of future events for the benefit of Posterity.

2

La verge en main, mise au milieu　　With divining rod in hand, I wet
　　des branches,　　　　　　　　　　　the limb and foot,
De l'onae je mouille & le limbe　　Set in the middle of the branches.
　　& le pied,　　　　　　　　　　Fearsome awe trembles my hand,
En peur j'escris tremissant par les　　　　I await,
　　manches;　　　　　　　　　　Heavenly Splendor! The Divine
Splendeur Divine; le Divine prez　　　　Genius sitteth by.
　　s'assied.

Evidently our author employed an instrument similar to the present forked, divining rod, now used for locating water. In a large brass bowl filled with water, various segments were marked off and, as the rod dipped to the proper significant areas, messages would emanate.

3

Quand la littiere du tourbillon versee, Et seront faces de leurs manteaux couvers, La Republique par gens nouveaux vexee, Lors blancs & rouges jugeront a L'envers.	When the litter shall be overthrown by a gust of wind, And faces shall be covered with cloaks, The Republic shall be vexed by new people, Then shall White and Red judge wrongly.

Nostradamus here forecasts the Russian Revolution of 1917 with the subsequent strife between the Red and White Russians.

4

Par l'Univers sera fait un Monarque, Qu'en paix & vie ne sera longuement, Lors se perdra la Piscature Barque, Sera regie en plus grand detriment.	In the world shall be a Monarch, Who will not leave peace, nor be long alive, Then will be lost the Fishing Boat, And shall be governed to its great detriment.

The Roman Catholic Church is often compared to a ship or boat, by Nostradamus. At a time when a Temporal Ruler shall reign over the entire earth, the Church shall be conspicuous by its absence.

5

Chassez seront sans faire long combat, Par le pais seront plus fort grevez, Bourg & Cite auront plus grand debat, Carcas, Narbonne auront coeurs esprouvez.	They shall be driven away without great fighting, Those of the country shall be greatly grieved, Town and City shall have a mighty debate, Carcassone, Narbonne shall prove their heart.

Here is nothing mysterious. It must be borne in mind that Nostradamus was a devout Catholic, and in keeping with the then current struggle between the Protestants and Catholics for power, he foretells a fraternal melee, centering about Carcassone and Narbonne in Languedoc.

6

L'oeil de Ravenne sera destitue,
Quand a ses pieds les aisles sailli-
ront;
Les deux de Bresse auront consti-
tue,
Turin, Verceil, que Gaulois foule-
ront.

The eye of Ravenna shall be desti-
tute,
When the wings shall rise at his
feet.
The two of Brescia shall have established Turin and Venice,
Which the French shall have trod
upon.

One who lives in Ravenna shall not find time for the pursuit of riches when the wings of inspiration arise.
The French shall ultimately have sovereignty.

7

Tard arrive, l'execution faite,
Le vent contrare, lettres au che-
min prinses,
Les conjurez quatorze d'une secte,
Par le Rousseau seront les entre-
prinses.

One arriving too late, the execution will take place,
The wind being contrary, and letters intercepted on the way.
The conspirators fourteen of a
separate body,
By the Red One, the enterprise
shall be undertaken.

Reference is made here to the assassinations of Nicholas and Alexandra with their royal children and fourteen retainers by the Reds.

8

Combien de fois prinse cite solaire,
Seras, changeant les loix barbares
& vaines,
Ton mal s'approche, plus seras tributaire,
Le grand Adrie recouvrira tes
veines.

How often taken, O city of the Sun
shall thou be?
Changing thy vain and barbarous
laws,
Thy Evil groweth nigh, Thou shalt
be more tributary,
The great Venice shall recover thy
veins.

Heliopolis, or Baalbec, an ancient city in Syria near Damascus, famous for its ruins, is used symbolically by Nostradamus to indicate the growing evil in the world.

9

De l'Orient viendra le coeur punique,
Fascher Adrie, & les hoirs Romulides,
Accompagne de la classe Libique
Trembler Melites, & proches Isles vuides.

From the East of Africa shall come the Lion-Heart,
To vex Venice and the heirs of Romulus,
Accompanied by the Libian Tribe,
Malta shall tremble and the neighboring islands shall be empty.

A remarkably prophetic description of the role of Emperor Haile Selassie, in World War II, who reconquered Ethiopia, in East Africa, and sent an expedition to aid the Allied Cause, eventually defeating the Fascists of Italy, self-styled "Heirs of Romulus."

10

Sergens transmis dans la Cage de Fer,
Ou les enfans septains du Roy sont pris,
Les vieux & peres sortiront bas d'enfer,
Ains mourir voir de son fruit mort & cris.

Sergeants sent into the Cage of Iron,
Where the seven children of the King are,
The old men and fathers shall see the death and cries of their first fruit,
And before they die, shall go through Hell.

A description of the incidents that came to pass during the "Reign of Terror" in the French Revolution. The daily roll calls of those proscribed for the guillotine are graphically portrayed.

11

Le mouvement de sens, coeur, pieds, & mains,
Seront d'accord, Naples, Leon, Sicile,
Glaives, Feux, Eaux, puis au Noble Romains,
Plongez, Tuez, Morts, par cerveau debile.

Naples, Spain and Sicily shall agree
To the movement with heart, feet hands and sense,
Swords, Fires, Water, then to the Noble Romans,
Plunged into death by a weak brain.

The active cooperation of Fascist Italy and Falangist Spain is foretold, predicting dire results to both Mussolini and his cohorts.

12

Dans peu ira fauce brute fragile,
De bas en haut ensleve prompte-
   ment,
Puis en estant desloyal & labile,
Qui de Verone aura gouvernment.

In a little while a treacherous brute
   shall be raised,
Quickly from a low to high estate,
Unfaithfully and swiftly,
He shall have the government of
   Italy.

A continuation of the previous quatrain, this depicts the rise of Mussolini from an insignificant rabble rouser to Duce, or Leader of the Italian
State.

13

Les exiles, par ire, haine intestine,
Feront au Roy grand conjuration,
Secret mettront ennemis par la
   mine,
Et les vieux siens, contre eux sedi-
   tion.

The exiles, by anger, shall spread
   internal strife,
And make against the King a great
   conspiracy,
Secret enemies shall they put in
   the mine,
And raise the old ones against
   them by sedition.

The progress of the Italian conspiracy is indicated—the rise of a fifth
column rife with internal dissensions, culminating with a plot against
King Victor Emmanuel.

14

De gens esclave, chansons, chants,
   & requestes,
Captifs par Princes, & Seigneurs
   aux prisons,
A l'aduenir par idiots sans testes,
Seront receus par divins oraisons.

Being kept prisoners, by Princes
   and Lords,
The slavish people petition for
   songs and books,
For the future, idiots without
   heads
Shall be received by divine prayers.

The forecast of a revolution in Russia. The Russian, or Slavonic,
people, held in subjection by their rulers, will seek enlightenment and
surcease from oppression.

15

Mars nous menace par la force bellique,
Septante fois fera le sang respandre,
Auge & ruine de l'Ecclesiastique,
Et par ceux qui d'eux rien ne voudront entendre.

Mars threatens us with a warlike
force,
Seventy times he shall cause blood
to be shed,
Causing the ruin of the Clergy
And those who will hear nothing
from them.

The Damoclean Sword of War shall hang over Humanity for a period
of Seventy Great Wars, eventually causing a debacle among the heedless
mortals as well as the Church.

16

Faux a l'Estang, joint vers la Sagit-
taire,
En son haut auge de l'exaltation,
Peste, Famine, Mort de main mili-
taire,
Le Siecle approcher de renovation.

When a fish pond that was a
meadow shall be mowed,
Sagittarius being in the ascendant,
Plague, Famine, Death by the mili-
tary hand,
The Century approaches renewal.

In 1999, as the old century is about to expire, between November 23rd
and December 21st, the climactic War of Wars shall be unleashed.

17

Par quarante ans l'Iris n'apparoistra,
Par quarante ans tous les jours sera
veu,
La Terre aride en siccite croistra,
Et grand deluge quand sera ap-
parceu.

For forty years the rainbow shall
not appear,
For forty years it shall be seen every
day,
The parched earth shall wax drier
and drier,
And a great flood when it shall
appear.

A continuation of the preceding stanza—the prediction depicts conditions during the Armageddon and forecasts the wasteland produced by
nuclear warfare and ultimate destruction.

18

Par la discorde, negligence Gau-
loise,
Sera passage a Mahomet ouvert,
De sang trempe la terre & mer
Senoise,
Le Port Phocen de voiles & nefs
couvert.

Through the discord and negligence of the French,
A passage shall be opened to Mahomet,
The land and sea of Italy shall be
bloody,
And the harbor of Marseilles shall
be covered with sails and ships.

The Arab Mohammedan Confederacy, dominated by the Mohammedan Church, shall find an entering wedge into geopolitics largely through French aid. There was the Moslem revolution in Iran in 1980, the construction of the nuclear reactor in Iraq, with French aid, in 1981, and its eventual destruction by the Israeli Air Force. Aggravation of the Middle East strife will bring warfare between the Moslems and non-Moslems of the world.

19

Lors que serpens viendront circuir
l'air,
Le sang Troien verse par les Espagnes,
Par eux; grand nombre en sera fait
tare,
Chef fuit, cache aux marets dans
les saignes.

When the serpents shall come to
encompass the air,
The French blood shall be angered
by Spain,
By them, a great number shall perish,
The chief flies, and hides in the
rushes of the marshes.

At the beginning of World War II, the air superiority of the Nazis was clearly demonstrated much to the chagrin of the French, who, threatened by Spain, were forced to maintain a strong force at their border. Eventually, the French President and his entourage were forced to fly from Paris.

20

Tours, Orleans, Blois, Angers,
Renes & Nantes,
Cites vexees par soudain change-
ment,
Par langues estranges seront ten-
dues tentes,
Fleuves, Darts, Rennes, Terre &
Mer tremblement.

Tours, Orleans, Blois, Angers,
Reims and Nantes,
Cities vexed by sudden change,
By strange languages tents shall be
set up,
Rivers, Darts, Rennes, Land and
Sea shall tremble.

The German Invasion continues, and the above-named cities are quickly changed over to Nazi rule. The strange German language becomes the official speech, and the rest of France trembles under bombardment from the air.

21

Profonde argile blanche nourrit rocher,
Qui d'un abysme istra l'acticineuse,
En vain troublez ne l'seront toucher,
Ignorant estre au fond terre argileuse.

A deep white clay a rock supports,
Which shall break out of the deep like milk,
In vain people shall be troubled, not daring to touch it,
Being ignorant that in the bottom there is a milky clay.

A prediction of a new and as yet undiscovered method of utilization of Nature's resources, producing powerful actinic properties, and also the mining of radioactive elements, and the development of water pollution by industrial waste disposal.

22

Ce qui vivra & n'aura aucen sens,
Viendra le fer a mort son artifice,
Autun, Chalons, Langres, & les deux Sens,
La guerre & la glasse fera grand malefice.

That which shall live shall leave no direction,
Its destruction and death will come by stratagem,
Autun, Chalons, Langres, and from both sides,
The war and ice shall do great harm.

A forecast of the use of supersonic weapons, traveling in the near absolute zero temperature above the stratosphere, i.e., satellites armed with nuclear warheads.

23

Au mois troisiesme se levant le Soleil,
Sanglier, Leopard, aux champs Mars pour combatre,
Leopard lasse au Ciel esttena son oeil,
Un Aigle autour du Soleil voit sesbatre.

In the third month at the rising of the sun,
The Wild Boar and Leopard in the fields of Mars battle,
The Leopard weary, lifts his eyes to Heaven
And seeth an eagle playing about the Sun.

The English Lion, or Leopard, doggedly holds off the German Boar, as the American Eagle gains altitude for his fateful swoop.

24

A Cite Nevue pensif pour condamner,
Loisel de Proie au ciel se vient off-
  rir,
Apres Victoire a captifs pardonner
Cremone & Mantoue grands maux
  auront ouffert.

In the New City, to condemn an
  idea,
The Bird of Prey shall offer himself
  to the sky,
After Victory the prisoners shall
  be forgiven,
After Cremona and Mantua have
  suffered much.

After many cities have received severe damage, and victory is achieved,
a trial shall be held in New City (Nu-Rem-Burg). Most of the prisoners
shall be given light sentences.

25

Perdu, trouve cache de si long sie-
  cle
Sera Pasteur demy-Dieu honore,
Ains que la Lune acheve son grand
  Siecle,
Par autre vents fera dishonore.

Lost, found again, hidden so great
  a while,
A Pasteur as Demi-God shall be
  honored,
But before the moon her great
  cycle ends,
By other ancient ones shall be dishonored.

Louis Pasteur, the great French physician, is shown here to be worshipped almost as a demi-god for his discoveries, until a resurgence of an
older school.

26

Le grande du Fondre tomb d'heure
  diurne,
Mal & predit par porteur populaire,
Suivant presage tombe d'heure
  nocturne,
Conflict Rheims, Londres, Etrusque, Pestifere.

The great man falleth by lightning
  in the day,
An evil foretold by the postulant
  one,
According to the forecast, another
  falls in hours of the night,
A conflict at Rheims and London,
  and a plague in Tuscany.

The taking over of Czechoslovakia by Hitler, the resignation of President Benes, the dissensions over the matter between France and England
and the dire warning of the consequences of this betrayal, are all remarkably outlined in this prophecy.

27

Des soubs le chesne Guyen du ciel
    frappe,
Non loin de la est cache le thresor,
Qui par long siecles avoir este
    grappe,
Trouve mourra, l'oeil creve de res-
    sor.

Underneath the cord, Guien struck
    from the sky,
Near where is hid a great treasure,
Which has been many years a
    gathering,
Being found, he shall die, the eye
    put out by a spring.

Paratroopers alight near the Nazi's plunder hoard and, captured, they
are executed.

28

La Tour de Bouk craindra fuste
    barbare,
Un temps, long temps apres barque
    Hesperique,
Bestial, gens, meubles tous deux
    feront grand tare,
Taurus & Libra quelle mortelle
    pique.

The Tower of Bouk shall be in awe
    of barbarous musty odor,
For a while, and a long time after
    afraid of Spanish craft,
Cattle, people and goods, both
    shall receive a great damage,
Taurus and Libra, oh, what a
    deadly feud!

The Tower of Bouk is a fortified place at the mouth of the Rhone. It
shall be attacked by gas, discharged from craft flying the Spanish flag,
sometime in April or October.

29

Quand le poisson, terrestre &
    aquatique,
Par forte vague au gravier sera mis,
Sa forme estrange suave & horri-
    fique,
Par mer aux murs bien tost ene-
    mies.

When the fish, that is both ter-
    restrial and aquatic,
By a strong wave shall be cast upon
    the shore,
With his strange, fearful, horrid
    form,
Soon after the enemy shall come
    to the walls by the sea.

A clear account of the D-Day Invasion of the Normandy beaches, with
an exact description of the amphibious tanks and ducks employed by
the Allies.

30

La Nef estrange par le tourment
Marin,
Abordera pres le port incognu,
Nonobstant signs due remeau pal-
merin.
Apres mort, pille, bon advis tard
venu.

The strange ship by the Seas torment,
Shall come near the unknown port,
Notwithstanding the signs given
to it of the bows and palms,
It shall die, be plundered, a good
advice come too late.

A prophetic description of France in the days preceding the War,
when the Ship of State was sabotaged and plundered by avaricious, selfish,
factional disputes.

31

Tant d'ans les guerras, en Gaule
dureont,
Outre la course du Castulon Mon-
arque,
Victoire incerte trois grands cou-
roneront,
Aigle, Coq, Lune, Lion Soleil en
Marque.

So many years the wars shall last in
France,
Beyond the course of the Castil-
lian monarch,
An uncertain victory three great
ones shall crown
The Eagle, the Cock, the Moon,
the Lion leaving the sun in its
mark.

At the conclusion of the war, an insecure truce is declared between
the victors—United States, France, China, and England—all of whom
will exact a penalty from the Land of the Rising Sun, or Japan.

32

La grand Empire sera tost translate,
En lieu petit qui bien tost viendra
coistre,
Lieu bien infime d'exigue comte,
Ou au milieu viendra poser son
scepter.

The great Empire shall soon be
translated
Which shall grow soon into an inferior place of small account,
In the middle of which he shall
come,
To lay down his scepter.

A continuation of the previous stanza. Great Japan will degenerate
into a minor power, with the Emperor abdicating the throne.

33

Pres d'un grand pont de plaine spa-
cieuse,
Le grand Lion par force, Cesarees,
Fera abatre hors cite, rigoureuse,
Par effroy portes luy seront reser-
rees.

At a great bridge, near a spacious
plain,
The great Lion, by Caesarous
forces,
Shall come to be pulled down before the rigorous city,
The gates which shall be shut to
him.

Winston Churchill will re-enter English politics to save the Tory
Party from Labor, but, by a coalition, shall be defeated.

34

L'oiseau de proye volant a la fe-
nestre,
Avant conflict, fait au Francois
parure,
L'un bon prendra, l'autre ambigue
sinistre,
La partie foible tiendra pour bonne
augure.

The bird of prey flying to the win-
dow,
Before battle shall appear to the
French,
One shall take good omen of it, the
other, an ambiguous one,
The weaker party shall hold it a
good sign.

A foreign Demagogue will cause intrigue by dividing the various
parties, and the faction weakest in numbers will be spurred to action.

35

Le Lion jeune le vieux surmontera,
En champ bellique par singulier
duelle,
Dans cage d'or loeil il lui crevera,
Deux plays une puis mourir mort
cruelle.

The young Lion shall overcome
the old one
In martial field by a single duel,
In a golden cage he shall put out
his eye,
Two wounds from one, then he
shall die a cruel death.

One of the most famous of Nostradamus' prophecies:—The Young
Lion, a Scottish Knight, in a tournament with King Henry II, the Old Lion,
accidentally pierced his golden helmet with a splinter of his wooden lance,
putting out his eye and penetrating his brain, causing the King to die "a
cruel death."

36

Tard le Monarque se viendra re-
    pentir.
De navior mis a mort son adver-
    saire,
Mais viendra bien a plus haut con-
    sentir,
Que tout son sang par mort fera
    deffaire.

The Monarch shall repent too late,
That he has not put his adversary
    to death,
But he shall give his consent to a
    greater thing than that,
Which is, to kill all his adversary's
    kindred.

Toussaint L'Overture, the great leader of the blacks of Haiti, and his
connection with Napoleon I, is here foreseen. Despite his fight on the side
of the French, L'Overture was eventually deposed as Governor of Haiti
by Napoleon, and brought to France where he died in prison.

37

Un peu devant que le Soleil saba-
    conse
Conflict donne, grand peuple du-
    bieux,
Profligez, port-marin ne fait re-
    sponce,
Pont & sepulchre en deux es-
    tranges lieux.

A little before the sun sets,
A battle shall be given, a great peo-
    ple shall be doubtful,
Of being foiled, the sea port makes
    no answer,
A bridge and sepulchre shall be in
    two strange places.

One of the numerous prophecies that refer to the events in the great
Armageddon.

38

Le sol & l'aigle victeur parois-
    stront,
Response vain au vaincu lon as-
    seure,
Par Cor ne cris, harnois n'arreste-
    ront,
Vindicte paix, par mort lacheve a
    l'heure.

The sun and eagle shall appear to
    be victorious,
A vain answer shall be made good
    to the vanquished,
By no means, arms shall not be
    stopped,
Peace, prosecuted by death, it shall
    be achieved.

A movement shall arise for the suppression of armament and wars.
War in itself will become so terrible that nations will achieve peace
through fear of Universal Death.

39

De nuit le lit le supresme estrange,
Pour avoir trop suborne blonde
esleu,
Partrois l'Empire subroge exancle,
A mort metra, carte ne pacquet
leu.

By night, in the bed, the chief one
shall be strangled,
For having corrupted too much the
fair elect,
By three the Empire subrogate
exancle.
He, devoted to death, reading
neither card nor packet.

The author purposely obscured this prophecy in the third line, because
the persons concerned were then alive, viz., King Phillip II of Spain, who
caused his only son, Don Carlos, to be strangled in bed, for suspicion of
being intimate with his wife, Elizabeth of France and daughter of Henry II.

40

La tourbe fausse dissimilant folie
Fera Bizance un changement de
loix,
Istra d'Egypt qui veus que l'on de-
slie,
Edict, changant monnoys & alloys.

The false troupe dissembling their
folly,
Shall make in Constantinople, a
change of laws,
One shall come out of Egypt who
will have untied the edict,
Changing the money and the
standards.

At a convention held in the Near East, the Nations will attempt to
draw up an economic and financial formula for the free flow of world
trade. Note the OPEC (Organization of Petroleum Exporting Countries)
meetings and their regulation of oil prices and consequent alteration of the
flow and value of money throughout the world.

41

Siege a cite & de nuit assaille,
Peu eschapez non loing de Mer
conflict,
Femme de joys, retour fils, de fail-
lie
Poison & lettres cache dedans le
plic.

A siege laid to a city, and assaulted
by night,
A few shall escape to fight not far
from the sea,
A woman swoons for joy to see her
son returned,
A poison hidden in the fold of
letters.

The siege of Leningrad brought starvation and death. A few escaped to
the Baltic Sea and Finland. "Woman" is Mother Russia. "Son" is victorious Stalin, who later became a "poison" to Russia and was subsequently
downgraded.

42

Les dix Calendes d'Avril de fait Gothique, *Rescuscite encor par gens malins,* *Le feu estaint, assemblee diabolique,* *Cherchand les os de d'amant & Psellin.*	The tenth of the Calends of April, Gothic account, Raised up again by malicious persons, The light put out, a diabolical assembly, Seek for the bones of the lovers and Psellus.

An account of a witches' assembly, on the twenty-third of April, old style—evil persons assemble and various diabolical acts are performed in the dark, all according to Psellus, a famed Byzantine writer on Black Magic.

43

Avant qu'avien le changement d'Empire, *Ill adviendra un cas bien merveilleux,* *Le champ mue, le pilier de Porphyre,* *Mis, translate sur le Rocher Noileux.*	Before the change of Empire comes, There shall be a strange accident, A field shall be changed, and a pillar of Porphyry Shall be transported upon the chalky cliffs.

England will change its course of Empire, when upon the chalky cliffs of Dover, shall appear a pillar, or adherent, of Porphyry (a famous anti-Christian philosopher of ancient Rome, A.D. 233–305).

44

En bref seront de retour sacrifices, *Contrevenans seront mis a martyre,* *Plus ne seront moins, abbez ne novices,* *Le miel sera beaucoup plus cher que cire.*	In a short time sacrifices shall return again, Opposers shall be put to martyrdom, There shall be no more monks, abbots, nor novices, Honey shall be dearer than wax.

A period of persecution against the Catholic Church is foretold, when Protestants will forbid the use of wax candles used in the Catholic ritual.

45

Secteur de Sectes, grand paine au delateur,
Beste en theatre, dresse le jeu scenique,
Du fait antique ennobly l'inventeur,
Par sectes, monde confus & schismatique.

Followers of Sects, great pains to the informer,
A beast on the stage prepares the scenes,
The inventor of that iniquitous fact shall be famous,
By sects the world shall be confused and schismatic.

Nostradamus, a confirmed Catholic, and a believer in the infallibility of the Church, releases a blast of condemnation at Martin Luther, whose appearance divided the Christian World into innumerable Sects.

46

Tout aupres d'Auch, de Lectoure & Mirande,
Grande feu du ciel en trois nuits tombera,
Chose adviendra bien stupende & mirande,
Bien peu apres al terre tremblera.

Near Auch, Lectoure and Mirande,
A great fire shall from the sky for three nights fall,
A thing shall happen stupendous and wonderful,
And shortly after the ground shall quake.

The forecast is of an extra-terrestrial sighting and landing with subsequent benefits to earth people.

47

Du Lac Lemans les sermons fascheront,
Des jours seront reduit par des sepmains,
Puis mois, puis an, puis tous dafalliront,
Les Magistrats damneront leurs Loix vaines.

The sermons of the Leman Lake shall be troublesome,
Some of the days shall be extended weeks,
Then into months, then into years, when they shall fail,
The magistrates shall condemn their own inept laws.

Lake Leman is the ancient name for Geneva. Here is clearly foretold the efforts and final failure of the League of Nations.

48

Vingt ans du regne de la lune passez,	Twenty years of the reign of the moon having passed,
Sept mil ans autre tiendra sa monarchie,	Seven thousand years another shall hold his monarchy,
Quand le soleil prendra ses jours laissez,	When the sun shall resume his days past,
Lors accomplit a fine ma Prophecie.	Then is fulfilled and ends my prophecy.

The end of the world is here explicitly prophesied by Nostradamus. In the year 7000 the Sun will destroy the Earth and again resume its undisputed sway.

49

Beaucoup, beaucoup avant telles menees,	Much, very much before these doings happen,
Ceux d'Orient par la vertu Lunaire,	Those of the East by virtue of the Moon,
L'An mil sept cens feront grands emmenees,	In the year 1700, shall carry away great multitudes,
Subjugant presque le coin Aquilonaire.	And shall subdue almost the whole northern section.

In the year 2025, by ritual, China, having completed her industrial and economic expansions, will absorb almost the whole of Northern Russia and Scandinavia.

50

De l'aquatique triplicite naistra,	From the aquatic triplicity shall be born,
Un qui fera Feudy pour sa feste,	One who shall make Thursday his holiday,
Son bruit, loz, regne & puissance croistra,	His fame, praise, rule, and power shall grow,
Par Terre & Mer, aux Orients tempeste.	By Land and Sea to become a tempest to the east.

Nostradamus predicts the origin of the United States 200 years before it existed. The "aquatic triplicity" refers to the Atlantic, the Pacific, and the Gulf of Mexico. Also the national holiday of Thanksgiving, always on Thursday (Thor) is noted.

51

Chef d'Aries, Jupiter and Saturn,
Dieu Eternal quelles mutations!
Puis apres long siecle son malin
   temps retourne,
Gaule & Italy quelles emotions!

Heads of Aries, Jupiter and Saturn,
O Eternal God, What changes
   there shall be!
After an era his evil time returns,
Gaule and Italy, what commotion!

A period of unrest in Italy shall culminate in the intervention of the French and a complete change in the social order.

52

Les deux malin de Scorpion conjoint,
Le Grand Seigneur meurtry dedans
   sa salle,
Peste a l'Eglise par le nouveau Roy
   jonts,
L'Europe basse & Septentrioanle.

The two evils of Scorpion being
   joined,
The Grand Seignior murdered in
   his hall,
Plague to the Church by a King
   joined to it,
Europe in the depths and dismem-
   bered.

The Church, as well as all Europe, is to be cut up by one born a member of the Catholic Church.

53

Las qu'on verra grand peuple tour-
   mente,
Et la Loy Saincte en totale ruyne,
Par autres loix toute la Chrestiente,
Quand d'or, d'argent trouve nou-
   velle mine.

Alas, how a great people shall be
   tormented
And the Holy Laws in total ruin,
By other laws, all Christianity
   troubled,
When new mines of gold and silver will be found.

The industrial revolution, the discovery of gold mines in Africa, Australia, etc., the rise of the God of Mammon, shall bring grief to all of Christendom.

54

Deux revolts faits du malin falci-
    gere
De regne & siecles fait permutation
Le mobil signe en son endroit s'in-
    gere,
Aux deux esgaux & d'inclination.

Two revolts shall be made by the
    evil torch bearer,
Which shall make a change of the
    reign and age,
The mobile sign to right shall med-
    dle,
And shall have an inclination to
    the two equals.

The evil genius of the age shall instigate two revolts, in the name of enlightenment; the Swastika shall make concessions to the right and to both leaders.

55

Soubz l'opposite climat Babylo-
    nique,
Grande sera de sang effusion,
Que terre & mer, air. ciel sera
    inique,
Sectes, faim, regnes, pestes, confu-
    sion.

In the climate opposite to the
    Babylonian,
There shall be a great effusion of
    blood,
So that the land and sea, air and
    heaven shall seem unjust,
Sects and famine shall rule over
    plague and confusion.

Cataclysmic destruction, with great loss of life, is promised to the land of the Pacific, far in the East (the antipodes of the Near East or Babylonia).

56

Vous verrez tost & tard faire grand
    change
Horreurs extresmes & vindications,
Que si la lune conduite par son
    ange,
Le ciel s'approche des inclinations.

Sooner or later, you shall see great
    changes,
Extreme horrors and persecutions,
The moon led by her angel,
The heaven draws near its inclina-
    tion.

This quatrain reflects, as do so many of Nostradamus' prophecies, his repeated prophetical conviction of the great changes to take place in the future, most of which will lead to strife among humans and the ultimate destruction of the Earth.

57

Par grand discord la trombe tremblera,	By great discord, the trumpet shall vibrate,
Accord rompu, dressant la teste au ciel,	Agreement broken, lifting the head to heaven,
Bouche sanglante dans le sang nagera,	A bloody mouth shall swim in blood,
Au sol sa face oingte de laict & miel.	The face turned to the sun anointed with milk and honey.

A clear and forthright prediction. Japan will treacherously break her agreement with the United States and, plunging into the bloody war, she will embark on her East Asia Co-Prosperity scheme, promising a future land of milk and honey to her cohorts.

58

Trenche le ventre, naistra avec deux testes	Slit in the belly, it shall be born with two heads,
Et quatre bras, quelques ans entiers viura,	And four arms, and shall live a few years,
Jour qui Aquilare celebrera ses festes,	The day that Aquila shall celebrate his feasts,
Foussan, Thurin, chef Ferrare suyura.	Fossan, Turin, the chief of Ferrara shall run away.

A monstrous thing shall be brought into being, but shall not exist long. When Aquila (a Jewish Proselyte who literally translated the Hebrew Scriptures into Greek) celebrates his feast, the Italians shall have much sorrow.

59

Les exilez deportez dans les Isles,	The exiles that were carried into the Isles,
Au changement d'un plus cruel Monarque,	At the whim of a most cruel monarch,
Seront meurtris, & mis deux des scintilles	Shall be murdered, and put in the sparks of fire,
Qui de parler ne seront este parques.	Because they had not been sparing of their tongues.

Hitler's wholesale extermination of the Jews and Poles, followed by the infamous cremation of their bodies, is indicated in this quatrain.

60

Un Empereur naistra pres d'Italie,	An Emperor shall be born in Italy.
Qui a l'Empire sera vendu bien cher,	Who shall cost the Empire dear,
Diront avec quels gens il se ralie	They shall say, with what peoples he keeps company!
Qu'on trouvera moins Prince que boucher.	He shall be found less a Prince than a butcher.

A presage of the coming of Napoleon, born in Corsica (then an Italian possession), and the subsequent wars and destruction he will bring to Europe.

61

La republique miserable infelice,	The miserable and unhappy republic
Sera vastee du nouveau Magistrat,	Shall be wasted by the new Magistrate,
Leur grand amas de l'exil malefice,	Their great number of broken refugees,
Fera Sueve ravir leur grand contract.	Shall cause Sweden to break her contract.

This refers to the dissipation of the resources of France, and the repudiation by Sweden of her treaty with France in favor of a Russian alliance, on December 3, 1804.

62

La grande perte las! que feront les lettres	Alas, what a great loss shall learning suffer
Avant le cicle de laton a parfaict,	Before the cycle of the moon is accomplished,
Feu, grand deluge, plus par ignares sceptres	By fire, great flood, and ignorant scepters,
Que de long siecle ne se verra refaict.	More than can be made good again in a long age.

The cycle of the moon shall end when, on the last cataclysmic day, it shall fall on the earth; until then much misery shall happen due to the ignorance of men.

63

Les fleaux passees diminue le monde,
Long-temps la paix, terres inhabitees,
Seur marchera par le ceil, terre, mer & Onde,
Puis de nouveau les guerres suscitees.

The scourge being past, the world shall be made smaller,
Peace for a long time, lands inhabited,
Everyone safe shall go by air, land and sea,
And then the wars shall begin anew.

In the period after the great influenza epidemic, that followed World War I, great progress was made in air travel, etc.; then after a brief time, World War was renewed.

64

De nuict soleil penseront auoir veu,
Quand le porceau demy homme on verra,
Bruit, chant, bataille au Ciel battre apperceu
Et bestes brutes a parler on orra.

They shall think to have seen the sun in the night,
When the hog half a man shall be seen,
Noise, singing, battles in the sky shall be perceived,
And brute beasts shall be heard to speak.

This presages modern mechanized warfare: searchlights, baby tanks, whistling bombs, dog fights in the air, and radio equipment.

65

Enfant sans mains, jamais veu si grand foudre
L'enfant Royal au jeu d'esteuf blesse,
Au puy brisez, fulgures allant moudre,
Trois sur le chaines par le milieu trousse.

A child without hands, lightning never so great was seen,
The Royal child, wounded at the tennis court,
Bruised at the well, lightning going to the ground,
Three in the midst of the field shall be struck thereby.

An allegorical attempt to show that when the "Oath of the Tennis Court" was taken by the French Revolutionists, the Royal Three were irretrievably struck down, viz; Louis XVI, Marie Antoinette, and the Dauphin.

66

Celuy qui lors portera les nouvel-
les,
Apres un peu il viendra respirer,
Vivers, Tournon, Montferrant &
Pradelles,
Gresle & tempeste, les fera sous-
pirer.

He that then shall carry the news,
A little while after shall draw his
breath,
Viviers, Tournon, Montserrant,
and Pradelles,
Hail and storm shall make them
sigh.

A continuation of the preceding quatrain—the mounting storm of
the Revolution rolls over all France.

67

La grand famine que je sens approcher,
Aouvent tourner puis estre univer-
selle,
Si grande & longue qu'on viendra
arracher,
Du bois racine, & l'enfant de ma-
melle.

The great famine do I see drawing
near,
Turning from one way to another
and then becoming universal,
So great and long, that they shall
come to pluck
The root from the wood and the
child from the breast.

Famine and drought are very prominent in the late twentieth century
in Europe, India, and Africa.

68

O quel horrible & malheureux
tourment!
Trois innocens qu'on viendra a
livrer,
Poison suspecte, mal garde tradi-
ment
Mis en horreur par bourreaux eny-
vrez.

O what a horrid and sad torment
Shall be put to three innocents,
Poison shall be suspected, evil
guards shall betray them.
They shall be put to horror by
drunken executioners.

Three innocent persons shall be suspected of a poison plot, and they
shall be tortured and put to death by drunken executioners.

69

La grand montagne ronde de sept estades,	The great mountain encompasses seven stadia,
Apres paix, guerre, faim, inondation,	After peace, war, famine, and inundation,
Roulera loing, abysmant grand contades,	Shall tumble a great way, sinking great countries,
Mesmes antiques, & grand fondation.	Even ancient houses and their great foundations.

Great institutions, after surviving the vicissitudes of war, etc., shall go down, carrying with them the long established order and the ruling castes.

70

Pluys, faim, guerre, en Perse non cessee,	Rain, famine, war in Persia having not ceased,
La foy trop grande trahira le Monarque,	Too great credulity shall betray the Monarch,
Par la finie en Gaule commencee,	Being ended there, it shall commence in France,
Secret augure pour a un estre parque.	A secret omen to one that he shall die.

The weak, vacillating policy of Louis XVI, and his too great faith in advisers, bring France to the brink of disaster, and an unheeded omen to the King himself:

71

La tour marins trois fois prinse & reprinse	The sea tower three times taken and retaken,
Par Espagnols, Barbares, Ligurins,	By Spaniards, Barbarians, and Italians,
Marseille & Aix, Arles par ceux de Pise	Marseilles, and Aix, Arles by those of Pisa,
Vast, feu, fer, pille, Avignon des Thurins.	Waste, fire, iron, pillage, Avignon by Piedmont.

Confirmation of Quatrain 28, Century One—wherein France is attacked by the Axis.

72

Du tout Marseille des habitans changee	Marseilles shall wholly change her inhabitants,
Course & pour fuitte jusques pres de Lyon,	These shall run and be pursued as far as Lyons,
Narbon, Tholoze par Bordeaux outragee,	Narbonne, Toulouse shall wrong Bordeaux,
Tuez, captifs, presque d'un million.	Killed and prisoners shall be almost a million.

The Vichy Regime of Marshal Petain occupied the territory of Tou-louse, Lyons, and Narbonne. German troops entered Paris (June 14, 1940) and the government fled to Bordeaux.

73

France a cinq parts par neglect as-saillie	France by neglect shall be assaulted by five sides,
Tunys, Argiels esmeuz par Persiens,	Tunis and Algiers shall be stirred by the Persians,
Leon, Seville, Barcelone faillie	Leon, Seville, Barcelona shall be missed,
N'aura la classe par les Venitiens.	And not be pursued by the Vene-tians.

By the pettiness of her political parties, France will be invaded, and in French Africa the Italians will cause unrest, while the cities of Spain remain untouched.

74

Apres sejourne vogueront en Epire	After a stay, they shall sail toward Epirus,
Le grand secours viendra vers An-tioche,	The great aids shall come toward Antioch.
Le noir poil crespe tendra fort a l'Empire,	The black hair curled, shall aim much to the Empire,
Barbe d'airain le rostira en broche.	The brazen beard shall be roasted on a spit.

An Axis expedition will be sent to Epirus (Greece) and the Mediter-ranean. Mussolini, the Black One, will aim at expansion of the Italian Empire.

75

Le tyran Siene occupera Savone,
Le fort gaigne tiendra classe ma-
rine,
Les deux armees par la marque
d'Ancone
Par effrayeur le chef s'en examine.

The tyrant of Sienna shall occupy
Savone,
The fort being won, shall hold a
fleet,
The two armies shall go by the
way of Ancona,
Where by fear the chief shall be
examined.

The tyrant of Italy shall occupy French Savoy, thereby tying up the
British fleet on the coast. Two Italian armies will proceed east, past
Ancona, on the Adriatic Sea. Marshal Balbo will be executed.

76

D'un nom farouche tel profere sera,
Que les trois soeurs auront fato le
Nom
Puis grand peuple par langue & fait
dira,
Plus que nul autre aura bruit &
renom.

By a wild name one shall be called,
So that three sisters shall have the
name of Fate
Afterward a great people by tongue
and deeds shall say,
He shall have fame and renown
more than any other.

Nostradamus very definitely feels that a Messiah will come.

77

Entre deux mers dressera promon-
toire
Que puis mourra par le mords du
cheval,
Le sien Neptune pliera voille noire,
Par Calpre & classe supres de Rocheval.

Between two seas shall a promontory be raised,
By him, who shall die by the biting
of the horse,
The proud Neptune shall fold the
black sail,
Through Calpre, and a fleet shall
be near Rocheval.

In Greek legend, according to the history of Theseus, the Greeks, in
order to please the Minotaur, sent him a tribute of Athenian children in a
ship with black sails.

78

D'un chef vieillard naistra sens he-
bete,
Degenerant par scavoir & par
armes,
Le chef de France par sa soeur re-
doute,
Champs divisez, concedez aux gens
L'armes.

An old head shall beget an idiot,
Who shall degenerate in learning
and in arms,
The head of France shall be feared
by his sister,
The fields divided and granted to
the people's army.

The long reign of Louis XV (1715–1774) yielded to his grandson, Louis
XVI, who was weak, irresolute, and awkward. The oncoming French Revolution spurred the rise of power of the masses.

79

Bazax, Lectore, Condon, Ausch,
Agine,
Esmeus par loix, querelles & mono-
pole,
Car Bourd, Tholouse, Bay mettra
en ruyne,
Renouveller voulant leur tauropole.

Bazax, Lectore, Condon, Auch,
Agine,
Being moved by laws, quarrels and
monopoly,
They shall put to ruin Bordeaux,
Toulouse, Bayonne,
Going about to renew their Tauro-
pole.

The Northern industrial districts of France will try to exploit the
agricultural regions.

80

De la sixiesme claire splendeur celeste,
Viendra tonner si fort eu la Bour-
gongne,
Puis naistra monstre de tres-hy-
deuse beste,
Mars, Avril, May, Juin grand char-
pin & rongne.

From the sixth bright celestial
splendor,
Shall come very great lightning to
Burgundy,
After which shall be born a monster of a most hideous beast,
In March, April, May and June
shall be great quarrelling and
muttering.

The sixth planet from the Sun, or Saturn, shall shed a clear light on
horrific events to occur in the above-named months.

81

D'humain troupeau neuf seront
mis a part;
De jugement & conseil separees,
Leur sort sera divise en depart,
Kappa, Theta, Lambda, morts,
bannis, egarez.

Of the human flock, nine shall be
set aside,
Being divided in judgment and
counsel,
Their destiny shall be to be divided,
Kappa, Theta, Lambda, dead, banished, scattered.

The Supreme Court of the United States, consisting of nine members
is here indicated, as well as the Politburo of the U.S.S.R. More than once
has death and dismissal involved both bodies.

82

Quand les colomnes de bois grande
tremblee,
D'auster conduicte couverte de rubriche,
Tant vuidera dehors une grand
assemblee,
Trembler Vienne & le pays d'Aus-
triche.

When the wooden columns shall
be shaken
By the stern wind and covered by
a ruby hue,
Then shall go out a great assembly,
And Vienna and the land of Austria shall tremble.

In July of 1934 there was an uprising in Vienna, Austria, followed by
the assassination of Chancellor Dolfuss. Anschluss followed with the an-
nexation of Austria by Nazi Germany in 1938.

83

La gent estrange divisera butins
Saturne & Mars son regard furieux,
Horrible estrange aux Toscans &
Latins,
Grec qui seront a frapper curieux.

The alien agent shall divide boo-
ties,
Saturn and Mars shall have his
aspect furious,
Horrid and strange to the Tuscans
and Latins,
The Grecians shall be curious tc
strike.

Extra-terrestrial aliens will land on earth and terrify southern Europe.

84

Lune obscur cie aux profondes te- nebres,	The moon shall be obscured in the deepest darkness,
Son frere passe de couleur ferrigine;	Her brother shall pass being of a ferruginous colour;
Le grand cache long temps soubs les tenebres,	The great one long hidden under shadows,
Tiendra fer dans la pluie sanguine.	Shall make his iron lukewarm in the bloody rain.

At a time when vision is obscured, the Sun shall take on a tinge of red, or iron rust, and this will be the signal for the great one to rise and whet his sword.

85

Par la response de dame, roy trouble,	A king shall be troubled by the answer of a lady,
Ambassadeurs mespriseront leur vie,	Ambassadors shall despise their lives,
Les grand ses freres contrefera dou- ble,	The great one being undecided, shall counterfeit his brothers,
Par deux mourront ire, hain envie.	They shall die by two, anger, hatred, and envy.

Note the mid-twentieth-century abdication of Edward VIII caused by his love affair with Wallis Simpson. Nostradamus also makes his first reference to the assassinations of the Kennedy brothers.

86

Le grande Royne quand se verra vaincue	When the queen shall see herself vanquished,
Fera excez de masculin courage;	She shall do a deed of masculine courage,
Sur cheval fleuve passera toute nue,	Upon a horse, she shall pass over the river naked,
Suitte par fer, a foy fera outrage.	Followed by iron she shall do wrong to her faith.

Here is an early reference to the women's movement and their drive for equality with men.

87

Ennosigee, feu du centre de terre,
Fera trembler autour de Cite Neu-
    fue;
Deux grands rocher long temps
    ferot la guerre,
Puis Arethusa rougira nouveau
    Fleuve.

Ennosigee, fire of the center of the
    earth,
Shall make an earthquake of the
    New City,
Two great rocks shall long time
    war against each other,
After that, Arethusa shall color red
    the fresh river.

This is a truly shattering prediction. The two great rocks at war can
only mean the East and West (the United States and the Soviet Union)
and the earthquake and fire in the New City refers to a nuclear holocaust
in New York (?) etc. (?). The "cold war" shall become a hot one.

88

Le divin mal surprendra le grand
    Prince,
Un peu devant aura femme es-
    pousee;
Son puy & credit a un coup viendra
    mince,
Conseil mourra pour la teste rasee.

The divine sickness shall surprise
    a great prince,
A little while after he hath married
    a woman,
His support and credit shall at
    once become slender,
Council shall die for the shaven
    head.

Napoleon's desire to found an empire led to his marriage to Marie
Louise, who bore him an heir. His quarrels with the Pope are also indicated here.

89

Tous ceux de Ilerde seront dedans
    Moselle
Mettans a mort tous ceux de Loyre
    & Seine,
Secours marin viendra pres d'haute
    velle.
Quand l'Espagnol ouvrira toute
    viene.

All those of l'Isle shall be in the
    Moselle,
Putting to death all those of Loire
    and Seine,
The sea chase shall come near the
    high city
When the Spaniard shall open all
    veins.

Quarrels and warfare among the provinces of France are here referred
to.

90

Bourdeaux, Poitiers, au son de la
    campane,
A grand classe ira jusques a l'An-
    gon,
Contre Gaulois sera leur tramon-
    tane,
Quand monstre hideux naistra pres
    d'Orgon.

Bordeaux, Poitiers, at the sound of
    the bell,
With a great navy shall go as far
    as Langon,
Against the French shall their Tra-
    montane be,
When a hideous monster shall be
    born near Orgon.

Tramontane, in Italian, is the North Wind; Orgon is a town in Gascony.—An implication that France will be pitted against Northern adversaries and native quislings.

91

Les Dieux feront aux humains ap-
    parence,
Ce qu'ile seront autheurs de grand
    conflit.
Avant ciel veu serain, espee &
    lance,
Que vers main gauche sera plus
    grand affliction.

The Gods shall make it appear to
    mankind,
That they are the authors of a great
    war,
The sky that was serene shall show
    sword and lance,
On the left hand the affliction shall
    be greater.

World leaders of East and West move toward confrontation. Air combat and space warfare with leftist (Communist) destruction is predicted.

92

Sous un la paix par tout sera clem-
    ence
Mais non long temps, pille & re-
    bellion
Par refus, ville, terre & mer entam-
    mee,
Morts & captifs, le tiers d'un
    million.

Under one shall be peace, and ev-
    erywhere clemency,
But not for a long while, then shall
    be plundering and rebellion,
By a denial shall town, land and
    sea be assaulted,
Dead and taken prisoner shall be
    the third part of a million.

The sneak attack on Pearl Harbor, by the Japanese, ushered the United
States into World War II, resulting in 350,000 American casualties.

93

*Terre Italique pres des monts trem-
blera,
Lyon & Coq, non trop confererez,
En lieu de peur, l'un l'autre s'ai-
dera,
Seul Castulon & Celtes moderez.*

The Italian land of the mountains
shall tremble,
The Lion and the Cock shall not
agree very well together,
And for fear shall help one another,
Only Spain and the Celts shall be
neutral.

The World War II alliance of France and England against Italy is
here foreseen. Also note Spanish and Irish neutrality in WW II.

94

*Au port Selim le tryan mis a mort
La liberte non pourtant recouvree
Le nouveau Mars par vindicte &
remort.
Dame par force de frayeur hon-
oree.*

In the port, Selim the tyrant shall
be put to death,
And yet, liberty shall not be recovered,
The new War by vengeance and
remorse begun,
A lady by force of fear shall be
honored.

The victorious Prime Minister Margaret Thatcher was honored after
the British and Argentine war in the Falkland Islands in 1982.

95

*Devant Moustier trouve enfant
besson
D'heroicq sang de moyne vestu-
tisque,
Son bruit par secte, langue & Puissance son,
Qu'on dira soit efleue le Vospique.*

Before the monastery shall one
twin be found
From heroic blood of a monk and
ancient,
His fame by sect, tongue and power
shall be founded,
So that they shall say, Vopisk is
highly raised.

One of a pair of illegitimate twins, found deserted in a church, shall
rise to great heights.

96

Celuy qu'aura la charge de destruire Temples & sectes changees par fan- tasie, Plus aux rochers qu'aux vivans viendra nuyre, Par langue ornee d'oreilles ressai- sies.	He that shall be in charge to de- stroy Churches and sects changed by fan- tasy, Shall do more harm to the stones than to the living, By a smooth tongue filling up the ears.

One shall undertake a campaign to destroy the Churches, but will not succeed, due to the firmness of the faithful, more durable than stone.

97

Ce que fer, flamme, n'a sceu para- cheuer, La douce langue au conseil viendra faire Par repos, songe, le roy fera resuer, Plus l'ennemy en feu, sang mili- taire.	What neither iron nor fire could achieve, Shall be done by a smooth tongue in a council, In sleep a dream shall make the king to think, The more the enemy in fire and military blood.

The United Nations is the council predicted as a deterrent to war.

98

Le chef qu'aura conduit peuple in- finy Loing de son ciel, de moeurs & langue estrange, Cinq mil en, Crete, & Thessale finy, Le chef fuyant sauve en la marine grange.	The leader who shall lead an in- finite number of people, Far from their country to one of strange manners and language, Five thousand in Candia and Thes- saly finished, The leader escaping, shall be safe in a barn on the sea.

Nostradamus forecasts a Sino-Soviet conflict. Lines one and two are very clear on this, but which leader, Chinese or Soviet, shall escape in a submarine or capital ship cannot be determined.

99

Le Grand Monarque qui fera compagnie,	Le Grand Monarque shall keep company,
Avec deux Roys unis par amitie,	With two kings united in friendship,
O quel souspir sera la grande mesnie,	Oh what fights shall be made by their followers,
Enfant Narbon a l'entour quel pitie.	Children, O what a pity about Narbonne,

"Le Grand Monarque" is Napoleon as Emperor of France. He won the Italian campaign in 1796 and made the King of Sardinia sue for peace. Further, Napoleon's Egyptian campaign ended with his stealthy and secret return to France near Narbonne (Carcassone).

100

Long temps au ciel veu gris oyseau,	For a long while shall be seen in the air a gray bird,
Aupres de Dole & de Tosquane terre,	Near Dola and the Tuscan land,
Tenant au bec un verdoyant rameau	Holding in his beak a green bough,
Mourra tost grand, & finira la guerre.	Then a great one shall die and the war be finished.

The role of Franklin D. Roosevelt is here clearly prophesied, indicating his untimely and tragic death just a few weeks before the close of the war in Europe.

CENTURY II

1

Vers Aquitaine par insuls Britaniques
Et par aux mesmes grandes incursions
Pluyes, gelees feront terroir iniques
Port Selyn fortes fera invasions.

Towards Gascony by English assaults
By the same shall be made great incursions,
Rains, frosts shall make the ground unrighteous,
Port Selyn shall make strong invasions.

The D-Day invasion of Europe in World War II by the Allied Expeditionary Forces took place in June, after winter frosts and spring rains.

2

La teste bleue fera la teste blanche,
Autant de mal que France a fait leur bien,
Mort a l'anthenne, grande pendu sur la branche
Quand des prins siens le Roy dira combien.

The blue law shall do the white law
As much harm, as France has done it good,
Dead on the antenna, a great one hanged on a branch,
When a king taken by his own shall say "How much?"

Mussolini, radio silenced, was trapped and hanged on a tree in northern Italy at the end of World War II. A plebiscite abolished the monarchy in 1946.

43

3

Pour la chaleur solaire sur la mer
De Negrepont les poissons demy
cuits,
Les habitans les viendront entemer
Quand Rhod & Gennes leur faudra
le biscuit.

By the heat of the sun upon the
sea,
At Black Bridge, the fishes shall be
half broiled,
The inhabitants shall come to cut
them up,
When Rhodes and Genoa shall
want biscuits.

Further volcanic eruptions are predicted along the Mediterranean coast-
line, viz., Vesuvius (1944), Aetna (1951), Stromboli (1951).

4

Depuis Monach jusqu'au pres de
Sicile,
Toute la plage demourra desolee
Il n'y aura faux-bourgs, cite, ne
ville,
Que par Barbares, pille soit & vol-
lee.

From Monaco as far as Sicily,
All the sea coast shall be left desolate,
There shall not be suburbs, cities
nor towns,
Which shall not be pillaged and
plundered by Barbarians.

The western Italian Sea Coast from Monaco to Sicily will be invaded
and sacked by barbarians.

5

Quand dans poissin fer & lettre
enfermee
Hors sortira qui pis fera la guerre,
Aura par mer sa classe bien ramee,
Apparoissant pres de Latine terre.

When in an iron fish, a letter shall
be shut up,
He shall go out, that shall afterwards make war,
He shall have his fleet by the sea
well provided,
Appearing by the Roman Land.

In a submarine, one bearing an important letter and military secrets
shall land and afterwards lead a nation to victory. Gen. Clark's daring feat
—culminating in the North African campaign—is clearly foreshadowed.

6

| Aupres des portes & dedans deux citez | Near the gates and within two cities, |

Aupres des portes & dedans deux
citez
Seront deux fleaux onc n'apperceu
yn tel,
Faim dedans peste, de fer hors gens
boutez,
Crier secours au grand Dieu immortel.

Near the gates and within two
cities,
Shall be two scourges, I never saw
the like,
Famine, within plague, people
thrust out by the sword,
Shall cry for help to the great God
immortal.

Clearly predicts the Berlin Wall which divides the city in two. "Two cities near the gate" (Brandenberg).

7

Entre plusieurs aux iles deportes
L'un estre nay a deux dents en la
gorge
Mourront de faim, les arbres es-
broutez.
Pour eux neuf Roy nouvel edict
leur forge.

Among many that shall be transported into the islands,
One shall be born with two teeth
in his mouth,
They shall die of hunger, the trees
shall be eaten,
They shall have a new king, who
shall make new laws for them.

As the British immigrated to Australia the aboriginal natives were down-graded by the government controlled by the British royal house.

8

Temples sacrez prime facon Romaine,
Reietteront les goffes fondemens,
Prenant leurs loix premieres & hu-
maines
Chassant, non tout, des saincts les
cultemens.

Temples consecrated and the early
Roman way,
Shall reject the tottering founda-
tions,
Sticking to their first humane laws,
Expelling, but not altogether, the
worshipping of saints.

The rise of the Reformation and split from the Catholic Church is here predicted; and the retaining in Protestant litany of only a few of the Saints.

9

Neuf ans le regne le maigre en paix tiendra	Nine years shall the lean one keep the kingdom in peace,
Puis il cherra en soif si sanguinaire	Then he will fall into such a bloody thirst,
Pour luy grand peuple sans foy & loy mourra,	That a great people shall die without faith or law,
Tue par un beaucoup plus debonnaire.	He shall be killed by one much wilder than himself.

The references here point to the reign of Louis XVI—the short period of peace at the start of his kingship, the bloody and lawless revolution, and his eventual execution before the eyes of the roaring mobs of Paris.

10

Avant long temps le tout sera range	Before long, all shall be arranged,
Nous esperons un siecle bien senestre	We look for an era most sinister,
L'estat des masques & des seule bien change,	The state of the masks and they alone shall be changed,
Peu trouveront qu'a son rang vueille estre.	They shall find few that will keep their rank.

A continuation of the preceding prophecy, describing the chaotic conditions to prevail during the Revolution.

11

Le prochain, fils de l'asnier paruiendra	The eldest son of L'Aisnier shall prosper,
Tant esleve jusques au regne des forts	Being raised to the degree for the great ones,
Son aspre gloire un chacun la eraindra,	Everyone shall fear his high glory,
Mais ses enfans du regne jettez hors.	But his children shall be cast out.

This is the famous prediction Nostradamus sent to the Lord of L'Aisnier, who had written him to know of his children's future.

12

Yeux clos ouverts d'antique fan-
tasie
L'habit des seules seront mis a
neant;
Le grand monarque chastira leur
frenaisie,
Ravir des temples le thresor par
devant.

Eyes shut, shall be opened by an
antique fancy,
The clothes of the solitary shall be
brought to nothing,
The great monarch shall punish
their frenzy,
For having ravished the treasure of
the temple before.

The Goddess of Justice, with blindfolded eyes, will be resurrected, and
shall mete out punishment to the ravishers of the people and the temple.

13

Le corps sans ame plus n'estre en
sacrifice,
Jour de la mort mis en nativite,
L'esprit divin fera l'ame felice
Voyant le verbe en son eternite.

The body without soul shall be no
more admitted in sacrifice,
The day of death placed on the
birthday,
The divine spirit shall make the
soul happy,
By seeing the voice in its eternity.

Correctly predicts the change in the language of the Mass from Latin to
the vernacular by authorization of the Second Vatican Council of 1964.

14

A Tours, Gien, garde gande seront
yeux penetrans,
Descouvriront de loing la grand'
sireine,
Elle & sa suitte au port seront en-
trans,
Combats poussez, puissance sou-
veraine.

At Tours, Gienn, on guard shall be
piercing eyes,
Who shall discover before long the
great queen,
She and her suite shall enter into
the port,
By the fight shall be thrust out the
reigning power.

Predicts the conflict in the Falkland Islands with Britain entering the
port (Stanley) and the queen thwarting the Argentines.

15

Un peu devant monarque trucide,
Castor, Pollux, en nef, astre crai-
nite,
L'Arain public, par terre & mer
vuide,
Pise, Ast, Ferrare, Turin, terre in-
terdicte.

A little before a monarch is killed,
Castor, Pollux, and a Comet in
the sky appears,
The public Brass, by land and sea
shall be emptied,
Pisa, Asti, Ferra, Turin shall be
forbidden countries.

A time of unrest is prophesied—great disturbances in Castor and Pollux, the constellations of the Twins or Gemini. Before the assassination of An-war Sadat, Israel and Egypt agreed to maintain peace and thus became the "twins" of a Mideast accord. Sadat was murdered in a public appearance.

16

Naples, Palerme, Sicile, Syracuse,
Nouveaux Tyrans, Fulgures, faex
celestes,
Force de Londres, Gand, Bruxelles
& Suise
Grand hecatombe, triomph, faire
festes.

Naples, Palermo, Sicily, Syracuse,
New tyrants, Lightnings, Celestial
Fires,
An Army from London, Ghent,
Brussels,
And Switzerland, a sacrifice, tri-
umph and feasts.

Forecasts many World War II events, viz., the rise of Mussolini, the deployment of the A.E.F., the neutrality of Switzerland, the opening of a second front in Italy with the invasion in the south at Anzio, Naples, etc.

17

Le camp du temple de la vierge
vestale,
Non esloigne d'Ethene & monts
Pyrenees;
Le grand conduit est cache dans
la male,
North, getez, fleuves, & vigues mas-
tinees.

The camp of the temple of the
vestal virgin,
Not far from Ethene and the Pyrenees Mountains,
The great passage is driven in the
wall,
Rivers overflow in the North and
the vines spoiled.

At Tivoli, the site of the antique temple of the Vestal Virgin, a great passage cuts through, and there will be a great flood.

18

Nouvelle pluie subite, impetueuse	A new rain, sudden, impetuous,
Empeschera subit deux excertites,	Shall suddenly hinder two armies,
Pierre, ciel, feux, faire la mer pier-	Stone, heaven, fire, shall make the
reuse	sea strong,
La mort de sept, terre & marin	The death of seven shall be sudden
subites.	upon land and sea.

At the D-Day Invasion of the Normandy Coast, the rain of missiles fired from new type rocket guns was most intense, also concrete floating docks were sunk at the beaches to form breakwaters and rallying points for the attack.

19

Nouveaux venus, lieu basty sans defence	Newcomers shall build a place without a fence,
Occuper place par lors inhabitable,	And shall occupy a place that was not then habitable,
Prez, maisons, champs villes prendre a plaissance,	They shall at their pleasure take fields, houses and towns,
Faime, peste, guerre, arpent long labourable.	There shall be famine, plague, war, and a long arable field.

Continuing the preceding stanza, the allied invaders occupy the unin-habited fortified coast and advance successfully inward.

20

Freres & Soeurs en plusieurs lieux captifs,	Brothers and sisters shall be slaves in various places,
Se trouveront passer pres du Monarque	And shall pass before the monarch,
Les contempler ses Deux yeux ententifs,	Who shall look upon them with attentive eyes,
Des plaisant voir, meton, frond, nez les marques.	They shall go in heaviness, witness their chin, forehead and nose.

The brutal enslavement of entire populations by the Nazis is explicitly foreshadowed.

21

L'Ambassadeur envoye par Birmes,
A my-chemin d'incogneus repoussez,
De Sel renfort viendront quartre
triremes,
Cordes & chaines en Negrepont
troussez.

The ambassador that was sent in
the small ship,
In the middle of the way, shall be
repulsed by unknown men,
And from the salt, to his rescue
shall come four great ships,
Ropes and chains shall be carried
to the Black Bridge.

Rudolph Hess, personal aide to the German Fuehrer, flew solo to England to contact influential British leaders with his unofficial peace terms which were rejected in a closed session of Parliament.

22

Le Camp Ascop d'Europe partira,
S'adioignant proche de l'isle sub-
mergee,
D'Arton classe phalange pliera
Nombril du monde plus grand voix
subrogee.

The Camp Ascop shall go from
Europe,
And shall come near the sub-
merged Island,
From Arton shall a phalange go
by sea and land
By the navel of the world, a greater
voice shall be subrogated.

Apparently a reference to the submerged continent of Atlantis, originally the Navel, which nourished all ancient human culture.

23

Palais oyseaux, par oyseau dechasse,
Bien tost apres le Prince parvenu,
Combien qu' hors fleuve ennemy
repousse.
Dehors saisi, trait d'oyseau sous-
tenu.

Palace birds, driven away by a bird
Soon after that, the Prince is come
to his own,
Although the enemy be driven beyond the river,
He shall be seized without, by a
trick of the bird.

Parasitic hangers-on will be expelled from the government, by one who is an Eagle, and a master of stratagem.

24

Bestes farouches de faim fleuves tranner,	Wild beasts for hunger shall swim over the rivers,
Plus part du camp encontre Ister sera,	Most of the field shall be near the Ister,
En cage de fer le grand sera traisner,	Into an iron cage he shall cause the great one to be drawn,
Quand rien enfant Germain observera.	When the child of Germany shall observe nothing.

A true prediction of the fate of Adolf Hitler. His demise in the bomb shelter bunker in Berlin is anticipated as his "iron cage."

25

La garde estrange trahyra for teresse,	The garrison of strangers shall betray the fort,
Espoir & ombre du plus haut mariage,	Under the game of hope of a higher union.
Garde deceue, fort prins dans la presse,	The garrison shall be deceived, and the fort taken quickly
Loire, Saone, Rhone, Gar a mort outragez.	Loire, Saone, Rhone, Gardone, outraged by death.

A garrison of extra-terrestrials arrives, defects, and seeks asylum in the "hope of a higher union." Anticipates the arrival of a breed of extra-terrestrials.

26

Pour la faveur que la cite fera,	Because of the favor, the city shall show
Au grand qui tost perdra champ de bataille	To the great one, who soon shall lose the battle,
Puis le sang Pau, Thesin versera	The Thesin shall pour blood into the River Po,
De sang, feux, morts, noyez de coupe de taille.	Of fire, blood, drowned, dead by the edge.

Because of disputes, a town on the River Thesin, a river which empties into the Po, shall see a great slaughter.

27

Le divin verbe sera du ciel frappe
Qui ne pourra proceder plus avant,
Du reserant le secret estoupe
Qu'on marchera par dessus & de-
vant.

The divine voice shall be struck by
heaven
So that he cannot proceed any
further,
The secret of close-mouthed one
shall be closed,
That people shall tread upon and
before it.

A voice, of celestial quality which will be perfection itself, shall appear,
the secret of which will be inviolate.

28

Le penultiesme du surnom de
Prophete,
Prendra Diane pour son jour &
repos,
Loing vauera par frenitique teste,
Et delivrant vn grand peuple d'im-
posts.

The last but one, of the surname
of Prophet,
Shall take Diana for his day and
his rest,
He shall wander far by reason of
his raving head,
Delivering a great people from im-
positions.

Universally, Monday will become a holiday, thereby creating a Satur-
day-Sunday-Monday, three-day holiday. Also, a demented leader will pro-
mote anarchy in a tax-free society.

29

L'Oriental sortira se son siege,
Passer les monts Appenins, voir la
Gaule,
Transpassera le ciel, les eaux &
neige,
En un chacun frappera de sa gaule.

The Oriental shall come out of his
seat,
Shall pass over the Apennines
Mountains and see France,
Shall go over the air, the waters and
the snow,
And shall strike everyone with his
staff.

Nostradamus predicts nuclear bombardment of France and Italy with
multi-warheads released from sites beyond the Urals (Orient?).

30

Un qui les dieux d'Annibal infernaux	One that shall cause the infernal gods of Hannibal
Fera renaistre, effrayeur des humains,	To live again, the terror of mankind,
Oncq plus d'horreur, ne plus dire journaux,	There never was more horror, not to say ill days,
Qu'advint viendra par Babel aux Romains.	Did happen, or shall, to the Romans by Babel.

Babel refers to Eurasia. Oil-rich kingdoms armed with nuclear weaponry terrorize Italy.

31

En Campania Cassilin fera tant	In Campania, the Castilian shall so behave himself,
Qu'on ne verra que d'eau les champs couverts	That nothing shall be seen but the fields covered,
Devant, apres, la pluye de long temps	Before and after, it shall not rain for a long time,
Hors mis les arbres rien l'on temps.	Except the trees, no green shall be seen.

In Campania, the Spaniard will strip the country of all wealth even to the verdure of the fields:

32

Laict, sang, grenovilles escondre en Dalmatie	Milk, blood, frogs shall rain in Dalmatia,
Conflt donne, peste preste, de baliene	A battle fought, the plague near Basel,
Cry sera grand par toute Esclavonie,	A great cry shall be through all Slovakia,
Lors naistra monstre pres & dedans Ravenne.	Then shall be born a monster, near and within Ravenna.

Dalmatia shall be in unrest, and Basel (Switzerland) and Czechoslovakia shall be in fear of an Italian monster.

33

Dans le torrent qui descend de Veronne,
Par lors qu'au Pau guidera son entree,
Un grand naufrage, & non moins
en Garonne,
Quand ceux de Gennes marcheront
leur contree.

In the torrent which descends from
Verona,
About the place where it enters
into the Po,
A great shipwreck, and no less in
Garonne,
When those of Genoa shall go into
their country.

When the Italians of Genoa invade France, they are foredoomed to
destruction and shipwreck.

34

L'ire insensee du combat furieux,
Fera a table par freres le fer luyre,
Les departir mort blesse curieux,
Le fier duelle viendra en France
nuyre.

The mad anger of the furious fight,
Shall cause by brothers the iron to
glisten at the table,
To part them, one mortally
wounded, curious,
The fierce duel shall do harm after
in France.

A quarrel between two allies shall be the cause of a misunderstanding
that will do France much harm.

35

Dans deux logis de nuict le feu
prendra,
Plusieurs dedans estouffez & rostis,
Pres de deux fleuves pour seur il
adviendra,
Sol, l'Arc & Caper, tous seront
amortis.

The fire shall take by night in two
houses,
Many shall be stifled and burnt by
it,
Near two rivers it shall for certain
happen
Sun, Arc, Caper, they shall all be
mortified.

In a town near two rivers, a momentous decision will be made, and
many shall suffer by it—all this to happen when the Sun is in the signs of
Arc (Sagittarius), and Caper (Capricorn).

36

Du grand prophete lettres seront prinses,	The letters of the great prophet shall be intercepted,
Entre les mains du tyran deviendront,	They shall fall into the hands of the tyrant,
Frauder son roy seront les entreprinses,	His undertakings shall be to deceive his king,
Mais ses rapines bien tost le troubleront.	But his extortions shall trouble him soon.

Before the great prophet shall triumph, his plans shall be betrayed by selfish, tyrannical interests.

37

De ce grand nombre que l'on envoyera	Of the great number which shall be sent,
Pour secourir dans le fort assiegez,	To relieve the besieged in the fort,
Peste & famine tous les deux devorera,	Plague and famine shall devour them all,
Hors mis septante qui seront profligez.	Except seventy that shall be beaten.

A warning that biological warfare and fearful destruction of both plant and animal life is imminent.

38

Des condamnez sera fait un grand nombre,	There shall be a great number of condemned men,
Quand les monarques seront conciliez;	When the monarchs shall be reconciled,
Mais l'vn d'eux viendra si mal encombre,	But one of them shall come to such a bad obstacle,
Que guerre ensemble ne seront raliez.	That their reconciliation shall not last long.

Forecasts the Hitler-Stalin non-aggression pact of August 24, 1939, which lasted till June 22, 1941, when Germany attacked Russia.

39

Un an devant le conflit Italique,
Germain, Gaulois, Espagnols pour
le fort,
Cherra l'escole maison de republic,
Ou, hors mis peu, seront suffoquez
morts.

One year before the Italian conflict,
German, French, Spaniards for the
fort,
The schoolhouse of the republic
shall fall,
Where except few, they shall be
suffocated to death.

One year before Italy enters World War III, Paris will be overwhelmed by a terrific onslaught of atomic-powered rockets.

40

Un peu apres non point longue in-
tervalle,
Par mer & terre sera fait grand
tumulte,
Beaucoup plus grand sera pugne
navalle,
Feux, animaux, qui plus feront
d'insulte.

A little while after, without any
great difference of time,
By land and sea shall a great tumult be made,
The sea fight shall be much greater,
Fire and beasts, which shall make
great affront.

Nostradamus forecasts a global conflict, World War III, with nuclear bombardments from ships and submarines.

41

La grand estoile par sept jours
bruslera,
Nue fera deux soliels apparior,
Le gros mastin toute nuict hurlera,
Quand grand pontife changera de
terroir.

The great star shall burn for the
space of seven days,
A cloud shall make two suns appear,
The big mastiff shall howl all night,
When a great Pope shall change
his country.

Pope John Paul II, from Poland, the first pontiff not of Italian birth, was installed in 1978. Also, see V. 79 wherein Nostradamus predicts the selection of a Frenchman as Pope.

42

Coq, chiens, & chats, de sang seront repeus,
Et de la playe du tyrant trouve
mort,
Au lict d'un autre jambes & bras
rompus,
Qui n'avoit pwu mourir de cruelle
mort.

A cock, dogs and cats shall be fed
with blood,
And with the wound of the tyrant
found dead,
In the bed of another with legs
and arms broken,
Who could not die before by a
cruel death.

The French Nation (the Cock), and the rabble of Paris (cats and dogs),
were satiated with the blood of the guillotine and the beheading of
Robespierre, the tyrant of the Revolution. He had been ordered seized by
the Convention, and in the struggle was dangerously wounded, tied on
a strange bed and executed the next morning.

43

Durant l'estoille cheuelue apparente,
Les trois grand princes seront faits
ennemys,
Frappez du ciel paix terre trembu-
lente,
Pau, Tymbre, Undans, serpens sur
le bord mis.

During the time when the hairy
star is apparent,
The three great princes shall be
made enemies,
Struck from heaven, place quaking
earth,
Arne, Tiber, full of surges, serpents
cast upon the shore.

The reappearance of Halley's Comet, due in 1985, will again presage
profound changes in human destiny.

44

L'aigle poussee entour des pavil-
lons,
Par autres oyseaux d'entour sera
chassee,
Quand bruit des cymbres, tubes et
sonnaillons
Rendront le sens de la Dame insensee.

The eagle flying among the tents,
By other birds shall be driven away,
When the voice of cymbals, trum-
pets, and bells
Shall make sense to the lady who
was insane.

The United States planes (eagles) fly over Arab lands (tent dwellers)
but are driven away by other nations who come to the aid of the Arabs.

45

Trop le ciel pleure l'Androgin procree	Heaven bemoaneth too much the Androgyn born,
Pres de ciel sang human respandu,	Near heaven human blood shall be spent,
Par mort trop tarde grand peuple recree,	By death too late a great people shall be diverted,
Tard & tost vient le secours attendu.	Late and soon cometh the help expected.

The Islamic revolution is anticipated but there will be much bloodshed after the death of Khomeini in the early- to mid-1980s.

46

Apres grand troche humain, plus grand s'appreste.	After a great human change, another greater is near at hand.
Le grand moteur les siecles renouvelle,	The great motor, reneweth the ages,
Pluye, sang, laict, famine, feu, & pest;	Rain, blood, milk, famine, sword, plague,
Au ciel veu, courant longue estincelle.	In the heavens shall be seen a running fire with long sparks.

After the great industrial age of steam and electricity, another stupendous revolution will be near. A new type of motive power will accelerate all human progress, but before this happens, there will be seen awesome aerial projectiles causing much suffering. Predicts nuclear space warfare.

47

L'ennemy grand vieil, dueil meurt de poison,	The great and old enemy grieveth, dieth by poison,
Les souverains par infinis subjuguez.	An infinite number of sovereigns conquered.
Pierres plouvoir cachez soubs la toyson,	It shall rain stones, they shall hide under rocks,
Par mort articles en vain sont alleguez.	In vain shall death assert articles.

The old enemy of mankind, war, shall no longer exist, nor will poverty and the allied ills. All this will happen after a period of human suffering.

48

La grand coppie qui passera les monts,	The great army shall pass over the mountains,
Saturne en l'arc tournant du poisson Mars,	Saturn, Aries, Mars turning to the fishes,
Venins chachez soubs testes de Saulmons,	Poisons hidden in the heads of Salmons,
Leurs chefs pendus a fil de polemars.	Their captain hanged with a string of the polemars.

An invasion over the mountains is indicated, with melancholy results, as this force will be driven into the sea and the captain slain.

49

Les conseillers du premier monopole,	The counselors of the first monopoly,
Les conquerans seduits par la Melite,	The conqueror being seduced by the Melite,
Rhodes, Bisance pour leur exposant pole	Rhodes, Bizance, for exposing their pole
Terra faudra le pour suivants de suite.	The ground shall fail the followers of the runways.

In the Latin tongue, Melites are classified as the inhabitants of the Island of Malta. The sense seems to be that Malta will successfully oppose its would-be conquerors who shall not be able to land planes on its runways.

50

Quand ceux d'Hinault, de Gand & de Bruxelles	When those of Hainault, of Gand and Brussels
Verront a Langres le siege devant mis,	Shall see the siege laid before Langres,
Derriere leurs flancs seront guerres cruelles,	Behind their sides shall be cruel wars,
La pluye antique, fera pis qu' ennemys.	The old wound shall be worse than enemies.

War shall devastate various cities of Holland, Belgium and Northern France.

51

Le sang du juste a Londres sera faute, Bruslez par foudres de vingt trois les six, La dame antique cherra de place haute, De mesme secte plusieurs seront occis.	The blood of the just shall be dry in London, Burnt by the fire of three times twenty and six, The ancient dame shall fall from her high place, Of the same sect many shall be killed.

The great Fire of London, 1666, three times twenty and six, with the subsequent falling of the statue of the Virgin from St. Paul's Steeple, is exactly predicted and occurred as forecast.

52

Dans plusieurs nuicts la terre trem-blera, Sur le printemps deux efforts feront suitte, Corinthe, Ephese aux deux mers nagers, Guerre s'esmeut par deux vailants de luitte.	During many nights the earth shall quake, About the spring, two great earth-quakes shall follow one another, Corinth, Ephesus shall swim in the twin seas, War shall be moved by two great wrestlers.

An era of earth-shaking events will occur in the region of Greece, caused by the actions of two great powers.

53

La grand peste de cite maritime Ne cessera que mort ne soit vengee; Du juste sang par pris damne sans crime, De la grand' dame par fainte n'out-rages.	The great plague of the maritime city, Shall not cease until the death be revenged, Of the just blood by price con-demned without crime, Of the great dame not feigned abused.

The great plague of London, 1665, shall be inflicted on the populace, as a revenge for the execution of Charles I.

54

Par gent estrange, & de Romains loingtaine,	By a strange people and a remote nation,
Leur grand cite apres eau fort troublee;	The great city near the water shall be much troubled,
Fille sans main trop different domaine,	The girl without great difference for an estate,
Prins, chef terreure n'auoit este riblee.	The chief frightened, at not having been warned.

This is Pearl Harbor of December 7, 1941, prior to which President Roosevelt had been deceived by the Japanese envoys at the White House.

55

Dans le conflit le grand qui peu valloit,	In the fight the great one, who was but little worth,
A son dernier fera cas merveilleux;	At his last endeavor shall do a wonderful thing,
Pendant qu'Hadrie verra ce qu'il falloit,	While Adria shall see what was wanting,
Dans le banquet pongnale l'orgueilleux.	In the banquet he shall stab the proud one.

The arch criminal seeing that the fight is lost shall go down in ruin, and drag his Italian fellow-conspirator with him.

56

Que peste & glaive n'a s'en definer,	He whom neither plague nor sword could destroy,
Mort dans le pluies sommet du ciel frappe,	Shall die in the rain being stricken by thunder,
L'abbe mourra quand verra ruyner	The abbot shall die when he shall see ruined
Ceux au naufrage, l'escueil voulant grapper.	Those in the shipwreck, striving to catch hold of the rock.

The destruction of Nazi Germany with the removal of Hitler to his bunker for his final hours and death.

57

Avant conflit le grand mur tombera,	Before the battle, the great wall shall fall,
Le grand a mort, mort trop subite & plainte,	The great one to death, too sudden and bewailed,
Nef imparfaict la plus part nagera,	The boat being imperfect the most part shall swim,
Aupres du fleuve de sang la terre tainte.	Near the river the earth shall be dyed with blood.

Anticipates a Sino-Soviet war with destruction of the Great Wall of China. The Yellow River intersects the Great Wall in Shansi Province where, on the outreaches of Peking, the great battle will be fought turning the Yellow River red with blood.

58

Sans pied ne main, dent aygue & forte	Without foot or hand, sharp and strong teeth,
Par globe au fort de port & l'aisne nay,	By a globe, in the middle of the port, and the first born,
Pres du portail desloyal se transporte,	Near the gate shall be transported by a traitor,
Seline luyt, petit grand emmene.	The moon shineth, the little great one carried away.

A kidnapping at night, by an alien, of an infant belonging to a great one, shall take place. This, of course, is the kidnapping of the Lindbergh baby allegedly by Hauptmann.

59

Classe Gauloise par appuy de grand' garde,	The French Fleet by the help of the great guards,
Du grand Neptune, & ses tridens soldats,	Of great Neptune, and his tridented soldiers,
Rongee Provence pour soustenir grand' bande,	Shall gnaw Provence by keeping great company,
Plus Mars, Narbon, par javelots & dards.	Also, Mars shall plague Narbonne by javelots and darts.

The French Fleet, with the aid of the British Navy, shall invade France, at the same time a heavy bombardment shall be kept up.

60

La Foy Punique en orient rompue,
Grand, Jud, & Rosne, Loyre &
    Tag, changeront,
Quand du mulet la faim sera re-
    peve
Classe espargie sang & corps na-
    geront.

The Punic Faith broken in the
    east,
Great Jud, and Rhone, Loire and
    Tagus shall be changed,
When the mule's hunger shall be
    satisfied,
The fleet scattered, blood and
    bodies shall swim.

The false faith broken in the East shall unleash a series of changes,
while the rivers shall be choked with bodies and the fields shall remain
uncultivated.

61

Agen, Tamins, Gironde & la Ro-
    chelle,
O sang Troien mort au port de la
    flesche,
Derriere le fleuve au fort mise l'es-
    chelle,
Pointes, feu, grand meurtre sus la
    breche.

Agen, Tomains, Gironde and Ro-
    chelle,
O Trojan blood, death is at the
    harbor of the arrow,
Beyond the river, the ladder shall
    be raised against the fort,
Points, fire, great murder upon the
    breach.

Civil Wars in France, between various cities, are predicted.

62

Mabus puis tost, alors mourra
    viendra,
De gens & bestes une horrible def-
    faite,
Puis tout a coup la vengeance on
    verra,
Sang, main, soif, faim, quand
    courra la comette.

Mabus shall come, and soon after
    shall die,
Of people and beasts shall be a
    horrible destruction,
Then on a sudden the vengeance
    shall be seen,
Blood, hand, thirst, famine, when
    the comet shall run.

The coming of the comet shall occur in the period of reconstruction,
and there will be vengeance for wrongs inflicted on humanity by selfish
interests.

63

Gauloise, Ausone, bien peu sub-
jugera,
Pau, Marne, & Seine fera perme
l'vrie,
Qui le grand mur contre eux dressera,
Du moindre au mur le grand perdra
la vie.

The French fleet shall a little subdue Ausonne,
Pau, Marne, and Seine shall make
permanent the truth,
Which shall raise a great wall
against them,
From the less to the wall the great
one shall lose his life.

Bordeaux is called Ausonne by Nostradamus because Ausonius, a Latin poet, was born there. During World War II part of the French fleet was sunk in the harbor of Bordeaux, thereby rendering it unfit for use by the Germans (creating a wall against them).

64

Seicher de faim, de soir gent Gene-
voise,
Espoir prochain viendra au defail-
lir,
Sur point tremblant sera loy Gehe-
noise,
Classe au grand port ne se peut
accueillir.

Those of Geneva shall be dried up
with hunger and thirst.
A near hope shall come when they
shall be fainting,
The Hellish law shall be upon a
quaking point,
The navy shall not be able to come
into port.

At Geneva men shall almost succeed in outlawing war and dismantling all navies, but those of Geneva shall have no support.

65

Le parc enclin grand calamite,
Par l'Hesperie & Insubre fera,
Le feu en nef, peste & captivite,
Mercure en l'arc, Saturne fenera.

The park inclineth to great calamity,
Which shall be through Hesperia
and Insubria,
The fire in the ship, plague and
captivity,
Mercury in Aries, Saturn shall
wither.

Spain and the House of Savoy (Italy) are due for a great calamity when the sun is in Mercury and Aries.

66

Par grand dangers le captif
eschappe,
Peu de temps grand la fortune
changee,
Cans le palais le peuple este attrape,
Par bon augure la cite assiegee.

The prisoner escaped through great
danger,
A little while after shall become
great, his fortune being changed,
In the palace the people shall be
caught,
And by a good sign the city shall
be besieged.

Once again, Napoleon's rise and fall. He escaped from Elba on March 1, 1815, and after 100 days re-entered Paris in triumph. His eventual defeat came at Waterloo on June 18, 1815.

67

La blonde au nez forche viendra
commettre
Par le duelle & chassera dehors.
Les exilez dedans fera remettre,
Aux lieux marins commettant les
plus forts.

The fair one shall fight with the
forked nose
In duel, and expel him forth.
The exiles shall be re-established,
Putting the stronger of them in
maritime places.

La Belle France—the Fair One—shall expel the intruder, regaining peace and a strong navy.

68

De l'aquilon les efforts seront
grande,
Sur l'ocean sera la porte ouverte,
Le regne en l'isle sera reintegrande,
Tremblera Londres par voile des-
couverte.

The endeavors of the north shall
be great,
Upon the ocean the gate shall be
open,
The kingdom in the island shall
be re-established,
London shall quake, for fear of sails
discovered.

A very remarkable prophecy. Charles II is re-established on the British throne; and the forays of the Dutch Fleet under Admiral Van Tromp against quaking London are predicted.

69

Le Roy Gaulois par la Celtique dextre
Voyant discorde de la Grand Monarchie,
Sur les trois parts fera fleurir son sceptre,
Contre la cappe de la grand Hierachie.

The French King, by the Celtic right hand,
Seeing the discord of the Great Monarchy,
Upon three parts of it, will make his scepter to flourish,
Against the cap of the great Hierarchy.

Henry II, King of France, seeing the discord in England under the Commonwealth, will aid in the restoration of Charles II.

70

Le dard du Ciel fera son estendue,
Morts en parlant grande execution,
La pierre en l'arbre la fiere gent rendue,
Bruit humain monstre, purge expiation.

The dart of heaven shall make his circuit,
Some die speaking, a great execution,
The stone in the tree, the fierce people humbled,
Human noise, a monster purged by expiation.

The blitz of London is herewith prophesied—blockbusters, scattering stones into trees, will cause instant death and terror, even to the mightiest.

71

Les exiles en Sicile viendront,
Pour deliverer de la gent faim estrange,
Au point du jour les Celtes luy faudront,
La vie demeure a raison Roy se range.

The banished persons shall come into Sicily,
To free the foreign nation from hunger,
In the dawning of the day the Celts shall fail them,
Their life shall be preserved, the King shall submit to reason.

The United Nations adopts the Palestine partition plan with the creation of the state of Israel. The immigrants (banished) flock to Israel and the King (Great Britain) removes its troops.

72

Armee Celtique en Italie vexee,
De toutes parts conflit & grande
  perte,
Romains fuis, o Gaule repousee,
Pres du Thesin, Rubicon pugne in-
  certe.

The French Army shall be vexed
  in Italy,
On all sides fighting, and a great
  loss,
The Romans run away, and though
  France, repulsed
Near the Ticino, by Rubicon the
  fight shall be doubtful.

A French Army will be routed from Italy. Two great battles will be
fought, one by the river Ticino, and one by the Rubicon; but so great will
be the slaughter that the victory will be a doubtful one.

73

Au Lac Fucin de Benacle rivage,
Prins du Leman ou port de l'Ori-
  guion,
Nay de trois bras predict belliq'
  image,
Par trois couronnes au grand Endy-
  mion.

At the Fucin Lake of the Benacle
  shore,
Near the Leman at the port of
  Lorguion,
Born with three arms, a warlike
  image,
By three crowns to the great Endy-
  mion.

Nostradamus confessed his inability to interpret this obscure stanza.
In this later day it becomes clearer. Fascism had its birth near Lake Fucino,
in Central Italy—the three-armed image indicates the strife and war that
will follow.

74

De Sens, d'Autun viendront jus-
  ques au Rhosne
Pour passer outre vers les monts
  Pyrenees,
La gent sortir de la marque d'Au-
  conne,
Par terre & mer le suyvra a grands
  trainnees.

They shall come from Sens and
  Autun, as far as the Rhone,
To go further to the Pyrenees
  Mountains,
The nation shall come from the
  mark of Ancona,
By land and sea shall follow speed-
  ily after.

Sens and Autun, two typical French towns, obviously represent the
spirit of the Maquis during World War II. Harassed by the Nazis,
the Maquis were forced to scatter, sometimes fleeing to the shelter of the
Pyrenees Mountains. The import of the remainder of this quatrain indicates quite clearly the eventual re-birth of France as a united nation.

75

La voix ouye de l'insolit oiseau,
Sur le canon du respiral estage;
Si haut viendra de froment le bois-
seau,
Que l'homme d'homme sera Antro-
pophage.

The noise of the unwanted bird
having been heard,
Upon the canon of the highest
story,
The bushel of wheat shall rise so
high,
That Man shall be a man-eater.

Nostradamus predicts aircraft and spacecraft with military implications of outer space warfare; worldwide famine, inflation, and eventual cannibalism.

76

Foudre en Bourgogne fera cas por-
tenteux,
Que par engin homme ne pourroit
faire,
De leur senat, Sacrifiste fait boy-
teux,
Fera scavoir aux ennemis l'affaire.

Lightning in Burgundy, with marvelous portents,
Which never could have been done
by art,
Of their senate, Sacriste being
lamed,
Shall make known the business to
the enemies.

The Sacriste, or clergy, shall betray the interests of the state to the enemies at a time of stress.

77

Par arcs, feux, poix, & par feu re-
poussez,
Crys, hurlemens sur la minuict
ouys;
Dedans sont mis par les ramparts
cassez,
Par cunicule les traditeurs fuis.

Being repulsed with bows, fires
and pitch,
Cries and howlings shall be heard
about midnight;
They shall get in through the
broken walls,
The betrayers shall run away
through the sewers.

By treason, some shall let in the enemy within the fortress, the betrayers themselves shall escape (the "fifth column" in Madrid).

78

Le grand Neptune du profond de
    la mer,
De gent Punique & sang Gaulois
    mesle,
Les isles a sang, pour le tardif ra-
    mer,
Pluy luy nuira que l'occult mal
    cele.

The great Neptune, in the deep of
    the sea,
Having joined African and French
    blood,
The islands shall be put to the
    sword and the slow rowing
Shall do them more harm than the
    concealed evil.

The threat of invasion of the British Isles by the Nazis in 1942–1943. Actually, their tardiness and turn toward the Russian front cost them the war, since it gave the British time to regroup and provide the United States with air bases from which U.S. aircraft bombarded Germany.

79

La barbe crespe & noire par engin,
Subjuguera la gent cruelle & fiere;
Le grand Chyren ostera du longin,
Tous les captifs par Seline baniere.

The frizzled and black beard by
    fighting
Shall overcome the fierce and cruel
    nation;
The great Henry shall free from
    bonds,
All the captives made by Selim's
    banner.

In 1571, five years after the death of Nostradamus, the Battle of Lepanto was fought. Don Juan of Austria, called the "Frizzled and Black Beard," defeated the Turks. Henry of France also redeemed many of the Christian slaves.

80

Apres conflit du leffe l'eloquence,
Par peu de temps se tramme saint,
    repos,
Point on n'admet les grands a deliv-
    rance,
Des ennemis sont remis a propos.

After the battle, the eloquence of
    the wounded man,
Within a little while shall procure
    a holy rest,
The great ones shall not be de-
    livered,
But shall be left to their enemies'
    will.

More clearly refers to Roosevelt paralyzed ("wounded"), and sustaining a stroke and dying in 1944 (holy rest). The Nazi leaders were left to the will of the victors at the Nuremberg trials.

81

Par feu du ciel la cite pres qu'-
   aduste,
Urna menace encor Deucalion,
Vexes Sardaigne par la Punique
   fuste,
Apres qu Libra lairra son Phaeton.
	By fire from heaven the city shall
	   be almost burnt,
	The waters threaten another Deu-
	   calion,
	Sardinia shall be vexed bv an Afri-
	   can fleet,
	After that Libra shall have left
	   her Phaeton.

Deucalion, a figure in Greek mythology, was the only human left after
the great flood.

A city shall be so destroyed from the air as to be nearly lifeless, all
this to occur when the sign of Libra has reached its last half.

82

Par faim la proye sera loup pris-
   sonnier,
L'assaillant hors en extreme de-
   tresse;
Un nay ayant au devant le dernier,
Le grand n'eschappe au milieu de
   la presse.
	By hunger, the prey shall make the
	   wolf prisoner,
	Assaulting him then in great dis-
	   tress;
	The eldest having got before the
	   last,
	The great one doth not escape in
	   the middle of the crowd.

The Wolf (Rome), being hungry, shall snatch at the prey offered to
it and become entrapped, while the greatest of all shall not escape the
vengeance of the mob.

83

Par le traffic du grand Lyon change,
Et la plus-part tourne en pristine
   ruine,
Proye aux soldats par pille ven-
   dange,
Par jura mont & Sueve bruine.
	The great trade of the great Lion
	   altered,
	The most part turns into pristine
	   ruin,
	Shall become a prey to soldiers and
	   reaped by wound
	In Mount Jura, and Suabia great
	   fogs.

The industrial supremacy of the British Lion shall be endangered. England shall become the scene of pillage and the home of wounded soldiers.
Mt. Jura and Suabia (Germany) shall have some relation to these events.

84

Entre Champagne, Sienne, Flora,
* Ostie*
Six mois neuf jours ne pleuvera une
* goutte;*
L'Estrange langue en terre Dalam-
tie,
Courira sus, gastant la terre toute.

Between Campania, Sienna, Pisa
  and Ostia,
For six months and nine days there
  shall be no rain,
The strange language in Dalmatian
  land,
Shall overrun, spoiling all the country.

There shall be a drought along the east coast of Italy; and adjacent Albania, a Soviet satellite, shall overrun Yugoslavia and possibly Greece.

85

Vieux plains de barbe sous le statut
* severe,*
A Lyon fait dessus l'Aigle Celtique,
Le petit grand trop outre persevere,
Bruit d'armes au ciel, mer rouge
* Lygustique.*

The old plain beard, under the
  severe statue,
Made at Lyon upon the Celtic
  Eagle,
The little great too far perseveres,
Noise of arms in the sky, and the
  Ligurian sea made red.

The power of the German Air Force will for a time sustain the big and little Fuehrers (obviously Hitler and his satellites), and war will rage in the air and on the sea.

86

Naufrage a classe pres d'onde ad-
* riatique,*
La terre esmeu sur l'air en terre
* mis;*
Egypte tremble augment Mahom-
metique,
L'Heraut se rendre a crier est com-
mis.

A fleet shall suffer a shipwreck near
  the Adriatic sea,
The earthquakes, a motion of air
  comes upon the land;
Egypt trembles for fear of the Mohammedan increase,
The Herald surrendering shall be
  commissioned to cry.

In the Mediterranean Seas a fleet will be wrecked, the earth will shake with the sound of terrible weapons, and the air will vibrate with a strange whirring. Mohammedan influence will increase to the detriment of the rulers of Egypt. The mouthpiece shall desert to the Victor and shall be commissioned under him.

87

Apres viendra des estremes contrees,
Prince Germain sur le throsne
dore.
En servitude & par eaux recontrees
La dame serve, son temps plus n'a
dore.

After that, shall come out of the
remote countries,
A German Prince upon a gilded
throne.
The slavery and waters shall meet,
The lady shall serve, her time no
more worshipped.

The accession of the Hanoverian Kings of England commencing with
George I is here indicated.

88

Le circuit du grand fait ruyneux,
Au nom septiesme le cinqueiesme
sera;
D'un, tiers plus grand estrange bel-
liquex,
Mouton, Lutece, Aix garantira.

The circuit of the great deed
ruined,
The seventh name shall be that of
the fifth,
From a third person, one greater,
a warlike man,
Aries shall preserve Paris nor Aix.

The reference here is to the French league against Henry III and Henry
IV, which numbers being joined together, make seven.

89

Un jour seront amis les deux grands
maistres,
Leur grand pouvoir se verra aug-
mente,
La terre nefue sera en ses hauts
estres,
Au sanguinaire, le nombre ra-
compte.

One day the two great masters
shall be friends,
Their great powers shall be in-
creased,
The new land shall be in a flourish-
ing condition,
The number shall be told to the
Bloody Person.

Nostradamus foresees a détente between East and West. China and
the U.S. become allies against their common enemy, Russia, here represented as the "Bloody Person."

90

Par vie & mort change regne d'-Hongrie,	By life and death the kingdom of Hungary shall be changed,
La loy sera sera plus aspre que service,	The law shall be more severe than the service,
Leur grand cite d'Urlemens, plaints & cris,	Their great city shall be full of howling and crying.
Castor and Pollux ennemis dans la lice.	Castor and Pollux shall be enemies in the lists.

Hungary is overrun by Soviet might and becomes a satellite with many repressive laws and civil war.

91

Soleil levant un grand feu on verra,	At the rising of the sun a great fire shall be seen
Bruit & clarte vers Aquilon tendant;	Noise and light tending to the north;
Dedans le rond mort & cris on orra,	Within the round, death and cries shall be heard,
Par glaive, feu, faim, mort les attendans.	Death by sword, fire, hunger watching for them.

Predicts the explosion of a nuclear device at sunrise with the attack coming from the north.

92

Feu, couleur d'or de ciel en terre veu,	Fire the color of gold, from heaven to earth shall be seen,
Frappe du haut n'ay, fait cas merveilleux;	Stricken of the high born, a marvelous event.
Grand meurtre humain, prinse du grand veveu,	Great murder of mankind, great loss of infants,
Morts d'expectacles, eschappe l'orgueilleux.	Some dead looking, the proud one shall escape.

Continues the previous stanza. The marvelous event refers to fission and/or fusion and satisfies Einstein's $E = mc^2$ formula. A savior shall become a great leader.

93

Bien pres du Tymbre presse la Ly-
bitine,
Un peu devant grand inondation;
Le chef du nef prins, mis en la
sentine,
Chasteau, palais en conflagration.

Near the Tiber, going towards
Libia,
A little before a great inundation,
The master of the ship being taken
shall be put into the well,
And a castle and a palace shall be
burnt.

An Italian prophecy. After a great flood the Pope will be disenfran-
chised and his summer residence, the castle (Gondolfo) and the Vatican
will be burned to the ground.

94

Grand Pau, grand mal pour Gau-
lois recevra,
Vain terreur au maritin Lyon,
Peuple infiny par la mer passera,
Sans eschapper un quart d'vn mil-
lion.

Great Po shall receive great harm
from the French,
A vain terror shall seize upon the
maritime lion,
Infinite people shall go beyond the
sea,
Which shall not escape even a
quarter million.

Italian cities shall receive great harm from the French, resulting in an
exodus of their inhabitants.

95

Les lieux peuplez seront inhabi-
tables,
Pour champs avoir grand division;
Regnes livrez a prudens incap-
ables,
Entre les freres mort & dissention.

The populous places shall be deserted,
A great division to obtain fields,
Kingdom given to prudent incapable
When the great brothers shall die
by dissension.

Civil War will cause the populace to leave congested places and seek
rural pursuits.

96

Flambeau ardant au ciel sera veu,
Pres de la fin & principe du
  Rhone,
Famine, glaive, tarde le secours
  poreu,
La Perse tourne envahir Mace-
  doine.

A burning shall be seen by night in
  Heaven,
Near the end and beginning of the
  Rhone,
Famine, sword, too late help shall
  be provided,
Persia shall come against Mace-
  donia.

Incendiary attacks will strike along the Rhone River in France, at the
same time that the war will continue in the East.

97

Romain Pontife garde de t'ap-
  pocher,
De la cite qui deux fleuves arrouse;
Ton sang viendras aupres de la
  cracher,
Toy & les tiens quand fleurira la
  rose.

Roman Pontiff take heed to come
  near,
To the city watered with two rivers,
Thou shall spit there thy blood,
Thou and thine when the rose
  shall bloom.

The attempted assassination of the Pope is forecast at a time when
the rose, the symbol of the French Socialist Party (of Mitterrand), as-
sumes power in 1981. The gunshot wound the Pope sustained tore
through his colon and caused him to spit much blood.

98

Celuy du sang resperse le visage,
De la victime proche sacrifice,
Venant en Leo augure presage,
Mais estre a mort lors pour la fi-
  ancee.

He that shall have his face bloody,
With the blood of the victims near
  to be sacrificed,
The sun coming into Leo shall be
  an augury by presage,
That then he shall be put to death
  for his confidence.

In the summer, one who is great oppressor of humanity shall be cut
down by death, before his bloody plans fully mature.

99

Terroir Romain qu'interpretatoit augure,
Par gens Gauloise par trop sera vexee,
Mais nation Celtique craindra l'-heure,
Boreas, classe trop loing l'avoir poussee.

The Roman country in which the augur did interpret,
Shall be too much vexed by the French nation,
But the Celtic nation shall fear the hour,
The North Wind had driven the navy in too far.

Rome, site of the ancient college of Augurs, shall be at cross swords with the nation of Celts (France).

100

Dedans le isles si horrible tumulte,
Rien on n'orra qu'une bellique brigue,
Tant grand sera des prediteurs l'insulte,
Qu'on se viendra ranger a la grand ligne.

In the islands shall be such horrible tumults,
That nothing shall be heard by a warlike surprise,
So great shall be the assault of the robbers,
That everyone shall shelter himself under the great line.

The London blitz, with all its horrid tumult due to the assault by the Nazis, is clearly foreshadowed even to the seeking of shelter by the populace in the London underground lines.

1

A pres combat & bataille navale,	After the fight and sea battle,
Le grand Neptun a son plus haut beffroy,	The great Neptune in his highest steeple,
Rouge adversaire de peur deviendra pasle	The red adversary shall wax pale with fear,
Mettant le grand Ocean en effroy.	Putting the great Ocean in a fright.

Adumbration of the Japanese attack on Pearl Harbor, December 7, 1941. The "red adversary" is the red circle of the flag of Japan with "great Neptune" represented by the United States fleet.

2

Le divin verbe pourra a la substance,	The divine word shall give to the substance
Comprins ciel, terre, or occult au fait mystique,	Heaven and earth, and gold hid in the mystic fact,
Corps, ame, esprit ayant tout puissance	Body, soul, spirit, having all power,
Tant soubs ses pieds comme au siege Celique.	As well under his feet, as in the Heavenly Seat.

A hermetic stanza, expounding the secret of the philosopher's stone, whereby medieval alchemists sought for a catalyst to convert base metals into gold.

3

Mars & Mercure & l'argent joint ensemble	Mars, and Mercury and silver joined together,
Vers le midy extreme siccite,	Towards the south a great drought,
Au fond d'Asie on dit a terre tremble,	In the bottom of Asia shall be a great earthquake
Corinthe, Ephese lors en perplexite.	Corinthe and Ephesus shall then be in perplexity.

The twentieth-century has already seen great earthquakes take their toll: 1935, India, 50,000 dead; 1939, northern Turkey, 100,000 dead; 1950, India, 30,000 dead; 1962, Iran; 1966, Turkey; 1975, Iran. And in the twenty-first century more natural disasters are forecast.

4

Quand seront proches le deffaut des lunaires,	When default of the luminaries shall be near,
De l'un a l'autre ne distant grandement,	Not being far distant one from another,
Froid, sicite, danger vers les frontieres,	Cold, drought, danger towards the frontiers,
Mesme ou l'oracle a prins commencement.	Even where the oracle had his beginning.

When two great lights shall be nearly eclipsed, privations will be increased, even where the oracle (Nostradamus) was born.

5

Pres loing defaut de deux grand luminaires,	Near the eclipse of the two great luminaries,
Qui surviendra entre Avril & Mars,	Which shall happen between April and March,
O quel cherte! mais deux grande debonnaires,	O what a dearth! But two great ones bountiful
Par terre & sea secourront toutes parts.	By land and sea shall succour them on all sides.

Verification of the preceding verse, naming the time of the event, and also the rehabilitation and relief of the stricken areas by two bountiful nations.

6

Dans temples clos le foudre y entrera,
Les citadins dedans leurs forts
grevez,
Chevaux, boeufs, hommes, l'onde
leur touchera,
Par faim, soif, soubs les plus foibles
armez.

In closed temples the lightning
shall fall,
The citizens shall be distressed in
their strength,
Horses, oxen, men, the water shall
touch the wall,
By hunger, thirst, down shall come
the worst provided.

The temples of learning shall be destroyed, but the citizens will hold
fast, even through much suffering and loss.

7

Les fugitifs feu du ciels aux les
piques,
Conflit prochain des corbeaux s'es-
tatans;
De terre on crie, aide secours ce-
liques,
Quand pres des murs seront les
combatans.

The fugitives, fire of heaven on the
pikes,
A fight near at hand, the ravens
croaking,
They cry from the land, Help, O
heavenly powers,
When near the walls shall be the
fighting men.

The European theatre of conflict in the late twentieth century with
nuclear installations and battles near the (Berlin) Wall. The raven appears
on the German emblem along with the black eagle.

8

Les Cimbres joints avec leurs vois-
ins,
Depopuler viendront presque l'Espagne,
Gens amaffez Guienne & Limou-
sins,
Seront en ligue & leur feront compagne.

The Welsh, joined with their
neighbors,
Shall come to depopulate most of
Spain,
People gathered from French
towns,
Shall be in league with them, and
keep them company.

Eighteenth-century colonizing rivalry between France and England.
Britain blockades the French channel seaports in 1759 preventing France's
reinforcing its troops in America. French and Indian war (seven-years
war, 1756–1763) ends with British domination of Canada and the other
American colonies.

9

Bordeaux, Rouen, & la Rochelle joints,
Tiendront autour de la grand mer Oceane,
Anglois, Bretons, & les Flamens conjoints,
Les chasseront jusques aupres de Rouane.

Bordeaux, Rouen and Rochelle joined together,
Will range about upon the great ocean,
English, Bretons and Belgians, joined together,
Shall drive them away as far as Rouane.

The great fleet of France will be driven from the seas by the British and Flemish fleets.

10

De sang & faim plus grand calamite,
Sept fois s'appreste a la marine plage,
Monech de faim, lieu pris captivite,
Le grand mene, croc, enferree cage.

Of blood and famine, what a great calamity,
Seven times is ready to come upon the sea coast,
Monaco by hunger, the place taken captivity,
The great one carried away, and shut up in a cage.

Monaco was annexed to France in 1793 after having been independent for over 800 years.

11

Les armes battre au ciel longue saison,
L'arbre au milieu de la cite tombe,
Vermine, rongue, glaive en face tyfon,
Lors le Monarque d'Adrie succombe.

Armies shall fight in the air a great while,
The tree shall fall in the middle of the city,
Vermin, scabs, sword, firebrand in the face,
When the Monarch of Venice shall fall.

Whatever else may be interpreted, to conceive of air battles and aircraft is remarkable. Nostradamus was aware of the work of Leonardo da Vinci (1452–1519).

12

Par la tumeur de Heb., Po, Tag.,
Tibre de Rome,
Et par l'estang Leman & Aretin,
Les deux grands chefs & citez de
Garonne,
Prins, morts, noyez, partir, humain
butin.

By the swelling of Heb., Po, Tag.,
Tiber of Rome,
And by Lake Leman, and cities of
Garonne,
The two great leaders will be taken,
Dead, drowned, the human booty
shall be divided.

Heb. is the river Hebrus in Thrace, the river Po is in Italy, and Tag. is the Tagus river in Portugal. Throughout Europe there will be a great disturbance, but the chief instigators will eventually meet violent deaths.

13

Par foudre en l'arche or & argent
fondu,
Des deux captifs l'un l'autre, man-
gera,
De la cite le plus grand estendu,
Quand submergee la classe nagera.

In the ark, lightning, gold and
silver melted,
Of two prisoners, one shall eat up
the other,
The greatest of the city shall be
laid down,
When the navy that was drowned,
shall swim.

When the ships that were sunk are afloat again, the greatest of the enemy's cities will be destroyed by a thunderbolt, leaving them with valueless money.

14

Par le rameau du vaillant personnage,
De France infirme, par le pere infelice,
Honneurs, richesses, travail en son
vieil age,
Pour avoir creu le conseil d'homme
nice.

By the branch of the valiant personage,
Of weak France, by the unfortu-
nate father,
Honours, riches, labour in his old
age,
For having believed the counsel of
a nice man.

Louis Philippe (whose father, descended from the brother of Louis XIV, was executed during the revolution) conspired with General Du-mouriez and was exiled from Paris on the discovery of their plot to over-throw the Republic in 1793. Returning as King in 1830, he later enjoyed great riches and honors.

15

Coeur, vigueur, gloire, le Regne changera,	Heart, vigour and glory shall change the Kingdom,
De tous points, contre ayant son adversaire,	In all points, having an adversary against it,
Lors France enfance par mort sujugera,	Then shall France overcome childhood by death,
Le grand Regent sera lors plus contraire.	The great Regent shall then be most contrary to it.

The courage, vigor and glory of France were reanimated by Napoleon. His greatest adversary was the Pope, "Regent of St. Peter's Temporal Rule."

16

Le Prince Angloise Mars a son coeur de ciel,	The English Prince Mars has his heart from Heaven,
Voudre pour suyure sa fortune prospere;	Will follow his prosperous fortune;
Des deux duels l'vn percera le fiel,	Of two duels, one shall pierce the gall,
Hay de luy, bien ayme de sa mere.	Being hated of him, and beloved of his mother.

Edward VIII, later the Duke of Windsor, abdicated the throne in 1936 in order to marry a commoner.

17

Mont Aventine brusler nuict sera veu,	Mount Aventine shall be seen to burn in the night,
Le Ciel obscur tout a un coup en Flandres;	The Heavens shall be darkened upon a sudden in Flanders,
Quand le Monarque chassera son neveu,	When the Monarch shall expel his nephew,
Lors Gens d'eglise commettront les esclandres.	Then churchmen shall commit scandals.

The burning of Mount Aventine, one of the seven hills of Rome, is probably one of the many symbolizations used by Nostradamus to indicate war.

18

Apres la pluye laict, assez longuette,	After a long rain of milk,
En plusieurs lieux de Reims le ciel touche,	In many places of Rheims the lightning shall fall,
O quel conflit de sang pres d'eux s'appreste!	O what a bloody fight is making ready for them,
Peres & Fils, Roys n'oseront approche.	Father and Son, both Kings, shall not dare to come near.

After a period of peace and plenty, France shall be involved in a bloody war.

19

En Luques sang & laict viendra pleuvoir,	In Lucca it shall rain blood and milk,
Vn peu devant changement de preteur,	A little before the change of the magistrate,
Grand peste & guerre, faim & soif fera voir,	A great plague, war, hunger and thirst shall be seen,
Loing ou mourra leur Prince & grand recteur.	Along where their Prince and great director shall die.

In Italy, there will be alternating periods of depression and prosperity, then a change of chief magistrate, who will bring a plague, followed by war and hunger. The leader will die near Lucca.

20

Par les contrees du grand fleuve Betique	Through the countries of the great River Betis,
Loing d'Ibere au royanne de Grenade,	Far off from Iberia, in the kingdom of Grenada,
Croix respoussees par gens Mahometiques,	Crosses beaten back by Mohammedan people,
Un de Cordobe trahyra la contrade.	One of Cordoba shall at last betray the country.

The River Betis (Latin name) is the River Guadalquivir in Spain, on whose banks is the city of Seville. There Christians shall be betrayed by a Spaniard of Cordova, who will bring in Moors to slaughter his own people.

21

Au Crustamin par Mer Adraitique,
Apparoistra vn horrible poisson,
De face humain & de corps aqua-
tique,
Qui se prendra dehors de l'hame-
con.

Among the Crustacea, near the
Adriatic Sea,
A horrid fish shall appear,
Having a man's face and a fish's
body,
Which shall be taken without a
hook.

The Manatee, an herbivorous aquatic mammal, inhabiting the African
and Amazonian Coasts, often wanders far from his haunts. It was fre-
quently mistaken for a human being, which its upper half resembles.

22

Six jours l'assaut devant citte
donne,
Livres sera forte & aspre bataille,
Trois la rendront & a eux par-
donne,
Le reste a feu & a sang tranche
taille.

Six days shall the assault be in front
of the city,
A great and fierce battle shall be
fought,
Three shall surrender it, and be
pardoned,
The rest shall be put to fire and
sword, cut and slashed.

In 1967 Israel threatened retaliation for Syrian border raids, whereupon
Syria asked for and received Egyptian aid. On June 5, with simultaneous
air attacks against Syrian, Jordanian, and Egyptian air bases, Israel totally
defeated her Arab enemies in what was to be called the Six Day War.
The three Arab nations surrendered and their prisoners of war were freed
and "pardoned."

23

Si, France, passe outre me Ligus-
tique,
Tu te verra en isles & mers enclos,
Mahomet contraire plus mer ad-
riatique,
Chevaux & d'asnes tu rongeras les
os.

If France goeth beyond the Li-
gustic Sea,
Thou shalt see thyself enclosed
with islands and seas,
Mahomet, against thee besides the
Adriatic Sea,
Of horses and asses thou shalt
gnaw the bones.

A warning to France not to advance beyond Corsica, or she will be
attacked on all sides, blockaded and will suffer want of food.

24

De l'entreprinse grande confusion,
Perte de gens, tresor innumerables;
Ty ny dois faire encores tension,
France, a mon dire fais que sois
   recordable.

From the undertaking great confusion,
Loss of people and innumerable
   treasure,
Thou ought not yet to tend that
   way,
France! Endeavor to remember my
   saying.

A continuation of the preceding stanza, and of the same general tenor.

25

Qui au royanne Navarrois parviendra,
Quande le Sicile & Naples seront
   joints,
Bigorre & Landes par Foix lors on
   tiendra,
D'un qui d'espagne sera par trop
   conjoints.

He that shall obtain the kingdom
   of Navarre,
When Sicily and Naples shall be
   joined,
Bigorre and Landes they by Foix
   shall be held,
Of one who shall too much be
   joined to Spain.

At a time when Italy is united, one who is deeply involved with Spain
shall also obtain his way in France.

26

Des Roys & princes dresseront si-
   mulachres,
Augures cruez, esclevez aruspices;
Corne victime doree, & d'azur d'-
   nacre,
Interpretez seront les estipices.

Some kings and princes shall set
   up idols,
Divinations and hollow raised di-
   vinators,
Victim with gilded horns, set with
   azure and mother of pearl,
The looking into the entrails shall
   be interpreted.

Oil-rich Arab kings and princes, idolizing modern technology, shall
soon be victimized. The kings and princes, with golden horns, shall have
their lands uprooted.

27

Prince Lybinique puissant en Occident,
Francois d'Arabe viendra tant enflammer;
Scavans aux lettres sera condescendent,
La langue Arabe en Francois translater.

A Libian Prince being powerful in the West,
The French shall love so much the Arabian language,
That he, being a learned man, shall condescend
To have the Arabian tongue translated into French.

An alliance is forecast between Libya and France with the construction of a nuclear reactor.

28

De terre foible & pauvre parentelle,
Par bout & paix parviendra dans l'Empire,
Long temps regner une jeune femelle,
Qu'onc q'en regne n'en furvint un si pire.

One weak in lands and of poor kindred,
By thrusting and peace shall attain to Empire,
Long time, shall reign a young woman,
Such as in a reign was never worse.

Nostradamus here refers to India in its poverty, ruled by Indira Gandhi.

29

Les deux neveaux en divers lieux nourris,
Navale pugne, terre peirres tombees.
Viendront si haut esleve enguerris,
Venger l'injure ennemys succombez.

The two nephews brought up in divers places,
A sea fight, fathers fallen to the earth.
They shall come highly educated and expert in arms,
To avenge the injury, their enemies shall fall down under them.

Two people of the same blood, from opposite sides of the ocean, shall unite and crush their common enemy. England and the United States fight their common enemy, Nazi Germany.

30

Celuy qu'en luitte & fer au fait bellique,	He who in wrestling and martial deeds,
Aura porte plus grand que luy le prix,	Had carried the prize before his better,
De nuit au lit six luy feront la pique,	By night six shall abuse him in his bed,
Nud sans harnois subit sera surprins.	Being naked and without harness he shall suddenly be surprised.

The Earl of Montgomery, who accidentally killed Henry II of France, in a sporting bout, was afterward beheaded for being one of the Protestant Party.

31

Aux champs de Mede, d'Arabe & d'armenie	In the fields of Media, Arabia and Armenia,
Deux grands copies trois fois s'assembleront,	Two great armies shall meet thrice,
Pres du rivage d'Araxes la mesnie,	Near the shore of Araxes, the people,
Du grand Soliman en terre tomberont.	Of great Solyman shall fall down.

In the Near East, two great armies will clash, the net result of which will be that the Jews will suffer thereby.

32

Le grand sepulchre du peuple Aquitanique,	The great grave of the Aquatanic people
S'approchera aupres se la Toscane,	Shall approach to Tuscany,
Quand Mars sera pres du coing Germanique,	When Mars shall be in the German corner,
Et au terroir de la gent Mantuane.	And in the territory of the Mantuan people.

When war shall be in Italian territory sponsored by the Germans, then the British shall suffer much loss of life in Tuscany.

33

En la cite ou le loup entrera, *Bien pres de la les ennemis seront;* *Copie estrange grand pays gastera,* *Aux monts & Alpes les amis pas-* *seront.*	In the city wherein the wolf shall go, Near the place the enemies shall be, An army of strangers shall spoil a great country, The friends shall go over the mountains of the Alps.

The city of the Italian Wolf shall be besieged and almost overcome by a great army of strangers until assistance shall be rendered by those on the other side of the Alps.

34

Quand le deffaut du soleil lors sera, *Sur le plain jour le monstre sera* *veu;* *Tout autrement on l'interpretera,* *Cherte n'a garde, nul n'y aura pour-* *veu.*	When the eclipse of the sun shall be, At noon day, the monster shall be seen, It shall be interpreted other ways. Then for a dearth, because nobody hath provided for it.

When the eclipse of Liberty shall be at its zenith, a monstrous movement shall arise, disguised as freedom; running its course it will cause great havoc.

35

Du plus profond de l'Occident d'- *Europe,* *De pauvres gens un jeune enfant* *naistra,* *Qui par sa langue seduira grande* *trouppe,* *Son bruit au regne d'orient plus* *croistra.*	Out of the deepest part of the west of Europe, From poor people a young child shall be born, Who with his tongue shall seduce many people, His fame shall increase in the Eastern Kingdom.

Adolf Hitler, born in Austria of poor parents, with his knowledge of mob psychology and powers of speech, was successful in seducing many people, even in the Eastern Empire of Japan.

36

Ensevely non mort apoplectique,
Sera trouve avoir les mains man-
 gees,
Quand la cite damnera l'heretique
Qu'avoit leurs loix ce leur sembloit
 changees.

One burned, not dead, but apo-
 plectical,
Shall be found to have eaten up
 his hands,
When the city shall damn the
 heretical man,
Who as they thought had changed
 their laws.

Former President Nixon's downfall predicted with Watergate scandal.
His "hands" repressed his aides, who suffered for his misdeeds.

37

Avant l'assaut l'oraison prononcee,
Milan prins d'Aigle par embusches
 deceus,
Muraille antique par cannons en-
 foncee.
Par feu & sang a mercy peu receus.

Before the assault, the prayer shall
 be said,
A kite shall be taken by the eagle,
 being deceived by an ambuscade.
The ancient wall shall be beaten
 down with cannons,
By fire and blood, a few shall have
 quarter.

A play on words, Milan being both the name of an Italian city and
a bird.

38

La gent Gaulois & nation estrange,
Outre les monts, prins & profligez;
Au moys contraire & proche de ve-
 dange,
Par les Seigneurs en accord redigez.

The French people and another
 nation,
Being over the mountains, shall die
 and be taken,
In a month contrary to them, and
 near the vintage,
By the Lords agreed together.

In September (grape harvest time), France and Britain give Hitler
an ultimatum and then on September 3, 1939, they declare war on Germany only to suffer great defeats and death in the ensuing three years.

39

Les sept en trois mis en concorde,
Pour subjuguer les Alpes Ape-
  ninnes,
Mais le tempeste & ligure courade,
Les profligent en subiets ruynes.

The seven shall agree together
  within three months,
To conquer the Apennine Alps,
But the tempest and the cowardly
  Genoese,
Shall sink them into sudden ruin.

Seven persons shall take three months to make an agreement to conquer the Italians, but the invasion shall be held up by bad weather.

40

Le grand theatre se viendra redres-
  ser,
Le dez jette & les rets ia tendus,
Trop le premier en glaz viendra
  lasser,
Par arcs prostraits de long temps ia
  fendus.

The great theatre shall be raised
  up again,
The die being cast and the net
  spread,
The first too much in tolling shall
  weary,
Beaten down by bows, who long
  before were split.

Allied reconstruction of Nazi Germany after World War II, United States reconstruction of Japan, as well as Vietnam in the 1970s. So it is with wars and reconstruction. The vanquished are helped by the victors and eventually the victor becomes the vanquished only to recycle the procedure.

41

Bossu sera esleu par le conseil,
Plus hydeux monstre en terre n'-
  aperceu;
Le coup volant prelat crevera l'oeil,
Le traistre au Roy pour fidelle re-
  ceu.

Crook-back shall be chosen by
  council,
A more hideous monster I never
  saw upon earth,
The flying blow shall put out one
  of his eyes,
The traitor to the King shall be
  admitted as faithful.

A hunchback will be elected to a position of power, but will turn out to be a traitor to the King.

42

L'enfant naistra a deux dents en la gorge,	A child shall be born with two teeth in his mouth,
Pierre en Tuscie par pluye tomberont;	It shall rain stones in Tuscany.
Peu d'ane apres ne sera bled ne orge,	A few years after there shall be neither wheat nor barley,
Pour faouller ceux qui de faim failleront.	To feed those that shall faint for hunger.

A world famine will occur after the birth of a prodigy and the falling of bombs in Tuscany.

43

Gens d'alentour de Tarn, Loth, & Garonne,	People that live about the Tar, Lot and Garonne,
Gardez les monts Apennines passer,	Take heed to go over the Apennine Mountains,
Vostre tombeau pres de Rome & d'Anconne	Your grave is near Rome, and Ancona,
Le noir poil crespe fera trophee dresser.	The black-haired ones shall set up a trophy.

The people of France, near the Tar, Lot and Garonne Rivers, are warned not to go into Italy, the home of the Black Shirts. The "trophy" refers to the dishonored corpse of the former duce—Mussolini.

44

Quand l'animal a l'homme domestique,	When the beast familiar to mankind,
Apres grand peine & saute viendra parler;	After great labour, and leaping shall come to speak,
Le foudre a vierge sera si malefique,	The lightning shall be so hurtful to a virgin,
De terre prinse & suspendue en l'air.	That she shall be taken from the earth and suspended in the air.

The dogs of war will be unleashed and shall come to "speak." An explosion in a church shall blow a Virgin skyward, and initiate a period of great uncertainty.

45

Les cinq estrangers entrez dedans le temple
Leur sang viendra la terre profaner;
Aux Thoulouseins sera bien dure exemple
D'un qui viendra les loix exterminer.

The five strangers having come into the church,
The blood shall profane the ground,
It shall be a hard example to those of Toulouse,
Concerning one that came to break their laws.

In Toulouse, five alien officials will be assassinated in a church, profaning the ground according to clerical opinion. The assassins shall be penalized heavily for it.

46

Le Ciel (de Plancus la cite) nous presage
Par clairs insignes & par estoilles fixes,
Que de son change subit s'approche l'aage,
Ne pour son bien ne pour les malefices.

The Heaven foretelleth concerning the city of Plancus,
By clear signs and fixed stars,
That the time of her sudden change is near at hand,
Neither because of her goodness nor wickedness.

The city of Plancus is Lyons, as Plancus was its founder. She is due for a sudden change in fortune.

47

Le vieux monarque dechasse de son regne,
Aux Orients son secours ira querre,
Pour peur de croix ployers son enseigne,
En Mitilens ira par port & par terre.

The old monarch being expelled out of his reign,
Shall go into the East to get assistance
For fear of the crosses he shall fold up his colours,
He shall go into Mitylene by sea and land.

The monarchy and regime in Greece in the twentieth century are noted for upheavals and change. In 1941 and 1967 the king was replaced by a military junta.

48

Sept cens captifs attachez rude-ment,	Seven hundred prisoners shall be tied together,
Pour la moitie meurdrir, donne le fort;	To murder half of them, the lot being cast,
La proche espoir si promptement,	The next hope shall come quickly,
Mais non si tost qu 'vne quinzi-esme mort.	And not so quickly, but fifteen shall be dead before.

An example of Nazi brutality to both civilians and combatants in World War II.

49

Regne Gaulois tu seras bien change,	French Kingdom, thou shalt be much changed,
En lieu estrange l'Empire translate,	The Empire is translated in an-other place,
En autres loix & moeurs seras range,	Thou shalt be put to other manners and laws,
Rouen & Chartres te fera bien du pire.	Rouen and Chartres shall do the worst they can to thee.

A prediction of the change of form of Government in France from Monarchy to Republic.

50

La Republic de la grande Cite	The Republic of the great City,
A grand rigueur ne voudra consen-tir;	With great harshness shall not con-sent,
Roy sortir hors par trompette cite,	That the king should go out being summoned by the city's trum-pet,
L'eschelle au mur la cite repentir.	The ladder shall be put to the wall and the city repent.

The government of Paris, with great harshness, summons and arrests the King and the Bastille is stormed.

51

Paris conjure un grand meurtre commettre *Blois le fera sortir en plain effect;* *Ceux d'Orleans voudront leur chef remmettre,* *Angiers, Troye, Langres leur foront grand forfait.*	Paris conspireth to commit a great murder, Blois shall cause it to come to pass, Those of Orleans will set up their head again, Angiers, Troyes, Langres will do them harm.

In Paris the Reign of Terror commences, and spreads to all France. The house of Orleans again will ascend the Throne, in the person of Louis Philippe.

52

En la campagne sera si longue pluye, *Et en l'Apoville si grande siccite,* *Coq verra l'Aigle mal acomplie,* *Par lyon mise sera en extremite.*	In the country shall be so long a rain, And in Apulia so great a drought, The cock shall see the eagle with his wing injured, And by him the lion brought to extremity.

The Gallic Cock shall see the American Eagle and the British Lion in great peril, during a long war.

53

Quand le plus grand emportera le pris, *De Nuremberg, D'usburg, & ceux de Basle,* *Par Agripine chef Frankfort repris,* *Traverseront par Flamens jusque'en Gale.*	When the great one shall carry the prize, Of Nuremberg, Augsburg and Basle, By Agrippina the Chief of Frankfort shall be taken, They shall go through Flanders as far as France.

When the Commander in Chief shall have captured other German cities, after the blasting of Cologne (ancient name, Agrippina), the German Commander shall be captured and imprisoned in France.

54

L'un des plus grands fuyra aux Espagnes,
Qu'en longue playe apres viendra feigner,
Passant copies par les hautes montainges,
Devastant tout & puis en paix regner.

One of the greatest shall run away into Spain,
That shall cause a wound to bleed long,
Leading armies over high mountains,
Destroying all, and afterwards shall reign.

Argentina's Juan Peron was sent into exile in 1955 and fled to Spain. Argentina was then thrown into chaos. Peron was brought back to power in 1973 subduing the junta.

55

En l'an qu'un ceil en France regnera,
La court sera en vn bien fascheux trouble,
Le grand de Bloys son amy tuera,
Le regne mis en mal & doubte double.

In the year that one eye shall reign in France,
The court shall be in the very same trouble,
The great one of Blois shall kill his friend,
The kingdom shall be in an evil way, and double doubt.

A King blind in one eye shall rule a court that is just as shortsighted.

56

Mantauban, Nismes, Avignon, & Besiers,
Peste, tonnerre, & gresle a fin de Mars,
De Paris pont Lyon mur, Montpellier,
Depuis six cens et sept vingt, trois parts.

Montauban, Nismes, Avignon and Besier.
Plague, lightning and hail at the end of March,
The Bridge of Paris, the Wall of Lyons, and Montpellier shall fall
From six hundred and seven score three parts.

Widespread destruction shall befall France in March, in 12,143 parts.

57

Sept fois changer verrez gent Britannique,	Seven times you shall see the English to change,
Taints en sang en deux cents nonante an;	Dyed in blood, in two hundred and ninety years,
France, non, point par appuy Germanique,	Not France, by the German support,
Aries double son Pole Bastarnan.	Aries doubles his Bastarnan Pole.

Thought to represent the period from 1555 to 1845, 290 years, and predicts greater English upheavals such as: (1) Protestant reversion under Elizabeth in 1558; (2) Stuart succession in 1663; (3) Commonwealth in 1649; (4) Restoration in 1660; (5) Bloodless revolution in 1688; (6) Hanoverian succession in 1714; and (7) The Reform Bill in 1832.

58

Aupres du Rhin des Montagnes Noriques,	Near the Rhine out of the Norick Mountains,
Naistra un grand de gens trop tard venu,	Shall be born a great one, though come too late.
Qui deffendra Saurome & Pannoniques,	Who shall defend the Poles and Hungarians,
Qu'on ne scaura qu'il sera devenu.	So that it shall not be known what is become of him.

Forecasts the birth and demise of Hitler. His burned body in the Berlin bunker was never found and his "defense" of Poland and Hungary were, in reality, conquests.

59

Barbare Empire par le iters usurpe,	A Barbarian Empire shall be usurped by a third person,
La plus part de son sang mettre a mort,	Who shall put to death the greater part of his kindred,
Par mort senile, par luy, le quart frappe,	By death of old age, the fourth shall be stricken by him,
Par peur que sang par la sang en soit mort.	For fear that blood should not die by blood.

Iran, under Khomeini, in a blood bath, shall end with the death of Khomeini in old age. Moslem revolution will be followed by a counterrevolution with the restoration of the monarchy.

60

Par toute Asie grande proscription,
Mesme en Mysie, Lysie, & Pam-
  phylie;
Sang versera par dissolution,
D'un jeunne noir remply de felon-
  nie.

Through all Asia shall be a great
  proscription,
The same as in Mysia, Lydia, and
  Pamphilia,
Blood shall be spilled by the de-
  bauchness
Of a dark young man, full of trea-
  son.

An Asiatic shall force the hordes of Asia into armies of conquest.

61

La grand bande & secte crucigere
Se dressera en Mesopotamie,
Du proche fleuve compagnie legere,
Que telle loy tiendra pour ennemis.

The great band and sect wearing
  a cross,
Shall rise up out of Mesopotamia,
Near the river shall be a light
  company,
Which shall hold that law for the
  enemy.

A great organization, with some kind of cross as its emblem, shall
emerge in a land between two rivers. Near one of those rivers, some traitors
shall give the enemy assistance.

62

Proche del Duero par mer Cyrene
  close,
Viendra percer les grands Monts
  Pyrenees,
La main plus courte & sa percee
  close,
A Carcassonne conduira ses me-
  nees.

Near the Duro, closed by the Cy-
  renian Sea,
Shall come to pierce the Pyrenees
  Mountains,
The shorter hand and his pierced
  criticism,
Shall in Carcassone lead his plot.

Near the Duro River, which rises in Spain near the Pyrenees Mountains, the one with a short hand shall lay a plot that will eventually embroil
the strongest fort of France, Carcassone.

63

Romain pouvoir sera du tout a bas,
Son grand voisin imiter ses vestiges;
Occultes haines civiles & debats
Retarderont aux bouffons leurs folies.

The Roman power shall be quite put down,
His great neighbor shall follow his steps,
Secret and civil hatreds and quarrels,
Shall stop the buffoon's folly.

The collapse of power under Mussolini, the Roman buffoon, was quickly followed by the downfall of his neighbor, Hitler.

64

Le chef de Perse remplira grands Olchades,
Classe trireme contre gent Mahometique,
De Parthe & Mede, & pilliers les Cyclades,
Repos long temps au grand port Ionique.

The head of Persia shall fill great merchant ships,
A fleet of warships against the Mohammedan folk,
From Parthia and Media they shall come to plunder the Cyclades,
A long rest shall be on the Ionic port.

A great potentate shall send a fleet of warships supported by a well-supplied group of commercial vessels against a Moslem League, and commerce in the Mediterranean shall be stagnant.

65

Quand le sepulcre du grand Romain trouve
Le jour apres sera esleu pontife,
Du senat gueres il ne sera prouve
Empoisonne son sang au sacre scyphe.

When the sepulcher of the great Roman shall be found,
The next day after a Pope shall be elected,
Who shall not be much approved by the Senate,
Poisoned, his blood in the sacred chalice.

On the election of a Pope, great turmoil will arise due to disapproval by the Senate, and he will be assassinated.

66

Le grand Baillif d'Orleans mis a
  mort,
Sera par un de sang vindicatif;
Demort merite ne mourra ne par
  fort,
Des pieds & mains mal le faisoit
  captif.

The great Bailiff of Orleans, shall
  be put to death,
By one of revengeful and vindictive
  blood,
He shall not die of a deserved death
  nor by chance,
But the disease of being tied hand
  and foot. hath made him prisoner.

The grim Rabelaisian humor of the age is well displayed here. A great personage of France will meet an untimely death at the hands of a vindic-tive enemy.

67

Une nouvelle secte de Philosophes,
Mesprisant mort, or, honneurs &
  richesses,
Des monts Germains seront fort
  limitrophes,
A les ensuyure auront appuy &
  presses.

A new sect of Philosophers shall
  rise,
Despising death, gold, honors and
  riches,
They shall be near the mountains
  of Germany,
They shall have abundance of others to support and follow them.

In Central Germany, near the Alps, a fanatical group shall arise and they will find much support and many followers throughout the world.

68

Peuple sans chef d'Espagne & d'-
  Italie,
Morts profligez dedans la Cherre-
  nosse,
Leur duict trahy par legere folie,
Le sang nager par tout a la traverse.

A people of Spain and Italy with-
  out a head
Shall die, being overcome in the
  Crimea,
Their saying shall be betrayed by
  their folly,
The blood shall swim all over at
  random.

The Blue Division, Fascist Spain's contribution to Hitler's invasion of Russia in World War II, was entirely exterminated on this front.

69

Grand exercite conduit par jou-
venceau,
Se viendra rendra aux mains des
ennemis;
Mais le vieillard nay au demy pour-
ceau.
Fera Chalon & Mascon estre amis.

A great army led by a young man,
Shall yield itself in the hand of
enemies,
But the old man born at the sign
of the Half Hog,
Shall cause Chalon and Mascon to
be friends.

Great French Armies shall be betrayed to the enemy by an inexperi-
enced leader, but the old man shall reunite all.

70

Le grand Bretagne comprinse d'An-
gleterre,
Viendra par eaux si fort a inondre,
La ligue neufue d'Ausonne fera
guerre,
Que contre eux il se viendront
bander.

Great Britain including all of England,
Shall suffer so great an inundation
of waters,
The new league of Italy shall make
wars,
So that they shall stand against
them.

Great Britain will be endangered by floods; and at the same time a
New League, under Italian leadership, will threaten her shores.

71

Ceux dans les Isles de long temps
assiegez,
Prendront vigueur force contre ennemis,
Ceux par behors morts de faim
profligez,
En plus grand faim que jamais
seront mis.

Those in the Islands that have long
been besieged,
Shall take vigour and force against
the enemies,
Those without shall die for hunger,
being overcome,
They shall be put in greater famine
than they were before.

The Dutch, being besieged, shall break the dikes to flood the country,
confronting the enemy with great danger and hunger.

72

Le bon vieillard tout ensevely,
Pres du grand fleuve par faux soup-
con,
Le nouveau vieux de richesse ennobly,
Prins a chemin tout l'or de la ran-
con.

The good old man shall be buried
alive,
Near the great river by a false suspicion,
The new old one made noble by
his riches,
The gold of his ransom shall be
taken in the way.

Winston Churchill, after leading Great Britain through its World
War II victory, was "buried alive" by a landslide election after the war.
Along the "great river" (Thames) this was predicted and occurred in
1945 with the ouster of Churchill and the Conservative Party.

73

Quand dans le regne parviendra le
boiteux,
Competiteur aura proche bastard,
Luy & le regne viendront si fort
rogneux
Qu'ains qu'il guerisse son fait sera
bien tard.

When the lame man shall attain
to the kingdom,
He shall have a bastard for his near
competitor,
He and his kingdom shall be so
scabby,
That before he be cured it will be
late.

An event that must have taken place in the days of Nostradamus, and
which has now lost its meaning.

74

Naples, Florence, Fayence, &
Imole,
Seront en termes de telles fascherie,
Que pour complaire aux malheu-
reux de Nole
Plaint d'avoir fait a son chef mo-
querie.

Naples, Florence, Fayenza and
Imola,
Shall be put into so much distress,
For being complacent to the un-
happy one of Nola,
Who was complained of for having
mocked his superior.

Italian factional disputes shall flourish because of the lack of unity
among the people.

75

Pau, Veronne, Vincence, Sara-
gousse,
De Glaives atteints terriors de sang
humides;
Peste si grande viendra a la grande
gousse,
Proches securs & bien loings les
remedes.

Pau, Verona, Vicenza, Saragossa,
Hit by the Sword, the country shall
be moist with blood,
So great a plague and so vehement
shall come
That though help be near, the
remedy shall be far off.

Italian cities, suffering from plague and famine, shall not be able to
avail themselves of assistance, due to lack of organization.

76

En Germanie naistront diverses
fectes,
S'approchant fort de l'heureux pa-
ganisme,
Le coeur captif, & petites receptes
Feront retour a payer le vray disme.

In Germany shall divers sects arise,
Coming very near to happy paganism,
The heart captivated and small re-
ceivings,
Shall open the gate to pay the true
tithe.

A prophetic description of the rise of the pagan doctrine of National
Socialism.

77

Le tiers climat sous Aries comprins,
L'ans mil sept cens vingt & sept en
Octobre,
Le Roy de Perse par ceux d'Egypte
prins,
Conflit, mort, perte, a la croix
grand opprobre.

The third climate comprehended
under Aries,
In the year 2025, the 27th of October,
The King of Persia shall be taken
by those of Egypt,
Battle, death, loss, a great shame
to the Christians.

In the year 2025, under a special chronology enumerated by Nostradamus, strange events are to take place in the Orient much to the shame
of Christians.

78

Le chef d'Escosse, avec six d'Alemagne, Par gens de mer Orientaux captifs, Traverseront le Calpre & Espagne, Present en Perse au nouveau Roy craintif.	The chief of Scotland with the six of Germany, Shall be taken prisoners by the seamen of the east, They shall go through the Calpre and Spain, And shall be made a present in Persia to the new fearful king.

A new King of the East shall arise and conquer many lands, and a British leader and six Germans shall be brought to him as hostages, by way of Calpre (the Straits of Gibraltar).

79

Le grand criard sans honte audacieux, Sera esle gouverneur de l'armee. La hardiesse de son contentieux, Le pont rompu, Cite de peur pasmee.	The great squawker proud without shame, Shall be erected governor of the army, The stoutness of his competitor, The bridge being broken, the city shall faint for fear.

A great demagogue, without shame or conscience, shall obtain control of the army, much to the citizens' helpless fear.

80

Erins, Antibe villes autour de Nice, Seront vastees fort, par mer & par terre, Les sauterelles terre & mer vent propice, Prins, morts, trossez, pillez sans loy de guerre.	Ervins, Antibes, and the towns about Nice, Shall be destroyed by land and sea, The grasshoppers shall have the land, the sea and wind favorable. They shall be taken, killed, thrust up, plundered, without law of war.

The tremendous air fleets used in the invasions of France are clearly indicated.

81

L'ordre fatal sempiternel per chaine,
Viendra tourner par ordre consequent;
Du port Phocen sera rompue la chaine,
La cite prinse l'ennemy quant & quant.

The fatal and eternal order by chain,
Shall come to turn by consequent order,
Of Port Phocen the chain shall be broken,
The city taken, and the enemy presently after.

Phocen is the ancient name for Marseilles. Her harbor chain shall be pierced by the enemy and the port captured.

82

Du regne Anglois l'indigne dechasser,
Le conseiller, par ite mis a feu;
Ses adherants iront si bas trasser,
Que le bastard sera demy receu.

From the English Kingdom the unworthy driven away,
The councillor through the anger shall be burnt,
His partners shall creep so low,
That the bastard shall be half received.

Rudolf Hess, as peace messenger to the Cliveden Set, was repudiated both by his master and also by his British partners, after the chief councillor of Britain, Winston Churchill, burnt with anger on the notification of his errand.

83

Les longs cheveux de la Gaule Celtique,
Accompagnez d'estranges nations,
Mettront captif la gent Aquitanique,
Pour succomber a leurs intentions.

The long hairs of the Celtic Gaul,
Joined with foreign nations,
Shall put in prison the Aquatanic agent,
To make him yield to their intentions.

The intellectuals of Northern France, with the support of foreign agents, shall stamp out and imprison their opponents that favor the opposite view.

84

La grand cite sera bien desoles,
Des habitans un seul ny demourra,
Mur, sexe, temple, & vierge violee,
Par fer, feu, peste, canon, peuple
  mourra.

The great city shall be made very
  desolate,
Not one of the inhabitants shall be
  left in it,
Wall, sex, church and virgin ravished,
By sword, fire, plague, cannon,
  people shall die.

Predicts the destructive removal of the Berlin Wall with fierce consequences.

85

La Cite prinse par tromperie &
  fraude,
Par le moyen d'un beau jeune at-
  trappe,
L'assaut donne, Raubine pres de
  Laude,
Luy & tours morts pour avoir bien
  trompe.

The City shall be taken by cheat
  and deceit,
By means of a fair young one
  caught in it,
Assault shall be given Raubins near
  Lande,
He and all shall die for having de-
  ceived.

A forecast of the Fifth Column as originally conceived during the
Spanish Civil War, 1936–1939. Later it was used by Hitler in his invasion
of the lowlands of Holland, Belgium, and Luxembourg.

86

Un chef d'Ausonne aux Espagnes
  ira,
Par mer fera arrest dedans Marseille,
Avant sa mort un long temps lan-
  guira,
Apres sa mort l'on verra grand
  merveille.

A chief man of Ausonne shall go
  into Spain,
By sea, he shall stay at Marseilles,
He shall languish a great while before his death,
After his death great wonders shall
  be seen.

Nostradamus makes constant reference to happenings connected with
Ausonne (the city of Bordeaux), and for the most part they are veiled
in obscurity.

87

Classe Gauloise n'approches de
Corsegne,
Moine de Sardaigne tu t'en repen-
tiras,
Trestous mourrez frustres de l'Aide
grogne,
Sang nagera captif ne me Croiras.

French Fleet, do not come near
unto Corsica,
Much less to Sardinia, thou shalt
repent it.
All of you shall die frustrate of the
help of the great ships,
Blood shall swim, being captive
thou shalt not believe me.

The French are warned to steer clear of Corsica, the birthplace of Napoleon.

88

De Barcelone par mer si grande
armee,
Toute Marseille de frayeur trem-
blera,
Isles saisies, de mer aide fermes,
Ton traditeur en terre nagera.

From Barcelona, shall come by sea,
so great an army,
That Marseilles shall quake for
fear,
The Islands shall be seized, help by
sea shut up
Thy traitor shall swim to land.

The victory of a force coming from Barcelona is predicted.

89

En ce temps la sera frustre Cypres,
De son secours de ceux de Mer Ae-
gee,
Vieux trucidez, mais par Mesles &
Lipre,
Seduict leur Roy, Royne plus out-
ragee.

At the time Cyprus shall be frus-
trated,
Of its help, those of the Aegean
Sea,
Old ones shall be killed, but by
Mesles and Lipre,
Their King shall be seduced, and
the Queen more wronged.

The island of Cyprus will be besieged and a constant source of conflict between the Turks and Greeks. In 1944 the (U.S.) ambassador was killed on Cyprus.

90

Le grand Satyre & Tygre d'Hycar-
nie,
Don presente a ceux de l'Ocean,
Un chef de classe iastra de Carmanie,
Que prendra terre au Tyrran Phocean.

The great Satyr and Tiger of Hir-
cania,
Shall be a gift presented to those
of the Ocean,
An admiral of a fleet shall come
out of Carmania,
Who shall land in the Thyrren
Phocean.

Hercynia, in ancient geography, is the mountain region of Germany.
The Tiger will be taken prisoner and turned over to a maritime people.
Carmania (now called Kerman) is in Persia, and the Thyrren Phocean
is Marseilles.

91

L'arbre qu'estoit nar si long temps
seche,
Dans une nuict viendra a reverdir;
Son Roy malade, prince pied
estache,
Craint d'ennemis fera voiles
bondir.

The tree that has been long dead
and withered,
In one night shall grow green again,
His king shall be sick, the prince
shall have his foot tied,
Being feared by his enemies, he
shall make his sail rebound.

A metaphorical description of a renaissance of human understanding
to take place in the future.

92

Le monde proche du dernier pe-
riode,
Saturne encor tard sera de retour;
Translat empier devers nation
Brodde,
L'oeil arrache a Narbon par autour.

The world being near its last period,
Saturn shall come yet late to his
return,
The empire shall be changed into
black nations,
Narbonne shall have her eye picked
out by a hawk.

Along toward the end of the world, the dark nations shall reign supreme. This presages the rise of the black (African) and third world
nations.

93

Dans Avignon tout le chef de l'Empire,
Fera appreste, pour paris desole;
Tricast tiendra l'Annibalique ire,
Lion par change sera mal console.

In Avignon all the chief of the Empire
Shall stay, by reason of Paris being desolate,
Tricast shall stop the Hanniballic anger,
The Lion by change shall be illcomforted.

Avignon, once the seat of the Papal government (1307–76), shall again have power, after Paris is desolate by reason of an African (Hanniballic) anger, and much to the disappointment of the British Lion.

94

De cinq cens ans plus compte l'on tiendra,
Celuy qu'estoit l'ornament de son temps,
Puis a un coup grande clarte donra,
Que par es siecle les rendra tres contens.

For five hundred years no account shall be made
Of him who was the ornament of his time.
Then of a sudden he shall give so great a light,
That for that age he shall make them to be most contented.

Nostradamus here refers to himself. After 500 years, i.e., in 2055, his predictions will all have been shown to bear fruit.

95

La Loy Moricque on verra deffaillir,
Apres une autre beaucoup plus seductive,
Boristhenes premier viendra faillir.
Par dons & langues une plus attractive.

We shall see the Moorish Law to decline,
After which another more seducing shall arise,
Boris Thenes shall be the first that shall fall,
By gifts and tongue that law shall be most seducing.

This forecasts the decline of Islam and the rise of Communism at the basin of the Dnieper (Boristhenes) River. A brilliant prediction in view of recent events in Afghanistan.

96

Chef de Fossan aura gorge couppes,
Par le ducteur du Limier & L'-
  curier,
Le fait patre par ceux du mont
  Tarpee,
Saturns en Leo treziesme Fevrier.

The chief of Fossan shall have his
  throat cut.
By the leader of Hunt and Grey-
  hound,
The act committed by those of the
  Tarpian Rock,
Saturn being in Leo, the Thir-
  teenth of February.

The chief man of Northern Italy shall be hunted down by those of
Rome and shall die an infamous death.

97

Nouvelle loy terre neuve occuper,
Vers la Syrie, Judee & Palestine,
Le grand Empire Barbare corruer,
Avant que Phebe son siecle deter-
  mine.

A new law shall occupy a new
  country,
Towards Syria, Judea and Palestine,
The great Barbarian Empire shall
  fall down,
Before Phoebe makes an end of
  her course.

The Arab Confederacy shall fall of its own weight and a new Judea
and Palestine shall occupy the place of Syria. This anticipates the origin
of the state of Israel and confusion within the Arab confederacy.

98

Deux Royals Freres si fort guer-
  royeront,
Qu'entre 'eux sera la guerre si mortelle,
Qu'un chacun places fortes occupe-
  ront,
De regne & vie sera leur grand querelle.

Two Royal Brothers shall war so
  much one against the other,
That the war between them shall
  be mortal,
Each of them shall seize upon
  strong places,
Their quarrel shall be concerning
  kingdom and life.

An incident to occur before the World Organization of Nations out-
laws wars for personal aggrandizement.

99

Aux champs herbeux d'Alein & du Varneigne,	In the meadow fields of Alein and Varneigre,
Du Mont Lebron proche de la Durance,	Of the brown mountains near the Durance,
Camp des deux parts conflit sera si aigre.	Armies on both sides, the fight shall be so sharp,
Mesopotamie deffaillira en la France.	That Mesopotamia shall be wanting in France.

France is to be the battleground for contending armies in a decisive engagement involving heavy losses.

100

Entre Gaulois le dernier honore,	He that least honored among the French,
D'homme ennemy sera victorieux,	Shall be conqueror of the man that was his enemy,
Force & terrior en moment explore,	Strength and terror shall in a moment be tried,
D'un coup de trait quand mourra l'envieux.	When the envious shall be killed with an arrow.

The underprivileged classes of France shall emerge victors after overthrowing a conspirator who will continue to be their greatest enemy. Also forecasts the rise of General de Gaulle and his victory over Hitler and the subsequent assassination of Admiral Darlin in 1942.

1

Cela du reste de sang non espande, Venise quiert secours esntre donne, Apres avoir bien long temps at- tendu, Cite livree au premier cornet sonne,	There shall be a remnant of blood unspilt, Venice shall seek for succour, After having long waited for it, The city delivered at the first sound of the trumpet.

This concerns the Siege of Candia which lasted for twenty years. The Venetians fought a losing battle with the Turks, expecting, but never receiving, help from the Christian Princes, until eventually the city was compelled to surrender.

2

Par mort la France prendra voyage a faire, Classe par mer, marcher monts Pyrenees. Espagne en trouble, marcher gent militaire, Des plus grand; dames en France emmences.	By reason of a death, France shall undertake a journey, They shall have a fleet at sea, and march towards the Pyrenees, Spain shall be in trouble by an army, Some of the greatest ladies in France carried away.

Conditions in France and Spain during a revolutionary period are forecast in this verse as it occurred in France in 1789 and in Spain in 1936 after which Franco assumed power in 1939.

3

D'Arras & Bourges de Brodes grands enseignes.
Unplus grand nombre de Gascons battre a pied,
Ceus long du Rhosne saigneront les Espagnes,
Proche du mont ou Sagonte s'assied.

From Arras and Bourges many colours of Dark men shall come.
A great number of Gascons shall go on foot,
Those along the Rhone shall let Spain blood,
Near the mountain where Saguntus is seated.

Saguntus, a city in Spain destroyed by the Romans, is here used symbolically. Men of the dark Mediterranean races shall roam widespread over Spain, to her detriment.

4

L'impotent prince fasche, plainte & querelles,
De raps & pilles par coqs & par Lybiques,
Grand est par terre, par mer infinies voilles,
Seule Italie sera chassant Celtiques.

The impotent prince angry complains and quarrels,
Concerning rapes and plunderings done by the cocks and Libiques.
Great trouble by land, by sea infinite sails.
Italy alone shall drive away the French.

Referring to France and Italy's African colonizing exploits; France in the northwest (Algeria and the Sahara and Italy in Ethiopia and Somaliland).

5

Croix paix soubs un, accomply divin verbe,
Espaigne & Gaule seront unis ensemble,
Grand clad proche, & combat tresacerbe,
Coeur si hardy ne sera qui ne tremble.

The cross shall have peace, under an accomplished divine word,
Spain and France shall be united together,
A great battle near hand and a most sharp fight,
No heart so stout but shall tremble.

A bold prophecy. Spain remained neutral in World War II and later was unallied to East and West in the political struggle in the latter half of the twentieth century, but is here visualized as joining with France and NATO (North Atlantic Treaty Organization). Spain and France shall have military, political, and eventually economic ties, i.e., the Common Market.

6

D'habits nouveaux apres fait la treuve,
Malice tramme & machination;
Premier mourra qui en sera la preuve,
Couleur Venise insidiation.

After the new clothes shall be found out,
There shall be malice, plotting and machination,
He shall die the first, that shall make trial of it.
Under cover of Venice, shall be a conspiracy.

A new form of government, by conspirators cast out by the Italians, shall destroy the innovators.

7

Le mineur fils du grand & hay prince,
De lepre aura a vingt ans grande tache;
De dueil sa mere mourra bien trist & mince,
Et it mourra la ou tombe chef lasche.

The younger of the great and hated prince,
Being twenty years old shall have a great touch of leprosy,
His mother shall die of grief, very sad and lean,
And he shall die of the disease loose flesh.

The King of Rome, Napoleon II, son of Napoleon and the ill-fated Marie Louise, died in 1832 after a wasting sickness lasting a year, at the age of twenty.

8

La grand cite d'assaut pront & re-pentin,
Surprins de nuict, gardes inter-rompus,
Les excubies & veilles saint Quin-tin,
Trucidez gardes & les portails rompus.

The great city shall be taken by a sudden assault,
Being surprised by night, the watch being beaten,
The court of guard and watch of St. Quentin,
Shall be killed, and the gate broken.

The battle of St. Quentin was one of the decisive fights in World War I. The Germans almost broke the Allied lines at this point in a surprise attack.

9

Le chef du camp au milieu de la presse,
D'un coup de flesche blesse aux cuisses.
Lors que Geneve en larmes & en detresse
Sera trahy par Lozan & Souysses.

The chief of the camp in the middle of the crowd,
Shall be wounded with an arrow through both his thighs,
When Geneva being in tears and distress,
Shall be betrayed by Lausanne and the Swiss.

The Treaty of Lausanne completely sabotaged the work of the League of Nations.

10

Le jeune Prince accuse feucement,
Mettra en trouble le camp & en querelles;
Meurtry le chef pour le sous Levement,
Scepter appraiser, puis guerur escrouelles.

The young prince being falsely accused,
Shall put the camp in trouble and in quarrels.
The chief shall be murdered by the tumult,
The scepter shall be appeased and later cure the king's evil.

Edward, Prince of Wales, was accused of being a Nazi sympathizer. He was feted by the Germans in the 1930s and later became an apologist for their aggressive behavior. His reign as King Edward VIII did not last very long.

11

Celuy qu'aura couvert de la grand cappe,
Sera induit a quelque cas patrer;
Le douze rouges viendront souiller la nape,
Soubs meurtre, meurtre se viendra perpetrer.

He that shall be covered with a great cloak
Shall be induced to commit some great act,
The twelve red ones shall soil the table cloth,
Under murder, murder shall be committed.

Evidently a phase of the activities of the Roman Catholic Church— the Twelve Red Ones, being Cardinals. and the Great Cloak, the Pope.

12

Le camp plus grand de route mis en suit,
Geures plus outre ne sera pourchasse;
Ost recampe & region reduicte
Puis hors de Gaule du tout sera chasse.

The greatest camp being in disorder shall be routed,
And shall be pursued not much after,
The army shall encamp again, and the troops set in order,
Then afterwards, they shall be wholly driven out of France.

The invasions of France by the Germans are here predicted. Nostradamus forecasts the eventual, and complete, victory of France.

13

De plus grand perte nouvelles rapportees,
Le rapport fait le camp s'eslongnera,
Bendes unies encontre revoltes,
Double phalange, grand abandonnera.

News being brought of a great loss,
The report divulged, the camp shall be astonished,
Troops being united and revolted,
The falange shall forsake the great one.

The revolt of the Spanish Army and Falangists against Franco's dictatorial power is predicted. The founder and chief Falangist spokesman, Jose Antonio Primo de Rivera, finally forsook Franco and was executed in November 1936.

14

La mort subiette du premier personnage,
Aura change & mis un autre au regne,
Tost, tard venu a si haut & bas age,
Que terre & mer faudra qu'on le craingne.

The sudden death of the chief man,
Shall cause a change, and put another in the reign soon,
Late come to so high a degree in a low age,
So that by land and sea he must be feared.

The sudden death of the president is here predicted with his successor being a younger vice-president. The assassination attempt on President Reagan in 1981 very closely approaches this forecast.

15

D'ou pensera faire venir famine,
De la viendra le rassassiement;
L'oeil de la mer par avare canine,
Pour de l'un l'autre donra huille
froment.

Whence one thought to make
famine to come,
Thence shall come the fullness,
The eye of the sea through a dog-
gish covetousness,
Shall give to both, oil and wheat.

Nostradamus here anticipated off-shore oil drilling and recovery of huge oil reserves from the "eye of the sea." Further, the sea provides many food products in the form of fish, vegetables, and minerals, but oil is the key to this quatrain.

16

La cite franche de liberte fait serue,
Des profligez & resueurs fait azyle;
Le Roy change a eux non si pro-
terue,
De cent seront devenus plus de
mille.

The free city from a free one shall
become slave,
And of the banished and dreamers
shall be a retreat,
The King changed in mind shall
not be so unfavorable to them,
Of one hundred, they shall become
more than a thousand.

The Free City of Danzig, enslaved by the Nazis, was nevertheless highly favored by them, even to the point of expansion.

17

Changer a Beaune, Nuis, Chalons,
Dijon,
Le Duc voulant amender la barree,
Marchant pres fleuve, poisson bec
de Plongeon,
Verra la queue port sera serree.

There shall be a change at Beaune,
Nuis, Chalons, Dijon,
The Duke going about to raise
taxes,
The Merchant near the river shall
see the tail
Of a fish, having the bill of a loon,
the door shall be shut.

A submarine shall be seen by a merchant, in a river near the above-mentioned French towns.

18

Des plus lettrez dessus les faits celestes,
Seront par princes ignorans reprou-
  vez,
Punis d'edit, chassez comme celestes,
Et mis a mort la ou seront trouvez.

The most learned in the celestial
  sciences,
Shall be found fault with by ignorant princes,
Punished by a proclamation, chased
  away as wicked,
And put to death where they shall
  be found.

The warnings of learned scientists shall be scoffed at by ignorant persons in power, even to the point of persecution.
    Nostradamus explicitly charges mankind to heed the warnings of science
and take atomic power under international control.

19

Devant Rouan d'insubres mis le
  siege,
Par terre & mer enfermez les passages,
D'Haynaut, & Flandres de Gand
  & ceux de liege,
Par dons levees raviront les rivages.

Before Rouen, a siege shall be laid
  by the Italians,
By sea and land the passages shall
  be shut up.
Those of Hianaut, Flanders, Ghent
  and Liege,
With them troops shall plunder
  the sea shore.

An incident in the many wars among the European nations is here
forecast.

20

Paix ubertre long temps Dieu
  louera,
Par tout son regne desert la fleur
  de lis
Corps morts d'eau, terre la l'on
  apportera,
Aperant vain heur d'estre la ense-
  velis.

Peace and plenty shall be not long
  praised,
All the time of his reign the Fleur
  de Lys shall be deserted,
Bodies shall die by water, earth
  shall be bought,
Hoping vainly to be there buried.

This predicts a great famine and flood in France, here signified by the
Fleur de Lys.

21

Le changement sera fort difficile,
Cite province au change gain sera,
Coeur haut, prudent mis, chasse
    luy habile,
Mer, terre, peuple, son estat chang-
    era.

The change shall be very hard,
The city and country shall gain by
    the change,
A high prudent heart shall be put
    in, the unworthy expelled,
Sea, land, people, its state shall
    change.

This is the forecast of a revolution that will bring great and good changes
to all.

22

La grand copie que sera dechassee,
Dans un moment fera besoin au
    Roy,
La foy promise de loing sera faus-
    see,
Nud se verra en piteux desarroy.

The great army that shall be re-
    jected,
In a moment shall be wanted by
    the King,
The faith promised afar off shall
    be broken,
So that he shall be left naked in a
    pitiful case.

A continuation of the preceding stanza, this tells of the disintegration of
the royal army and their desertion from the King to the cause of revolution. Note the changes in Iran.

23

La Legion dans la Marine classe,
Calcine, Magne, souphre & poix
    bruslera,
Le long repos de l'asseuree place,
Port Selyn chercher feu les con-
    sumera.

The Legion in the Maritime Fleet,
Calcining greatly, shall burn brim-
    stone and pitch,
After a long rest in the secure
    place,
They shall seek Port Selyn, but
    fire shall consume them.

A terrific assault by a great fleet equipped with weapons employing
potent chemical agents, shall attack a country which has long enjoyed
peace and security. They shall attack the great Port of LES N. Y. but
will be repulsed by weapons even more terrible.

24

Ouy sous terre saincts d'ame voix
  fainte,
Humains flamme pour divin voir
  luire,
Fera des seuls de leur sang terre
  tainte,
Et les saints temples pour les im-
  pure destruire.

Underground, shall be heard the
  feigned voice of a holy dame,
A human flame to see a divine one
Shall cause the ground to be dyed
  with their own blood,
And the holy temples to be destroyed by the wicked.

Under the guise of a so-called reform movement, humanity shall suffer
much and the holy temples shall be destroyed.

25

Corps sublimes sans fin a l'oeil visi-
  bles,
Obnubiler viendra par ses raisons,
Corps, front comprins, sense, chef
  & invisibles,
Dimineant les sacrees oraisons.

The celestial bodies that are always
  visible to the eye,
Shall be darkened for these reasons,
The body with the forehead, sense
  and head invisible,
Diminishing the sacred prayers.

The occult knowledge of "prophets" shall flourish during this period,
keeping alive the hope of the world.

26

Lou grand cyssame le levera d'al-
  belhos,
Que non sauran don, te signen ven
  guddos,
Denech l'embousq, sou gach sous
  las treilhos,
Cuitad trahido per cinq lengos non
  nudos.

The great swarm of bees shall rise,
And it shall not be known whence
  they come,
Towards the ambush, the jay shall
  be under a trellis,
A city shall be betrayed by five
  tongues not naked.

"Bees" refers to the emblem Napoleon used for his dynasty, and
the "five" relates to the Directory which gave way to Napoleon's Consulate.

27

Salon, Mansol, Tarascon de Sex l'arc,
Ou est debout encor la pyramide;
Viendront livrer le prince d'Denemark,
Rachapt honny au temple d'Artemide.

Salon, Mansol, Tarascon of six arches
Where is still standing the pyramids,
Shall come to deliver the Prince of Denmark,
A shameful ransom shall be paid into the temple of Artemis.

Provincial towns are named here and the arches mentioned are the ruins of ancient triumphal monuments erected by the Romans. Artemis is another name for Diana.

28

Lors que Venus du Sol sera couvert;
Soubs l'esplendeur sera forme occulte;
Mercure au feu les aura descouvert,
Par bruit bellique sera mis a l'insulte,

When Venus shall be covered by the Sun,
Under the splendor it shall be an occult form,
Mercury in the fire shall discover them,
And by a warlike rumor shall be provoked.

An allegorical stanza, wherein is expressed a hidden formula, having to do with the preparation of the elixir to make the hermetic Philosophers' Stone. The same occult directions are given also in the three stanzas following.

29

Le Sol cache eclipse par Mercure,
Ne sera mis que pour le ciel second;
De Vulcan Hermes sera faite pasture,
Sol sera veu pur rutilant & blond.

The Sun shall be hid and eclipsed by Mercury,
And shall not be set but for the second heaven,
Hermes shall be made a prey to Vulcan,
And after that the Sun shall be seen pure, shining and yellow.

The Sun refers to gold, the second heaven means a furnace. "Hermes a prey to Vulcan" indicates the elixir to be put upon the fire in a furnace.

30

Plus unze fois Lune Sol ne voudre,
Tous augmentez & baissez de de-
gree;
Et si bas mis que peu d'or le secret,
Qu'apres faim, peste, decouvert le
secret.

The Moon will not have the Sun
above eleven times.
Then both shall be increased and
lessened in degree,
And put so low, that a little gold
shall be sewed up,
So that hunger and plague, the
secret shall be discovered.

Alchemical formulae and processes are clearly expressed for the adept,
but are most confusing for the uninitiated.

31

Le lune au plain de nuict sur le
haut mont
Le nouveau sophe d'vn seul cerveau
l'a veu,
Par ses disciples estre immortel se-
mond,
Yeux au midy, en sens mains corps
au feu.

The moon at full by night upon
the high mount,
The new Sophe with only one
brain has seen it,
Invited by his disciples to become
immortal,
His eyes to the south, his hands
and body to the fire.

The Sophe, or wise man, has mastered the secret. Invited to reveal
the secret to the world, by his disciples, he refuses, and does not become
immortal.

32

Es lieux & temps chair au poisson
dorna lieu.
La loy commune sera faite au contraire,
Vieux tiendra fort, puis este du
milieu,
Le Panta, Choina Philon, mis fort
arriere.

In places and times, flesh shall give
way to flesh,
The common law shall be made
against it;
The old man shall stand fast, then
being taken away,
Then all things common among
friends, shall be set aside.

Panta, Choina Philon are Greek words expressed best in English as
"All things are common among friends."

33

Jupiter joint plus Venus qu'a la
Lune,
Apparoissant   de   plentitude
blanche;
Venus cachee sous la blancheur
Neptune,
De Mars frappee par la grande
branche.

Jupiter being more joined to Venus
than to the Moon,
Appearing in a full whiteness,
Venus being hid under the whiteness of Neptune,
Stricken by Mars through the en-
graved branch.

Those in power shall give more time to the pleasures of Venus than to
other activities, until the sudden onslaught of a war.

34

Le grand mene captif d'estrange
terre,
D'or enchaine au Roy Chyren of-
fert;
Qui dans Ausonne, Milan perdra la
guerre,
Et tout son ost mis a feu & a fer.

The great one brought prisoner
from a far country,
And chained with gold, shall be
presented to Henry, the ruler,
Being then at Ausonne, Milan shall
lose the war,
And all its host put to fire and
sword.

Nostradamus interprets this literally, thus: When a great one from a
far country shall be brought prisoner chained with gold, and presented to a
King called Henry (for Chyren by transposition of letters is Henryc) who
then shall be at Bordeaux (Ausonne), Milan shall lose a great army.

35

Le feu estaint les vierges trahyront,
La plus grand part de la bande vou-
velle;
Poudre a fer, lance les seule Roy
garderont,
Etrusque & Corse de nuict gorge
allumelle.

The fire being put out, the virgins
shall betray,
The greatest part of the new troup,
Gunpowder, lance, shall keep only
the King,
In Etruria and Corsica by night,
throats shall be cut.

An insurrection in Italy (Etruria) is predicted, which shall take place at
night and be betraved by Virgins.

36

Les jeux nouveaux en Gaule redressez,	The new plays shall be set up again in France,
Apres victoire de l'Insubre campagne,	After the victory obtained in Piedmont,
Monts d'Esperie, les grands liez troussez,	Mountains of Spain, the great ones tied and carried away,
De peur trembler la Romaine & Espagne.	Romania and Spain shall quake for fear.

France again will be triumphant after a victory over the Italians. Over the mountains of Spain the great ones will be carried away, and Romania and Spain shall be in terror.

37

Gaulois par sauts, monts viendra penetrer.	The French by leaping shall go over the mountains,
Occupera le grand lieu de l'Insubre; Au plus profond son ost fera entrer,	And shall seize the great mount of the Savoyard, He shall cause his army to go to the furthermost,
Gennes, Monech pousseront classe rubre.	Genoa, and Monaco shall set out their red fleet.

This prophecy concerns Henry IV, King of France, who went over the Alps and conquered the dukedom of Savoy.

38

Pendant que Duc, Roy, Roynes occupera,	While the Duke shall keep the King and Queen busy,
Chef Bizantin captif en Samothrace;	A great man of Constantinople shall be prisoner in Greece;
Avant l'assaut l'vn l'autre mangera,	Before the assault one shall eat up the other,
Rebours ferre suyura de sang la trace.	Rebours armored shall trace one by the blood.

A great tumult and riot will occur before the city is captured by the heavily armored enemy.

39

Les Rodiens demanderont secours,	The Rhodians shall ask for aid,
Par le neglet de ses hoirs delaisses,	Being forsaken by the neglect of her heirs,
L'empire Arabe revalera son cours,	The Arabian Empire shall slack his course,
Par Hesperies la cause radressee.	By means of Spain the care shall be mended.

The current dominance of Saudi Arabia in the world of petro-dollars is seen to decline.

40

Les forteresses des assiegez ferrez,	The strong places of the besieged shall be pressed.
Par poudre a feu profondes en abysme;	By gunpowder they shall be plunged into a pit,
Les proditeurs seront tous vifs ser-rez,	The traitors shall be shut up alive,
Onc aux Sacristes n'advint si pit-eux scisme.	Never did happen so pitiful a schism to the Sacristes.

By Sacristes, the author means that part of the Roman Catholic Church that is in charge of the books and property. There seems to be a warning implicit in this quatrain—probably slanted against those whom Nostradamus considered heretics.

41

Gynique sexe captive hostage,	Gynical sexe being captive by hostage,
Viendra de nuict custodes dece-voir;	Shall come by night to deceive her keepers,
Le chef du camp deceu par son lignage,	The chief of the camp being deceived by her language,
Liarra le genre, fera piteux avoir.	Shall keep her folks, a thing pitiful to behold.

Clearly foretells the trials and tribulations of Patti Hearst in America in 1974–1975. Ransom and gifts in millions were provided before this radical group was disbanded.

42

Geneve & Langres par ceux de Chartre & Dole	Geneva and Langres by those of Chartres and Dole,
Et par Grenoble captif au Montli-mar,	And by one of Grenoble captive at Montlimar,
Seysset, Losanne par fraudulente dole,	Seisset, Lausanne by a fraudulent deceit,
Les trahyront par or soixante marc.	Shall betray them for thirty pounds weight of gold.

The sense is plain, and this apparently refers to struggles among various towns in France.

43

Seront ouys au ceil les armes battre,	There shall be heard in the air the noise of weapons,
Celuy an mesme les divins enne-mis,	And in that same year, the divines shall be enemies,
Voudront Loix Sainctes injuste-ment debatre,	They shall unjustly put down the Holy Laws,
Par foudre & guerre bien croyants a mort mis.	And by thunder and the war, true believers shall die.

A religious war shall break out, during which many true believers will suffer again. Also, once again, Nostradamus forecasts aerial warfare.

44

Deux gros de Mende de Rhodes & Millaud,	Two great ones of Mendes, of Rhodes and Millaud,
Cahors, Limoges, Castre malo sep-mano,	Cahors, Limoges, Castres, an evil week,
De nuech l'intrado, de Bordeaux an cailhau,	By might the entry shall be from Bordeaux one cailhau,
Par Perigort au toc de la Campano.	Through Perigort at the ringing of the bell.

Towns near the home of Nostradamus are spoken of here, and a rising against tax collectors is indicated.

45

Par conflit Roy Regne abandonnera,
Le plus grand chef faillira au besoing,
Morts profligez, peu en rechappera,
Tous destranchez, un en sera tes-
moin.

By a battle the King shall forsake
his kingdom,
The great commander shall fail in
time of need,
They shall be killed and routed,
few shall escape,
They shall be cut off, one only shall
be left for a witness.

The Battle of Waterloo is prognosticated. His defeat in this battle, due
to the failure of Marshal De Grouchy, caused Napoleon to lose his Empire.

46

Bien deffendu le fait par excellence,
Garde toy Tours de ta proche
ruyne;
Londres & Nantes par Rheims fera
deffence
Ne passez outre au temps de la
bruyne.

The fact shall be defended excel-
lently well,
Tours beware of thy approaching
ruin,
London and Nantes by Rheims
shall stand upon their defence,
Do not go further in foggy weather.

Tours, a city in France, is warned of a fog, and told to beware of her
approaching ruin.

47

Le noir farouche quand aura essaye,
Sa main sanguine par feu, fer arcs,
tendus,
Trestout le peuple sera tant effraye,
Voir les plus grands par col & pieds
pendus.

The wild black one, after he shall
have tried,
His bloody hand by fire, sword,
bended bows,
All the people shall be so fright-
ened,
To see the greatest hanged by neck
and feet.

Astonishingly accurate prophecy of the fate of Mussolini, Leader
of the Black Shirts. After his death, he was hung by his feet for the mob to
spit upon.

48

Plannure, Ausonne fertille, spacieuse,	The plain about Bordeaux fruitfu? and spacious,
Produira tahons si tant de sauterelles,	Shall produce so many hornets and so many grasshoppers,
Clarte solaire viendra nubileuse,	That the light of the sun shall be darkened,
Ronger le tout, grand peste venir d'elles.	They shall fly so low, a great plague shall come from them.

The prediction here is of the D-Day invasion of France by the Allies in World War II; at that time the sky was darkened by the tremendous concentration of Air Power.

49

Devant le peuple sang sera respandu,	Before the people, blood shall be spilt,
Que du haut ciel ne viendra eslongner;	Who shall not come far from high heaven,
Mais d'un long temps ne sera entendu,	But it shall not be heard of for a great while,
L'esprit d'un seul le viendra tesmoigner.	The spirit of one shall come to witness it.

Foretells the assassination of a great leader, John F. Kennedy, later followed by his alter ego (spirit) brother, Robert Kennedy. The "great while" implies some passage of time between the death of Robert Kennedy and the attempt on the life of the last brother, Edward Kennedy.

50

Libra verra regner les Hesperies,	Libra shall see Spain to reign,
De Ciel & Terra tenir la monarchie,	And have the monarchy of Heaven and Earth,
D'Asie forces nul ne verra peries,	Nobody shall see the forces of Asia to perish,
Que sept ne tiennent par rang la Hierarchie.	Till seven have kept the Hierarchy successively.

A Spaniard shall attain to the office of Pope, Monarch of Heaven and Earth, and after seven of the Spanish faction have reigned successively then the Asiatic forces will be overcome.

51

Un Duc cupide son ennemy ensuyvre,	A Duke being earnest in the pursuit of his enemy,
Dans entrera empeschant la phalange,	Shall come in, hindering the falange,
Hastez a pied si pres viendront poursuyvre,	Hastened on foot shall follow them so close,
Que la journee conflit pres de Gange.	That the day of the battle shall be near Ganges.

Lord Louis Mountbatten was appointed Viceroy of India in 1947. Later strife between India and Pakistan is predicted as well as the murder of Mountbatten. His yacht was blown up by terrorists.

52

En cite obsessee aux murs hommes & femmes,	In a besieged city, men and women being upon the walls,
Ennemys hors le chef prest a soy rendre,	The enemy without, the governor ready to surrender,
Vent sera fort encontre les gens-d'-armes,	The wind shall be strong against the soldiers
Chassez seront par chaux, poussiere & cendre.	They shall be driven away by lime, dust and cinders.

Urban America has become a series of besieged cities whose militia is under constant harassment by urban guerrillas fighting with stones, debris, etc.

53

Les fugitifs & bannis revoquez,	The fugitive and banished men being rescued,
Peres & fils grand garnissant les haut poits;	Fathers and sons garnishing the high walls,
Le cruel pere & les siens suffoquez,	The cruel father and his retinue shall be suffocated,
Son fils plus pire submerge dans le puis.	His son, being worse, shall be drowned in the well.

The reappearance of evil men, banished because of their part in the making of war, once again shall usher in a period of destruction.

54

Du nom qui onc ne fut au Roy Gaulois,	Of a name that a French King never was,
Jamais ne fut un foudre si craintif,	There was never a lightning so much feared,
Tremblant l'Italie l'Espagne & les Anglois,	Italy shall tremble, Spain and the English
De femme estrangers grandement attentif.	He shall be much taken with women strangers.

This concerns Napoleon Bonaparte, even to his many amours.

55

Quand la Corneille sur tour de brique jointe,	When the Crow on a tower made of brick
Durant sept heures ne fera que crier,	For seven hours shall do nothing but cry,
Mort presagee de sang statue tainte,	Death shall be foretold and the statue dyed with blood,
Tyran meurtry, aux Dieux peuple prier.	Tyrant shall be murdered and the people pray to the Gods.

A tyrant will be murdered after a "crow on a tower of brick" (broadcast studio?) shall cry out the news.

56

Apres victoire de raibeuse langue,	After victory over a raging tongue,
L'esprit tempte en tranquil & repos;	The mind that was tempted shall be in tranquility and rest,
Victeur sanguin par conflit fait harangue,	The bloody emperor by battle shall make a speech,
Rostir la langue, & la chair & les os.	And roast the tongue, the flesh and the bones.

Adolf Hitler was known to have had a raging tongue. Line 4 predicts the extermination ovens of Nazi Germany. A grim but true prediction.

57

Ignare envie du grand Roy sup-
portee,
Tiendra propos deffendre les escrits;
Sa femme non femme par un autre
tentee,
Plus double deux ne feront ne cris.

Ignorant envy being supported by
the great King
Shall talk of prohibiting the writings,
His wife no wife, being tempted
by another,
Shall no more than they two prevail by crying.

Envious persons, in favor with the King, shall attempt to suppress
learning. But the King's mistress shall persuade him to the contrary, and
shall prevail.

58

Soleil ardant dans le gosier coller,
De sang humain arroser terre
Etrusque;
Chef seille d'eau mener son fils
filer,
Captive dame conduite en terre
Turque.

Burning sun shall pour into the
throat,
This human blood shall wet the
Etruscan ground,
The chief pail of water shall lead
his son to spin,
A captive lady shall be carried into
the Turkish country.

Molten gold shall be poured into a throat and human blood shall
flow. Because of this, a great water carrier shall make his son effem-
inate, and a captive lady shall be exiled.

59

Deux assiegez en ardante fureur,
De soif estaints pour deux plaines
tasses,
Le fort limen & vn viellard resueur,
Aux Genois de Nizza monstrera
trasse.

Two besieged, being in a burning
heat,
Shall die for thirst, want of two
cups full,
The fort being filed, an old doting
man,
Shall show to the Genoese the way
to Nice.

Nice shall be taken by the Italians through the help of an old dotard.

60

Les sept enfans en hostage laissez,
Le tiers viendra son enfant trucider;
Deux par son fils seront d'estoc percez,
Gennes, Florence, lors viendra enconder.

The seven children being left in hostage,
The third shall come to kill his child,
Two by their sons shall be run through,
Genoa and Florence shall second them.

Evidently this indicates an event which occurred during the time of Nostradamus, and according to him should be understood by all.

61

Le vieux mocque, & prive de sa place,
Par l'estranger qui le subornera;
Mains de son fils mangees devant sa face
Les freres a Chartres, Orleans, Rouen trahyra.

The old man shall be baffled and deprived of his place,
By the stranger that shall have instigated him,
But his sons shall be eaten before his face,
The brother at Chartres, Orleans shall betray Rouen.

Foretells the downfall and disgrace of President Nixon. His "sons" refers to his party colleagues who were soundly defeated after the Watergate scandal.

62

Un coronel machine ambition,
Se saisira de la plus grande armee;
Contree son prince fainte invention,
Et descouvert sera sous sa ramee.

A colonel intrigues a plot by his ambition,
He shall seize upon the best part of the army,
Against the prince he shall have a feigned invention.
And shall be discovered under the harbour of the vine.

Nostradamus here predicts the downfall of the dictator of Libya, Col. Muammar el-Qaddafi. His rivalry with the Saudi princes shall remain fierce until his demise.

63

L'armee Celtique contre les Mon-
  tagnars,
Qui seront sceus & prins a la pipee;
Paysans irez pouseront tost faug-
  nars,
Precipitez tous au fil de l'espee.

The Celtic army shall go against
  the Highlanders,
Who shall stand upon their guard,
  and being taken with trickery,
The peasant being angry, shall roll
  down the stones,
They shall be all put to the edge
  of the sword.

The heroic peasant rebellion of the Austrian Tyrol, under Andreas
Hofer, against the French Republican Army, is here prophesied by our
author.

64

Le deffaillant en habit de bou-
  geois,
Viendra le Roy tempter de son offense,
Quinze soldats la plus part osta-
  gois,
Vie derniere & chef de sa chevance.

The guilty, in a citizen's habit,
Shall come to tempt the King concerning his offense,
Fifteen soldiers the most part hostages,
Last shall be his life and the best
  part of his estate.

Note the Iranian crisis with the United States in 1979–1980. The King
(Shah) had to abdicate under the pressure of the citizenry and the American hostages were taken and eventually freed.

65

Au deserteur de la grand forteresse,
Apres qu'aura son lieu abandonne;
Son adversaire fera si grand pro-
  vesse,
L'Empereur tost mort sera con-
  damne.

To the deserter of the great for-
  tress,
After having forsaken his place,
His adversary shall do great feats,
That the Emperor shall soon be
  condemned to death.

Treachery shall play a prominent part in the destruction of a future
emperor who will be condemned to a living death.

66

Soubs couleur fainte de sept'testes
    rasees,
Seront semez divers explorateurs;
Puys & fontaines de poison arrou-
    sees,
Au fort de Gennes humaine devora-
    teurs.

Under the feigned colour of seven
    shaven heads,
Shall divers spies be framed,
Wells and fountains shall be sprin-
    kled with poison,
In the fort of Genoa shall be hu-
    man devourers.

Seven priests or monks shall poison the well of public opinion, and in Genoa shall be those that live on human flesh.

67

L'an que Saturne & Mars eagaux
    combust,
L'air fort seiche, longue trajection;
Par feux secrets, d'ardeur grand lieu
    adust
Peu pluye, vent, chaud, guerres,
    incursions.

In the year that Saturn and Mars
    shall be fiery,
The air shall be very dry, in many
    countries,
By secret fires, many places shall
    be burnt with heat,
There shall be scarcity of rain, hot
    winds, wars, wounds.

A prognostication that Saturn (Commerce) and Mars (War) shall have a Roman Holiday.

68

En l'an bien proche eslongue de
    Venus,
Les deux plus grands de L'Asie &
    d'Affrique;
De Rhin, & Hyster, qu'on dira sont
    venus.
Cris, pleurs a Malte & coste a Ly-
    custique.

In the year that is to come soon,
    and not far from Venus,
The two greatest ones of Asia and
    Africa,
Shall be said to come from the
    Rhine and Ister,
Crying and tears shall be at Malta
    and on the Italian Shore.

From the shores of the Rhine and Danube shall come those who will bring woe on Malta and also to the Italian shores.

69

La cite grande les exilez tiendront,
Les citadins morts meurtris & chassez;
Ceux d'Aquilee a Parmee promet-
tront,
Monstrer l'entree par les lieux non
trassez.

The banished shall keep the great
city,
The citizens being dead, murdered
and expelled,
Those of Aquelia shall promise to
Parma,
To show the entrance by unknown
paths.

Aquelia and Parma are Italian cities and, according to Nostradamus,
they will be involved in inter-city warfare.

70

Bien contigue des grands monts
Pyrenees,
Un contre l'Aigle grand copie ad-
dresser;
Ouvertes vaines, forces extermi-
nees,
Que jusque a Pau, le chef viendra
chasser.

Near the great Pyrenees Mountains,
One shall raise a great army against
the Eagle,
Veins shall be opened, forces
driven out,
So that the chief shall be driven
as far as the Po.

Near the Spanish border one shall raise an army against an Emperor,
whose emblem is the Eagle, but to no avail, as the chief of the army will
flee and his forces will be scattered.

71

En lieu d'espouse les filles truci-
dees,
Meurtre a grand faute ne sera su-
perstile;
Dedans le puys vestuies inondees,
L'espouse estaint par hauste d'-
Aconite.

Instead of the bride, the maid shall
be killed,
The murder shall be a great fault,
none shall be surviving,
In the well they shall be drowned
with their clothes,
The bride shall be disposed of by
high Aconite.

This tells of the tragic aftermath of a marriage, in which the bridesmaids
shall be drowned in their wedding finery and the bride poisoned by Aconite.

72

Les Artomiques par Agen & Lectoure,
A saint Felix feront leur parlement,
Ceux de Basas viendront a la malheure,
Saisir Condon & Marsan promptement.

The Artomiques, through Agen and Lectoure,
Shall keep their parliament at Saint Felix,
These of Bazan shall come in an unhappy hour,
To seize Condon and Marsan speedily.

By Artomiques, our author means the Protestants, who take the Communion with leavened bread, called in Greek, Artos. The towns mentioned are all in Gascony.

73

Le nepveu grand par forces prouvera,
Le peche fait du coeur pusillanime;
Ferrare & Ast le Duc esprouvera,
Par lors qu'au soir fera la pantomime.

The great nephew by force shall provoke,
The sin committed by a pusillanimous heart,
Ferrari and Asti shall make a trial of the Duke,
When the pantomime shall be in the evening.

While the performance of a comedy is being enacted, a cowardly person, provoked by his nephew, shall go on a rampage.

74

Du lac Leman & ceux de Brannonices,
Tous assemblez contre ceux d'Aquitaine,
Germains beaucoup encor plus souisses,
Seront defaicts avec ceux d'Humaine.

From Lake Geneva and to Verona,
They shall be gathered against those of England,
Great many Germans and many more mercenaries,
Shall be routed together with many people.

The Germans and their allies shall be decisively beaten by the English-speaking allies during a great campaign in Italy.

75

Prest a combattre fera defection,
Chef adversaire obtiendra la vic-
toire,
L'arriere garde fera defension,
Les deffaillans mort au blanc terri-
toire.

One being ready to fight shall faint,
The chief of the adverse party shall
obtain the victory,
The rear guard shall fight it out,
Those that fall away shall die in the
white country.

A prediction of the conflict in the Pacific between the U.S. and Japan.
After the original naval feint at islands other than Pearl Harbor, Japan
made its attack on the American fleet. Later, American victories developed
from rear guard actions against Japanese resistance on many islands.

76

Les Nictobriges par ceux de Peri-
gort,
Seront vexez tenant jusques au
Rhosne,
L'associe de Gascons & Bigorre,
Trahir le temple, le prestre estant
au prosne,

The Nictobriges by those of Pe-
rigort,
Shall be vexed as far as the Rhone,
The associate of the Gascons and
Bigorre,
Shall betray the church while the
priest is in his pulpit.

Nictobriges, in Greek, signifies a people of a dark and moist country.
—Perigort and Bigorre are towns in France.

77

Selyn monarque, L'Italie pacific-
que,
Regnes unis Roy Chrestien du
monde;
Mourant voudra coucher en terre
belsique,
Apres pyrates avoir chasse de l'-
onde.

Selyn being monarch, Italy shall be
in peace,
Kingdoms shall be united, a Christian King of the world,
Dying, shall desire to be buried
in Europe.
After he shall have driven the pirates from the sea.

During a time of peace, all the world will be united under a great
and noble king who will be a Christian.

78

La grand armee de la pugnee civille,
Pour de nuict Parme a l'estrange
  trouvee
Septante neuf meurtris dedans la
  ville,
Les estrangers passez tous a l'espee.

The great army belonging to the
  civil war,
Having found by night Parma possessed by strangers,
Shall kill seventy-nine in the town
And put all the strangers to the
  sword.

Great civil wars are promised for Parma and other Italian cities.

79

Sang Royal fuis, Monheurt, Mas
  Aiguillon,
Remplis seront de Bourdelois les
  Landes,
Navarre, Bigorre, pointes & eguil-
  lons,
Profonds de faim, vorer de liege,
  glandes.

Royal Blood run away from Monheurt, Marsan, Aiguillon,
The Landes shall be full of Bourdelois,
Navarre, Bigorre, shall have points
  and pricks,
Being deep in hunger, they shall
  devour the cork and acorns.

Bourdelois refers to the people of Bordeaux. Landes is a desert region in France near the towns of Navarre and Bigorre. As in quatrain 76, there seems to be no deeper significance beyond Nostradamus' concern with these French towns and their current troubles.

80

Pres du grand fleuve grand fosse
  terre egeste
En quinze part sera l'eau divisee,
La cite prinse, feu, sang cris, conflit mestre,
Et la plus part concerne au colli-
  see.

Near the great river, a great pit,
  earth dug out,
In fifteen parts, the water shall be
  divided,
The city taken, fire, sword, blood,
  cries, fighting,
The greatest part concerns the Col-
  osseum.

In Rome there shall be a great tumult and fighting, concerning in most part a revival of ancient ideas.

81

Pont on fera promptement de na-
celles,
Passer l'armee du grand prince Bel-
gique;
Dans profondrees & non loing de
Bruxelles,
Outre passez, destrenchex sept a
picque.

A bridge of boats shall suddenly
be made,
To pass over the army of the great
Belgian Prince.
In deep places, and not far from
Brussels,
Being gone over, there shall be
seven cut with a pike.

A prophecy of the Siege of Antwerp by the Spanish under the Prince
of Parma, who eventually erected a pontoon bridge over the River Schelde
and captured the city.

82

Amas s'approche venant d'Escla-
vonie,
L'Olestant vieux cite ruynera;
Fort desclee vera sa Romaine,
Puis la grand flamme estaindre ne
scaura.

A great troop gathered shall come
from Russia,
The old Olestant shall ruin a city,
He shall see his Romania very
desolate,
And after that, shall not be able
to quench that great flame.

Russia will dominate a bloc of neighboring countries but the flame of
freedom shall not be extinguished. After uprising after uprising, Russia
shall be in big trouble—see Yugoslavia, Poland, Czechoslovakia, Rumania,
East Germany.

83

Combat nocturne le vaillant capitaine,
Vaincu fuyra, peu de gens profli-
gee;
Son peuple esmeu, sedition non
vaine,
Son propre fils le tiendra assiege.

In a fight by night, the valiant captain
Being vanquished shall run away,
overcome by few.
His people being moved, shall
make no small mutiny,
His own son shall besiege him.

An event in Nostradamus' time which he felt needed no explanation.

84

Un grand d'Auxerre mourra bien miserable,	A great man of Auxerre shall die very miserably,
Chasse de ceux qui soubs luy ont este,	Being expelled by those who have been under him,
Serre de chaisnes, apres d'un rude cable,	Bound with chains, and after that, with a strong cable,
En l'an que Mars, Venus, Sol mis en este.	In the year that Mars, Venus, and Sol shall be in conjunction.

Auxerre is a city in France about fifty miles from Paris. And this stanza merely concerns the unhappy fate of one of its chief men—many, many years ago.

85

Le charbon blanc du noir sera chasse,	The white coal shall be expelled by the black one,
Prisonnier fait mene au tumbereau,	He shall be made prisoner carried in a dung cart,
More chameau sus pied estrelassez,	His feet twisted on a black camel,
Lors le puisne fillera l'aubereau.	Then the youngest, shall suffer the Falcon to have more freedom.

A white prince shall be overcome by a black one, and carried to his execution in a dung cart. According to Nostradamus, this is both "allegorical and metaphorical, and the judgment must be left to the reader."

86

L'an que Saturne en eau sera conjoinct,	In the year that Saturn in Aquarius shall be in conjunction
Avec Sol, le Roy fort & puissant,	With Sol, the King being strong and powerful,
A Rheims & Aix sera receu & oingt,	Shall be received and anointed at Rheims and Aix,
Apres conquestes meurtrura innocens.	After conquest he shall murder innocent persons.

Rheims, a city in France, and Aix, a city in Germany, shall both be the scene of the coronation of a common ruler. Afterwards his actions shall be ominous.

87

Un fils du Roy tent de langues
  aprins,
A son sisne au regne different,
Son pere beau au plus beau fisz
  comprins,
Fera perir principe adherent.

A son of a King having learned
  divers languages
Shall fall out with his elder brother
  for the kingdom,
His father-in-law being more concerned with his elder son,
Shall cause the principal adherent
  to perish.

A King having two sons, the elder shall succeed him. The younger, being well educated, shall rebel against the King, his father, but shall be slain by his own father-in-law.

88

Le grand Anthoine du moindre
  fait sordide,
De Phytriase a son dernier ronge,
Un qui de plomb voudra estre cu-
  pide,
Passant le Port d'Esleu sera plonge.

The great Anthony by name, but,
  in effect sordid,
By lice, shall at last be eaten up,
One that shall be covetous of lead,
Passing the Port Esleu shall fall
  into the water.

One who pretends to greatness shall at last realize his failure. He shall commit suicide by drowning himself.

89

Trente de Londres secret conjur-
  eront,
Contre leur Roy, sur le pont l'en-
  treprinse,
Les satalites la mort degousteront,
Un Roy esleu blonde, natif de
  Frize.

Thirty of London shall secretly
  conspire,
Against the King, upon the bridge
  the plot shall be made,
These satellites shall taste of
  death,
A King shall be elected, fair, and
  born in the low countries.

The Guy Fawkes gunpowder plot against the British Throne is clearly outlined here.

90

Les deux copie aux murs ne pour-
ront joindre,
Dans cest instant trembler Milan
Ticin,
Faim, soif, doutance si fort les
viendra poindre,
Chair, pain, ne vivres, n'auront un
seul bouncin.

The two armies shall not be able
to join by the walls,
At the instant Milan and Ticin
shall tremble
Hunger, thirst, and fear shall so
seize upon them
They shall not have a bit of meat,
bread nor victuals.

A description of conditions in Italy during a war is here given, referring
specifically to the city of Milan.

91

Au Duc Gaulois constranet battre
au duelle,
La nef Mole Monech n'appro-
chera,
Tort accuse prison perpetuelle,
Son fils regner auant mort taschera

A French Duke compelled to fight
a duel,
The ship of Mole shall not approach Monaco,
Wrongfully accused, shall be perpetually imprisoned,
His son shall endeavor to reign before his death.

Publication of the private papers of Louis XIV revealed that the "Man
in the Iron Mask" was Count Girolamo Mattioli. In 1678 he had acted
treacherously against Louis XIV and was subsequently imprisoned and
masked.

92

Teste trenchee du vaillant Capitaine,
Sera jette devant son adversaire,
Son corps pendu de sa classe a l'an-
tenne,
Confus furia par rames a vent contraire.

The head cut off of the valiant
Captain,
Shall be thrown down before his
adversary,
His body hanged from the ship's
antenna,
Confused, they shall fly with oars
against the wind.

This quatrain caused confusion in the mind of Nostradamus. To us,
there is an obvious reference to radio in it—but the event itself remains
obscure.

93

Un serpent veu proche du lit Royal,
Sera par dame, nuict chiens n'ab-
    bayeront;
Lors naistre en France un Prince
    tant Royal
Du ciel venu tous les Princes ver-
    ront.

A serpent shall be seen near the
    Royal bed,
By a lady of the night, the dogs
    shall not bark,
Then shall be born in France a
    Prince so much royal,
Come from heaven all the Princes
    shall see it.

All the princes of the world will acknowledge a French Prince as the greatest of them all. The serpent is an allusion to his greatness, as when Alexander was born, a serpent was seen near his mother's bed.

94

Deux grands freres seront chassez
    d'Espaigne,
Laisne vaineu soubs les monts Py-
    renees;
Rougir mer, Rosne sang Leman d'-
    Alemagne,
Narbon, Blyterres, d'Agath, con-
    taminees.

Two great brothers shall be driven
    from Spain,
The elder of them shall be over-
    come under the Pyrenean Moun-
    tains,
Bloody sea, Rhone, bloody Geneva
    of Germany,
Narbonne, the Land of Agath con-
    taminated.

The two great brothers in crime, Nazism and Fascism, will be driven from Spain, but not before a great struggle takes place near the border of France.

95

Le regne a deux laisse bien peu
    tiendront,
Trois ans sept mois passez feront
    la guerre;
Les deux vestales contre rebeller-
    ont,
Victor puis nay en Armorique
    terre.

The reign left to two they shall
    not keep it long,
Three years and seven months be-
    ing past,
The vestals shall rebel against
    them,
The youngest shall be the con-
    queror of the Armorick country.

This signifies a Kingdom that shall be left to two, who shall keep it but a short while. Their title will be challenged by two Nuns.

96

La soeur aisnee de l'Isle Britannique,
Quinze ans devant le frere aura
  naissance,
Par son promis moyennant verri-
  fique,
Succedera au regne de Balance.

The eldest sister of the Britannic
  Island
Shall be born fifteen years before
  her brother,
By what is promised her and by
  help of truth,
She shall succeed in the Kingdom
  of Libra.

The eldest sister of Britain, the U. S. A., was born in 1776. Fifteen
years later, 1791, the Republic of France (brother) came into being.

97

L'an que Mercure, Mars, Venus
  retrograde,
Du grand Monarque la ligne ne
  faillir,
Esleu du peuple lusitant pres de
  Pactole,
Que'n paix & regne viendra fort
  envillir.

When Mercury, Mars and Venus
  shall retrograde,
The line of the great Monarch shall
  be wanting,
He shall be elected by the Portuguese near Pactole,
And shall reign in peace a good
  while.

This signifies the change of state in Portugal, when they threw off
the yoke of Spain, and chose their own King.

98

Les Albanois passeront dedans
  Rome,
Moyennant Langres dimiples affu-
  blez,
Marquis & Duc ne pardonner a
  homme,
Feu, sang morbile, point d'eau,
  faillir les bleds.

The Albanians shall pass through
  Rome,
By means of Langres covered with
  half helmets,
Marquis and Duke shall spare no
  man,
Fire, blood, smallpox, water shall
  fail us, also corn.

The Albanians shall conquer a large territory and take Rome, and
desolation shall follow in their wake.

99

L'aisne vailland de la fille du Roy,
Repoussera si avant les Celtique,
Qu'il mettra foudres, combien en
tell arroy,
Peu, & loing puis profondes Hes-
perique.

The valiant eldest son of the
daughter of the King,
Shall beat back so far, those of
Flanders,
That he shall employ lightnings,
how many in such order,
Little and far, after shall go deep
in Spain.

An able leader of noble birth shall show great skill in employing the
forces of nature in conquering Flanders and Spain.

100

De feu celeste au Royal edifice,
Quand la lumiere du Mars deffail-
lira,
Sept mois grand' Guerre, mort
gent de malefice,
Rouen Eureux, au Roy ne faillira.

Fire shall fall from the skies on
the King's palace
When Mar's light shall be eclipsed,
Great war shall be for seven
months, people shall die by
witchcraft,
Rouen and Eureux shall not fail
the King.

A seven months' war, of tremendous destructive force such as the
world has never seen before, shall terrify mankind.

1

Avant venus du uyne Celtique,
Dedans le temple aeux parlemente-
   ront,
Poignart coeur, d'un monte au
   coursier & pique,
Sans faire bruit le grand enterre-
   ront.

Before the coming of the ruin of
   the Celts,
Two shall discourse together in the
   church,
Dagger in the heart of one, on
   horseback and spurring,
Without noise they shall bury the
   great one.

Nostradamus accurately predicts the conflict in Northern Ireland between the Catholics and the Protestants. As an aside, the British ambassador to Ireland was assassinated in 1976.

2

Sept conjurez au banquet feront
   luyre,
Contre les trois le fer hors de na-
   vire,
L'un les deux classes au grand fera
   conduire,
Quand par le mail denier au front
   luy tire.

Seven conspirators at a banquet
   shall make their iron glisten
Against three, out of a ship,
One shall carry the two fleets to
   the great one,
When in the promenade, the last
   one shall shoot him in the forehead.

At a banquet a conspiracy of seven shall succeed against three. A
naval officer shall deliver two fleets to a great one, and for his treachery
shall be shot in the forehead.

145

3

Le successeur de la Duche viendra,
Beaucoup plus outre que la mer de
Toscanne,
Gauloise branche la Florence
tiendra,
Dans son giron d'accord nautique
Rane.

The successor to the Dukedom
shall come
Far beyond the Tuscan sea,
A French branch shall hold Florence,
In its lap, to which the Sea Frog
shall agree.

Il Duce, after his fall, shall be succeeded by a non-Italian. Florence
will be under French influence.

4

Le gros mastin de cite dechasse,
Sera fasche de l'estrange alliance,
Apres aux champs avoir le chef
chasse,
Le loup & l'ours se donneront de-
fiance.

The great mastiff being driven from
the city,
Shall be angry at the strange alliance,
After he shall have hunted the hart
in the fields,
The wolf and the bear shall defy
one another.

England shall be angry at a strange alliance, whereby the helpless
are hunted down. The Italian Wolf and the Russian Bear shall defy one
another.

5

Sous ombre saincte d'oster de servitude,
Peuple & cite l'usurpera luy-mes-
mes,
Pire fera par faux de jeune pute,
Libre au champ lisant le faux pro-
esme.

Under the feigned shadow of free-
ing people from slavery,
He shall usurp the people and city
for himself,
He shall do worse by the deceit of
a young whore,
For he shall be betrayed in the field
reading a false proem.

This prognosticates the "final" days and actions of Hitler, his false
marriage to the actress Eva Braun, and his spurious will at his supposed
death.

6

Au Roy l'augure sur le chef la
  main mettre,
Viendra prier pour la paix Italique,
A la main gauche viendra changer
  le sceptre,
De Roy viendra Empereur pacifique.

The augur shall come to put his
  hand on the King's head,
And pray for the peace of Italy,
In the left hand he shall change
  the scepter,
From a King he shall become a
  pacific Emperor.

The Latin word augur may mean one who foretells events, or may also
be taken for a clergyman. Here the significance is, that a priest shall put
his hand upon a King's head (Napoleon) and, praying for the peace of Italy,
shall place a scepter in his hand, and install him as Emperor.

7

Du triumvir seront trouvez les os,
Cerchant profond tresor enigma-
  tique,
Ceux d'alentour ne seront en repos,
De concaver marbre & plomb me-
  talique.

The bones of the triumvirate shall
  be found out,
When they shall seek for a deep
  and enigmatical treasure,
Those there about shall not be in
  rest,
This concavity shall be of marble
  and metallic lead.

This delves into Roman history, and tells of the plot of Octavius Caesar,
Marcus Antonius and Lepidus to make themselves masters of the Roman
Empire and to divide the spoils among the three of them.

8

Sera laisse le feu mort vif cache,
Dedans les globes horribles espou-
  ventable
De nuict a classe cite en poudre
  lache,
La cite a feu, l'ennemy favorable.

The fire shall be left burning, the
  dead shall be hid,
Within the globes terrible and
  fearful,
By night the fleet shall shoot
  against the city,
The city shall be on fire, the enemy
  shall be favorable to it.

Terrible new weapons launched from ships shall create fearful destruction and cause unquenchable fires; and so complete will be the havoc,
it will be impossible to count the dead. Between the U.S. and Japan at
Pearl Harbor at the outset of World War II and Hiroshima and Nagasaki
at the end. Foretells a nuclear holocaust.

9

Jusques au fond la grand arq de malve	At the bottom of the great evil arch,
Par chef captif l'amy anticipe,	By a chief that is a captive, the friend shall be anticipated,
Naistra de dame front face chevelue,	One shall be born of a lady with hairy face and forehead,
Lors par astuce Duc a mort attrapppe.	Then by craft shall a duke be put to death.

These words are too veiled in obscurity for either Nostradamus or myself to render a clear interpretation.

10

Un chef Celtique dans le conflit blesse,	A Celtic leader wounded in battle,
Aupres de cave vouant siens mort abbatre,	Near a cellar, seeing death about to overthrow his people,
De sang & playes & d'ennemis presse,	Being much oppressed with blood, wounds and enemies,
Et securs par incogneuz de quatre.	Is succoured by four unknown.

A European leader seriously wounded, and his country severely pressed, will be helped by his allies.

11

Mer par solaires seure ne passera,	Sea by solars, she shall pass safely,
Ceux de Venus tiendront toute l'Affrique;	Those of Venus shall hold all Africa,
Leur regne plus Sol, Saturne n'occupera,	Saturn shall hold their kingdom no longer,
Et changera la mort Asiatique.	And shall change the Asiatic port.

Those of Venus, born to the sea, are the English; as a maritime nation they shall hold great colonial possessions.

12

Aupres de Lac Leman sera conduite,
Par garse estrange cite voulant
  trahir,
Avant sen meurtre a Aspurg la
  grand suitte,
Et ceux du Rhin la viendront envahir.

Near Lake Geneva shall be a plot,
By a strange whore to betray a city,
Before she be killed, her great reti-
  nue will come to Augsburg,
And those of the Rhine shall come
  to invade her.

The corrupting influence of Fascism had its inception in northern Italy, close to Lake Geneva. Before it ran its mad course it also ruined the Germans.

13

Par grand fureur le Roy Roman
  Belgique,
Vexer voudra par phalange barbare,
Fureur grincent chassera gent Ly-
  bique,
Depuis Pannons jusques Hercules
  la Bare.

By great fury, the Roman-Belgic
  Kingdom,
Shall come to vex, by their bar-
  barian falange,
Gnashing fury shall pursue the
  Savage people,
From Hungary as far as the Straits
  of Gibraltar.

The shaky peace between the Warsaw Pact nations and NATO will be tested. The alignment of nations dividing Europe into two camps will not hold, to the vexation of both sides.

14

Saturne & Mars en Leo Espagne
  captive,
Par chef Libique au conflit attrape;
Proche de Malte, heredde Prinse
  vive,
Et Romain sceptre sera par coq
  frappe.

Saturn and Mars being in Leo,
  Spain shall be captive,
By an African general taken in
  battle,
Near Malta, a hereditary Prince
  shall be taken alive,
And the Roman sceptre shall be
  struck by the cock.

Under the joint influence of Saturn (commerce) and Mars (war) Spain shall suffer great defeat. France (the cock) shall contribute to her downfall.

15

En navigant captif prins grand
  pontife;
Grands apprestez saillir les clercs
  tumultuez,
Second esleu absent son bien de-
  bise,
Son favory bastard a mort tue.

In sailing a pope shall be taken
  captive,
After which, shall be a great uproar
  amongst the clergy,
A second absent elected, consumed
  his goods,
His favorite bastard shall be killed.

A controversy shall arise in the Catholic Church, caused by the election of a Pope who is in disfavor with the clergy.

16

A son haut prix la lerme Sabee,
D'humains chair pour mort en cen-
  dre mettre,
A l'isle Pharos par croisars pertur-
  bee,
Alors qu'a Rhodes paroistra dure
  espectre.

The Sabean tear shall be no more
  at its high price,
To turn human flesh by death into
  ashes,
The island Pharos shall be troubled
  by croisars,
When at Rhodes shall a hard
  phantom appear.

Sabean tear, a term used to describe frankincense, was a vegetable product extensively used in embalming. Pharos, an island opposite Alexandria, shall be troubled by Christians (croisars) when a vision appears in Rhodes.

17

De nuict passant le Roy pres d'une
  Andronne
Celuy de Cypres & principal
  guerre,
Le Roy failly la main fuit long du
  Rhosne,
Les conjurez l'iront a mort mettre.

The King going by night near an
  Andronne,
He of Cyprus and chief of war,
The King having missed the hand,
  along by the Rhone,
The conspirators shall put him to
  death there.

A noted military figure shall conspire against France, but in southern France he shall meet his just fate.

18

De dueil mourra l'infelix proflige,
Celebrera son vitrix l'heccatombe;
Pristine loy, franc edit redige,
Le mur & Prince au septieme jour
    tombe.

The unhappy one, being overcome,
    shall die of grief,
His victrix shall celebrate the heca-
    tomb,
The former law and free edict shall
    be brought again,
The wall and seventh Prince shall
    go to the grave.

Victrix is a Latin word, the feminine gender of the word victor; Heca-tomb was a Grecian sacrifice whereby 100 oxen were killed.

19

Le grand Royal d'or, d'airain aug-
    mente,
Rompu la pache, par ieune ouverte
    guerre,
Peuple afflige par unchef lamente,
De sang barbare sera couvert de
    terre.

The great golden Royal, being in-
    creased with copper,
The agreement being broken by a
    young man, there shall be open
    war,
People afflicted by the loss of a
    chief lamented,
The ground shall be covered with
    barbarous blood.

An alliance between a rich nation with one of little wealth shall result in an open warfare, in which the chief will lose his life.

20

De la les Alpes grande armee pas-
    sera,
Un peu devant naistra monstre va-
    pin;
Prodigieux & subit tournera,
Le grand Toscan a son lie plus pro-
    pin.

Beyond the Alps shall a great army
    go,
And a little while before shall be
    born a vapin monster,
Prodigious and suddenly the great
    Tuscan,
Shall return to his own nearest
    place.

Napoleon shall cross the Alps with a great army, and Nostradamus also forecasts his exile to Elba with his return to "his own nearest place," i.e., Corsica.

21

Par les trespas du Monarque Latin,
Ceux qu'il aura par regne secourus;
Le feu livra divuse le butin,
La mort publique au hardis in-
corus.

By the death of the Latin Monarch,
Those that he shall have succoured
in his reign,
The fire shall shine, the booty shall
be divided,
The bold comers in, shall be put
to public death.

A people shall be pillaged after the death of a monarch of Latin origin.
However, the persecutors will eventually be publicly executed.

22

Avant qu'a Rome grand aye rendu
l'ame,
Effrayeur grand a l'armee estrang-
ere;
Par escadrons l'embusche pres de
Parme,
Puis des deux rouges ensemble fer-
ont chere.

Before a great man renders up his
soul at Rome,
The army of strangers shall put
into a great fright,
By squadrons the ambush shall be
near Parma,
After that, the two red ones shall
make good cheer together.

Most likely, the "two red ones" represent Communist leaders rejoicing
at the death of the Pope.

23

Les deux contents seront unis ensemble,
Quand la pluspart a Mars sera con-
jonct,
Le grand d'affrique en effrayeur &
tremble,
Duumvirat par la classe des joints.

The two contested shall be united
together,
When the most part shall be joined
to Mars,
The great one of Africa shall be in
fear and terror,
Duumvirat shall by the pursuit be
disjointed.

The alliance between Israel and Egypt shall not last long. The alliance
(duumvirat) will be disrupted by Saudi Arabia, Libya, Syria, and the
P.L.O.

24

Le Kegne & Roy soubs Venus esleve,
Saturne aura sur jupiter empire,
Be loy & regne par le Soleil leve,
Par Saturnius endurera le pire.

The Kingdom and King being joined under Venus,
Saturn shall have power over Jupiter,
The law and reign raised by the Sun,
Shall be put to the worse by the Saturnians.

The frivolous court of Louis XV, led by Madame Du Barry, made a farce of law and order, by their Saturnine revels.

25

Le prince Arabs, Mars, Sol, Venus, Lyon,
Regne d'Eglise par mer succombera,
Devers la Perse bien pres d'un million,
Bisance, Egypte, Ver. Serp. invadera.

The Arab Prince, Mars, Sol, Venus, Leo,
The Kingdoms of the Church shall be overcome by the sea,
Towards Persia very near a million,
Turkey, Egypt, Ver. Serp. shall invade.

Christian ideals will be overcome by Oriental ideology (Ver. Serp. meaning true serpents).

26

La gent esclave par un heur martiel,
Viendra en haut degre tant esleve,
Changeront prince, naistra un provincial,
Passer la mer, copie aux monte leve.

The Slavic Nation shall by martial luck,
Be raised to so high a degree,
That they shall change their Prince and elect one among themselves,
They shall cross the sea with an army raised in the mountains.

Russians, by a military revolution, shall change their form of government and they will grow to be a great power and invade many countries.

27

Par feu & armes non loing de la
    Mer Negro,
Viendra de Perse occuper Trebi-
    sonde;
Trembler Pharos Methelin, Sol ale-
    gro,
De sang Arabe d'Adrie covert
    l'onde.

By fire and sword not far from the
    Black Sea,
They shall come from Persia to
    seize upon Trebisonde,
Pharos and Methelin shall quake,
    Sun be merry,
The sea of Adria shall be covered
    with Oriental blood.

A Russian invasion, coming through Iran, shall seize Mediterranean
ports. In the Adriatic Sea they shall be driven back with great losses.

28

Le bras pendu & la jambe liee,
Visage pasle, au sein poignard
    cache;
Trois qui seront jurez de la meslee,
Au grand de Gennes sera le Fer
    lasche.

The arm hanging and the leg
    bound,
With a pale face, a dagger in the
    bosom,
Three shall be sworn to the fray,
To the great one of Genoa the Iron
    shall be darted.

In July 1944, an assassination of Hitler was attempted but this only
resulted in arm and leg injuries to him. Thereafter he walked with a limp,
and his arm was in a sling. By this time in Italy, Mussolini was already
captured.

29

La liberte ne sera recouvres,
L'occupera noir, fier, vilain inique;
Quand la matiere du pont sera
    ouvree,
D'Hister, Venise faschee la repub-
    lique.

Liberty shall not be recovered,
It shall be occupied by a black,
    fierce and wicked villain,
When the work of the Danube
    bridge shall be ended,
The Italian commonwealth shall
    be angry.

The black-shirted villain shall destroy Italian liberty. When the wreck
of the German alliance is complete, then Italy will really show her anger.

30

Tout a l'entour de la grande cite,	Round about the great city,
Seront soldats logez par champs & villes,	Soldiers shall be in fields and towns,
Donner l'assaut Paris, Rome incite,	Paris shall give the assault, Rome shall be incited,
Sur le pont lors sera faite grand pille.	Then upon the bridge shall be great plunderings.

The capture and sacking of Rome by the French Duke of Bourbon is here described.

31

Par terre Attique chef de la sapience,	In the country of Attica which is the head of wisdom
Qui de present est la Rose du Monde;	And now is the Rose of the World,
Pont ruyne & sa grand preeminence,	A bridge shall be in ruins with its great preeminence,
Sera subdite & naufrage de undes.	It shall be subdued and made a wreck by the waves.

The country of Attica, or Greece, famed for its wisdom, shall be corrupted by the usages of mankind.

32

Ou tout bon est, tout bien Soleil & Lune,	Where all well is, are good Sun and Moon,
Est abondent, sa ruyne s'approche,	Is existent, its ruin approaches near,
Du ciel s'advance vaner ta fortune,	The heaven is making haste to change thy fortune,
En mesme estat que la septiesme roch.	Into the same state as the seventh rock.

This dark stanza seems to predict the bad times that shall exist during a civil war between the Catholics and Protestants.

33

Des principaux de cite rebellee,
Qui tiendront fort pour liberte
    r'avoir,
Detrencher masses infelice meslee,
Cris hurlemens a Nante; piteux
    voir.

Of the principal men in a rebelled
    city,
Who shall stand out to recover
    their liberty,
The males shall be cut in pieces, O
    unhappy quarrels!
Cries and howlings, it shall be pity
    to see at Nantes.

Nantes in France, shall be the seat of a rebellion against the rest of
France. Tremendous massacres of the natives shall follow. And so it was
in Nantes, 250 years after Nostradamus wrote this quatrain. Males were
guillotined; women, children, and priests were drowned in the Loire in
1793.

34

Du plus profond de l'occident An-
    glois,
Ou est le chef de l'isle Britannique;
Entrera classe dans Garonne par
    Blois,
Par vin & sel, feux cachez aux bar-
    riques.

From the most westerly part of
    England,
Where the chief of the British Is-
    land is,
A fleet shall come into the Ga-
    ronne by Blois,
By wine and salt, fire shall be hid-
    den in barrels.

A British Fleet shall plant mines (barrels) in French waters.

35

Par cite franche de la grand Mer
    Seline,
Qui porte encore a l'estomach la
    pierre;
Angloise classe viendra sous la bru-
    ine,
Un rameau prendre du grand ou-
    verte guerre.

By a free city of the Mediterranean
    Sea,
Which carries yet the stone in the
    stomach,
An English Fleet shall come under
    a fog,
To take a branch of great open
    war.

The Free City of Venice in the Mediterranean, shall be invaded by an
English Fleet under cover of a fog.

36

De soeur le frere par simulte fain-
tise,
Viendra mesler rosee en mineral;
Sur la placente donne a vieille tar-
dive,
Meurt le goustant sera simple &
rural.

The brother of the sister, by
feigned simulation,
Shall mix dew with mineral;
The aftermath being given to a
slow old woman,
She died tasting, the deed shall
be simple, and rural.

A brother shall poison his sister during childbirth.

37

Trois sens seront d'un vouloir &
accord,
Qui pour venir au bout de leur
attainte,
Vingt mois apres tous & records,
Leur Roy trahir simulant haine,
fainte.

Three hundred shall be of one
mind and agreement,
That they may attain their ends.
Twenty months after by all of
them and their partners,
Their King shall be betrayed by
simulating a feigned hatred.

The Legislative Assembly after a period of deliberation finally ordered
King Louis XVI to stand trial for treason.

38

Ce grand monarque qu'an mort
succedera,
Donnera vie illicite & lubrique;
Par nonchalance a tous concedera,
Qu'a la parfin faudra la loy Salique.

The great monarch that shall succeed to the great one,
Shall lead a life unlawful and
lecherous,
By carelessness he shall give to all,
So that in conclusion, the Salic
law shall fail.

The Salic law, most famous for its chapter on succession to private
property, which declares that daughters cannot inherit land, is here referred
to in an incident which seems to indicate the degeneracy of the males of
a royal line, which eventually led to the enthroning of a woman.

39

Du vray rameau des fleurs de lys issu,	Issued out of the true branch of the city,
Mis & loge heritier d'Hetrurie;	He shall be set for heir of Etruria;
Son sang antique de longue main tissu,	His ancient blood weaned by a long while,
Fera Florence florir en l'Armoirie.	Shall cause Florence to flourish in the coats of arms.

A reference to the Medici family and their alliance with the Crown of France—Catherine de Medici, wife of Henry II, was Queen of France when Nostradamus lived.

40

Le sang Royal sera si tresmesle,	The Royal blood shall be so much mixed,
Contrainct seront Gaulois de l'-Hesperie;	The French shall be constrained by the Spaniards,
On attendra que terme soit coule,	They shall stay till the term is past,
Et que memoire de la voix soit perie.	And the remembrance of the voice is over.

This merely signifies the alliance between France and Spain by reason of royal intermarriages.

41

Nay sous les umbres & journee nocturne,	Being born in the shadows and nocturnal time,
Sera en regne & bonte souveraine,	He shall be a sovereign in kingdom and bounty,
Fera renaistre son sang de l'antique urne,	He shall cause his blood to be born again from the antique urn,
Renouvellant siecle d'or pour l'airain.	Renewing a golden age instead of a brass one.

A great king, born in a time of darkness, shall reign with a bountiful sceptre and lead the land to a golden age.

42

Mars esleve en son plus haut bef-
froy,
Fera retraire les Allobrox de France,
La gent Lombarde fera si grand
effroy,
A ceux de l'aigle compris sous la
Balance.

Mars being raised in its highest
watch tower,
Shall cause the Allobrox to retreat
from France,
The people of Lombardy shall be
in so great fear
Of those of the eagle, comprehended under Libra.

The Allobrox are those of Savoy, or Italians; retreating from France,
they shall cause great havoc.

43

La grand ruyne des sacrees ne
s'eslongne,
Provence, Naples, Sicile, Seez &
Ponce,
En Germanie, au Rhin & la Co-
logne,
Vexez a mort par tous ceux de Mo-
gonce.

The great ruin of the sacred things
is not far off.
Provence, Naples, Sicily, Sez and
Ponce,
In Germany towards the Rhine
and Cologne,
They shall be vexed to death by
those of Moguntia.

Great damage to sacred monuments of art and religion is predicted.
There will be religious troubles in the regions mentioned. Here is forewarn-
ing of what became an early one-thousand-plane bombing of Cologne
with great destruction by the Allies in World War II.

44

Par mer le rouge sera prins des pyrates,
La paix sera par son moyen troublee;
L'ire & l'aure commettra par sainct
acte,
Au grand pontife sera l'armee dou-
blee.

By sea the red one shall be taken
by pirates,
The peace by that means shall be
troubled,
He shall commit anger by a feigned
act,
The high priest shall have a double army.

Very clearly, Nostradamus predicts the threat to Joseph Cardinal
Mindszenty in 1956 during the Hungarian uprising, at which time he
sought and received asylum in the U.S. legation.

45

Le grand Empire sera tost desole,
Et translate pres d'Arduenne silve;
Les deux bastards pres l'aisne de-
colle,
Et regnera Aeneodarb, nes de
milve.

The great Empire shall soon be
made desolate,
And shall be transplanted near the
Forest of Arden,
The two bastards shall have their
heads cut off by the eldest son,
And he that shall reign shall have
a reddish beard and a hawk's
nose.

The great Empire of Germany shall be broken up and its lands, especially near the borders of France, will be divided and ruled by many strangers.

46

Par chappeaux rouges querelles &
nouveaux scismes,
Quand on aura esleu le Sabinois,
On produira contre luy grands
sophismes,
Et sera Rome lesee par Albanois.

By red hats, quarrels and new
schisms,
When the Sabine shall be elected,
Great sophisms shall be produced
against him,
And Rome shall be damaged by the
Albanians.

The cardinals of Rome shall raise great quarrels and schisms when a man of Sabine (a region near Rome) is chosen Pope. Rome will further be endangered by the war-like advances of the Albanians.

47

Le grand Arabe marchera bien
avant,
Trahy sera par les Bisantinoise,
L'antique Rhodes luy viendra au
devant,
Et plus grand mal par austre Pan-
nonois.

The great Arab shall proceed a
great way,
He shall be betrayed by the Turks,
Ancient Rhodes shall come to
meet him,
Great evil by a south wind from
Hungary.

The latter half of the twentieth century has Turkey with NATO on one side and the Arab League with Syria, Jordan, Saudi Arabia, Lebanon, and the P.L.O. on the other.

48

Apres la grande affliction du sceptre,	After the great afflictions of the sceptre,
Deux ennemis par eux seront defaits,	Two enemies shall be overcome by themselves,
Classe d'Affrique aux Pannonois viedra naistre,	A fleet of Africa shall go toward the Hungarians,
Par mer & terre seront horribles faits.	By sea and land shall be horrid facts.

This has relation to the preceding stanza; due to a falling out between two enemies, the Hungarians will be the gainers.

49

Nul de l'Espagne, mais de l'antique France,	None out of Spain, but of the ancient France,
Ne sera esleu pour le tremblant nacelle;	Shall be elected to govern the tottering ship.
A l'ennemy sera faicte fiance,	The enemy shall be trusted,
Qui dans son regne sera peste cruelle.	Who to his kingdom shall be a cruel plague.

Nostradamus predicts that a Frenchman will be chosen Pope. With the selection of John Paul I of Poland in 1978, the first non-Italian Pope since Nostradamus's writing in 1555, the forecast of this quatrain cannot be far distant.

50

L'an d'eux les freres du lys seront en aage,	In the year that the brothers of the lilies shall be of age,
L'un d'eux tiendra la grande Romanis,	One of them shall hold the great Romany,
Trembler les monts, ouvert Latin passage,	The mountains shall tremble, the Latin passage shall be opened,
Pache marcher contre fort d'Armenie.	A Pascha shall march against the fort of Armenia.

One of France's generals will occupy Rome after crossing the Alps with a mighty army. At the same time an Oriental ally will assist the French by marching in from the Near East.

51

La gent de Dace, D'Angleterre & Polonne,	The people of Romania, England, and Poland,
Et de Bohesme seront nouvelle ligue;	And of Bohemia shall make a new league,
Pour passer outre d'Hercules la Colonne,	To go beyond the Pillars of Hercules,
Barcyns, Thyrrens dresser cruelle brigue.	Barcins and Thyrrens shall make a cruel plot.

Romania, England, Poland and Czecho-slovakia shall attempt a united invasion beyond Gibraltar, but will meet with great resistance.

52

Un Roy sera qui donrra l'opposite,	A King shall be, who shall be of the opposite,
Les exilez eslevez sur le Regne,	To the banished persons raised upon the Kingdom,
De sang nager la gent caste hypolite,	The chaste Hippolite nation shall swim in blood,
Et florira long temps soubs telle enseigne.	And shall flourish a great while under such a design.

The recurrent turmoil of the Greek government is forecast here. Recall that from 1832 to 1967, Greece has had four different kings with intermittent bloody strife until Constantine II was removed in 1967.

53

La loy de Sol, & Venus contendans,	The law of the Sun and Venus contending,
Apparopriant l'esprit de prophetie,	Appropriating the spirit of prophecy,
Ne l'un ne l'autre ne seront entendans,	Neither one nor the other shall be heard,
Par Sol tiendra la loy du grand Messie.	By Sol the law of the great Messiah shall subsist.

The forces of light and darkness, struggling for domination over the spirit of man, shall both be superseded by the new law of the great Saviour.

54

Du pont Euxine & la grand Tar-
taric,
Un Roy sera qui viendra voir la
Gaule,
Transpercera Alane & l'Armenie,
Et dans Bisance lairra sanglante
Gaule.

From the Black Sea and great Tar-
taria,
A King shall come to see France,
He shall go through Alanea and
Armenia,
And shall leave a bloody rod in
Constantinople.

An Asiatic power shall come to France, by way of Armenia and Turkey.
Constantinople will be governed by one of his tools.

55

De la felice Arabie contrade,
Naistra puissant de loy Mahome-
tique,
Vexer l'Espagne, conquester la
Grenade,
Et plus par mer a la gent Lygus-
tique.

Out of the country of greater
Arabia,
Shall be born a strong master of
Mohammedan law,
Who shall vex Spain and conquer
Grenada,
And by sea shall come to the
Italian nation.

From a country of Mohammedan law (Morocco), shall come one who
is a strong master of their law—the sword: Khomeini and the Moslem
revolution in Iran.

56

Par le trespas du tres vieillard
pontife,
Sera esleu Romain de bon aage;
Qu'il sera dit que le siege debiffe,
Et long tiendra & de picquant
courage.

By the death of the very old high
priest,
Shall be elected a Roman of good
age,
Of whom it shall be said, that he
dishonors the seat,
And shall live long, and be of fierce
courage.

Always deeply concerned with matters of the Church, Nostradamus
here discusses one of the many schisms then current among the clergy.

57

Istra du mont Gaulsier & Aventine, *Qui par le trou advertira l'armee;* *Entre deux rocs sera prins le butin,* *De Sext. Mansol faillir la renommee.*	One shall go out of the mountains Gaulsier and Aventine, Who through a hole shall give notice to the army, Between two rocks shall be taken the prize, And the glory of the Sun shall lose its renown.

One of Nostradamus's most incredible predictions. Mount Gauffier is really Montgolfier, the inventor of the hot air balloon. Originally used for military reconnaissance with a hole in the bottom of the gondola. Also, "de Sext" is the only Pope since Nostradamus's time with the number VI after his name; Pius VI reigned during the time of the Montgolfier brothers, 1775–1799.

58

De l'Aqueduct d'Uticense, Gardoing, *Par la forest & mont inaccessible,* *Emmy du pont sera tasche ou poing,* *Le chef Nemans qui tant sera terrible.*	From the Aqueduct of Uticense and Gardoing, Through the forest and inaccessible mountains. In the middle of the bridge shall be tied by the wrist, The chief Nemans, that shall be so terrible.

An incident in a future war, in France, is here obscurely described. The various places mentioned are probably points of attack.

59

Au chef Anglois a Nimes trop sejour, *Dever l'Espagne au secours Aenobarbe,* *Plusieurs mourront par Mars ouvert ce jour,* *Quand en Artois faillir estoille en barbe.*	The chief English shall stay too long at Nismes, A red-haired man shall go to the help of Spain, Many shall die by open war that day, When in Artois the star shall fail in the beard.

A play on words, this appears to have no deep significance, and the only clear reference concerns a bearded comet, or *cometa barbatus* as it is known in Latin.

60

Par teste rase viendra bien mal
  eslire,
Plus que sa charge ne porte passera;
Si grand fureur & rage fera dire,
Qu'a feu & sang tout sexe tran-
  chera.

By a shaven head shall be made
  an ill choice.
That shall go beyond his commis-
  sion,
He shall proceed with so great fury
  and rage,
That he shall put forth both sexes
  to fire and sword.

Six years after the death of Nostradamus, on St. Bartholomew's Day,
August 24, 1572, a massacre of the Huguenots began in Paris. Spurred on
by the high clergy of the Catholic Church, it spread to many provinces
of France, and before it was checked many, many thousands of people
were killed.

61

L'enfant du grand n'estant a sa
  naissance,
Subjuera les hauts monts Apen-
  nins,
Fera trembler tous ceux de la bal-
  ance,
Et des Monts Feurs jusques a Mont
  Cenis.

The child of the great one that was
  not at his birth,
Shall subdue the high Apennine
  Mountains,
Shall make all those under Libra
  to quake,
From Mount Feurs, as far as
  Mount Cenis.

A person, of illegitimate but noble birth, shall attain great heights as
a military figure and shall cause havoc in both France and Italy by reason
of his conquests.

62

Sur les rochers sang on verra pleu-
  voir,
Sol Orient, Saturn Occidental,
Pres Orgon guerre, a Rome grand
  mal voir,
Nefs parfondrees & prins le Tri-
  dental.

It shall rain blood upon the rocks,
The sun being in the east, and Saturn in the west,
War shall be near Orgon and a
  great evil at Rome,
Ships shall be cast away, and the
  trident be taken.

This quatrain carries on Nostradamus' repeated warnings of a future
war between the Orient and Occident, and the horrible consequences
thereof.

63

De vaine emprinse l'honneur in-
deue plainte,
Gallots errants, par Latins froid,
faim vagues;
Non loing du Tybre de sang terre
tainte,
Et sur humaine seront diverses
plagues.

Honor brings a complaint against
a vain undertaking,
Galleys shall wander through the
Latin seas, cold, hunger, wars,
Not far from Tiber, the earth shall
be dyed with blood,
And upon mankind shall be vari-
ous plagues.

Tiber is the river on which Rome is situated; and the rest of the verse indicates incidents which shall come to pass.

64

Les assemblez par repos du grand
nombre,
Par terre & mer, conseil contre-
mande;
Pres de l'Autonne, Gennes, Nue
de l'ombre,
Par champs & villes le chef contrebande.

The assembly by the rest of the
great number
By land and sea shall recall their
council.
Near Autonne, Gennes, Cloud of
the shadow,
In fields and towns, the chief shall
be one against another.

Here we have a prognostication of the dissensions among the heads of nations gathered ostensibly for a council of peace.

65

Subit venu l'effrayeur sera grande,
Des principaux de l'affaire cachez,
Et dame en braise plus ne sera veus,
Et peu a peu seront les grands
fachez.

One coming upon a sudden shall
cause a great fear,
To the principals that were hidden
and concerned in the business,
And the fiery lady shall be seen no
more,
And little by little the great ones
shall be angry.

Consternation shall seize the betrayers of the people when they perceive the growing strength of the masses and their insistence upon a voice in their destiny.

66

Soubs les antiques edifices estaux,
Non eslonguez d'aqueduct ruyne,
De Sol & Luna mont les luysants
    metaux,
Ardante lampe Trajen d'or burine.

Under the ancient edifices of the
    vestals,
Not far from a ruined aqueduct,
Are the bright metals of sun and
    moon,
A burning lamp of Trajan, of en-
    graved gold.

Near a ruined aqueduct will be found ancient articles of gold and silver,
including a Roman lamp of gold, inscribed with Trajan's name.

67

Quand chef Perousse n'osera sa
    tunique,
Sens au couvert tout nud s'expo-
    lier,
Seront print sept faict aristocra-
    tique,
Le pere & fils morts par points au
    collier.

When the chief of Perouse shall
    not dare without a tunic,
To expose himself naked in the
    dark,
Seven shall be taken for setting up
    an aristocracy,
The father and son shall die by
    pricks in the collar.

Perugia is a city in Italy, which will be the seat of an unsuccessful attempt at setting up a revolution.

68

Dans le Danube & du Rhin viendra
    boire,
Le grand Chameau, ne s'en repen-
    tira;
Trembler du Rhosne & plus fort
    ceux de Loire,
Et pres des Alpes Coq les ruynera.

In the Danube and Rhine shall
    come to drink,
The great camel and shall not re-
    pent,
The Rhone shall tremble and more
    those of Loire,
And near the Alps the Cock shall
    ruin him.

A Turkish invasion shall reach Germany as far as the Rhine and
Danube. France shall be in danger for a while, but shall finally triumph
in a battle near the Alps.

69

Plus ne sera le grand en faux sommeil,
L'inquietude viendra prendre repos;
Dresser phalange d'or, azur & vermeil,
Subjuger Affrique la ronger jusque aux os.

The great one shall be no more in a false sleep,
The restlessness shall take rest,
He shall raise an army of gold and azure
He shall conquer Africa and gnaw it to the bone.

A great nation shall awake from its false sense of security and isolationism, and raise an immense amount of gold and a great navy. With its newfound strength it will invade the African shore. The isolation and neutrality of the United States prior to World War II is changed (false sleep) into war preparedness (raise an army), subsequently gaining a foothold in North Africa, from which, as Churchill said, to "attack the soft underbelly of Europe."

70

Les regions suvjettes a la Balance,
Feront trembler les monts par grande guerre;
Captif tout sexe deu & toute Bisance,
Qu'on criera a l'aube terre a terre.

The regions under the sign of Libra,
Shall make the mountains quake with great war,
Slaves of all sexes, with all Constantinople,
So that in the dawn, they shall cry from land to land.

The European nations shall embark on a universal war, with the complete destruction of Constantinople promised.

71

Par la fureur d'un qui attendra l'eau,
Par la grand rage tout l'exercite esmeu,
Charge de nobles a dix-septe batteaux,
Au long du Rhosne tard messager venu.

By the fury of one looking forward to the water,
By his great rage the whole army shall be troubled,
There shall be seventeen boats full of noblemen,
Along the Rhone the messenger shall come too late.

The fury and rage of an invader driving his legions toward English shores, shall result in a great destruction of navies.

72

Pour le plaisir d'edict voluptueux,	By the pleasure of a voluptuous edict,
On meslera la poison dans la loy,	The poison shall be mixed with the law,
Venus sera en cours si vertueux,	Venus shall be in so great request,
Qu obsuquera du Soleil tout aloy.	That it shall darken all the alloy of the sun.

Pornography and a liberalization of all moral codes is foreseen here. Nostradamus, however, although he anticipates this, is unhappy with the results it produces.

73

Persecutee de Dieu sera l'Eglise,	The church of God shall be persecuted,
Et les saints temples seront expoliez;	And the holy temples shall be spoiled,
L'enfant la mere mettra nud en chemise,	The child shall turn out his mother nude in her shirt,
Seront Arabes aux Polons railez.	Arabians shall agree with Polonians.

The Catholic Church shall be persecuted and its temples despoiled. Anti-Semitism shall be rampant among the Arabs and Poles.

74

De sang Troy en naistra coeur Germanique,	Of Trojan blood shall be born a German heart,
Qui de viendra en si haute puissance,	Who shall attain to so high a power,
Hors chassera gent estrange Arabique,	That he shall drive away the Eastern people,
Tournant l'Eglise en pristine pre-eminence.	Restoring the church to pristine pre-eminence.

A German of great courage shall attain great eminence by destroying the influence of Oriental power and re-establishing the Church.

75

Montera haut sur le bien plus a dextre,	Mounting high on the good, more to the right,
Demourra assis sur la pierre carree;	He shall remain sitting upon the square stone,
Vers le midy pose a sa fenestre,	Towards the South, being set on the left hand,
Baston tortu en main bouchee serree.	A crooked stick in his hand and his mouth shut.

This predicts and describes the hectic sessions of the National Assembly during the French Revolution, where the parties of the left and the right contended for the power.

76

En lieu libere tendra son pavillon,	He shall pitch his tent in the open air,
Et ne voudra en citez prendre place;	Refusing to lodge in the city,
Aix, Carpen, l'Isle, Volce, Mont Cavaillon	Aix, Carpentres, Lille, Volce, Mont Cavaillon,
Par tout les lieux abolira la trasse.	In those places, he shall abolish his trace.

All the places mentioned in this stanza are in Provence. The event referred to has no current interest.

77

Tous les degrez d'honneur Ecclesiastique,	All the degrees of Ecclesiastical honor
Seront changez en Dial Quirinal;	Shall be changed into a Quirinal Dial,
En Martial Quirinal flaminique,	Into Martial Quirinal, Flaminus,
Puis un Roy de France le rendra Vulcanal.	After that, a King of France shall make it Vulcanal.

This is another discussion of clerical affairs in the Catholic Church in Nostradamus' time.

78

Les deux unis ne tiendront longuement.	The two united shall not hold long,
Et dans treze ans au Barbare Sattrappe;	Within thirteen years to the Barbarian Satrap,
Aux deux costez feront tel perdement,	They shall cause such loss on both sides,
Qu'un benira la barque & sa cappe.	That one shall bless the boat and its covering.

Adolf Hitler and Von Hindenburg first became associated (historically) in 1920, the year that the Nazi Party was founded. Thirteen years later, just prior to Hindenburg's death, Hitler assumed full power, resulting in the ultimate ruin and destruction of the German State.

79

Le sacree pompe veindra baisse les aisles	The sacred pomp shall bow down her wings,
Par la venue du grand Legislateur;	At the coming of the great law giver,
Humble haussera, vexera les rebelles,	He shall raise the humble and vex the rebellious,
Naistra sur terre aucun semulateur.	No emulator of his shall be born.

The advent of Abraham Lincoln is plainly prophesied here.

80

L'Ogmion grand Bisance approchera,	The Ogmion shall come near great Constantinople,
Chasses sera la Barbarique Ligue,	And shall expel the Barbarian League,
Des deux loix l'une l'unique laschera,	Of the two laws, the wicked one shall yield,
Barbare & France en perpetuelle brigue.	The Barbarian, and the French shall be in perpetual friction.

A King of France shall go to Constantinople, and shall break the Barbarian League; that is, Christian principles shall triumph over the Mohammedan law.

81

L'Oyseau Royal sur la cite Solaire,
Sept mois devant fera nocturne augure,
Mur d'Orient cherra tonnerre es-
claire,
Sept jours aux portes les ennemis
a l'heure,

The Royal Bird upon the city of
the Sun,
Seven months together shall make
a nocturnal augury,
The Eastern wall shall fall, the
lightning shall shine,
Then the enemies shall be at the
gate for seven days.

The Royal Bird (eagle) shall fly for many months over an Eastern city. When it unlooses its most deadly weapon (which shines with the brilliance of lightning) the Eastern wall will crumble.

82

Au conclud pache hors de la forteresse,
Ne sortira celuy en desespoir mis,
Quand ceux d'Arbois, de Langres,
contre Bresse,
Auront monts Dolle bouscade d'-
ennemis.

On the conclusion of the pact
made, out of the fortress,
Shall not come he that was in de-
spair,
When those of Arbois, of Langres,
against Brescia,
Shall put in Dolle an ambus-
chade of foes.

During a war a truce will be declared, but the commander of the besieged city shall refuse its terms.

83

Ceux qui auront entrepris subvertir,
Nompareil regne puissant & invin-
cible,
Feront par fraude, nuicts trois ad-
vertis
Quand le plus grand a table lire
Bible.

Those that shall have undertaken
to subvert,
The kingdom that has no equal in
power and victories,
Shall cause by fraud, notice to be
given for three nights together
When the greatest shall be reading
a Bible at the table.

A subversive movement within a great nation shall have its inception on a Sunday night.

84

Naistra du gouphre & cite emme-
    suree,
Nay de parens obscurs & tene-
    breux;
Quand la puissance du grand Roy
    reveres,
Voudre destruire par Rouen &
    Eureux.

One shall be born out of the gulf
    and immeasurable city,
Born of parents obscure and dark,
Who, by means of Rouen and Eu-
    reux,
Will go about to destroy the power
    of the great King.

A person of obscure and dark parentage is predestined to destroy the power of a great King.

85

Par les Sueves & lieux circonvoi-
    sins,
Seront en guerre pour cause des
    neuus.
Gamp marins locustes & cousing,
Du Leman fautes seront bien des-
    nuees.

Through Switzerland and the
    neighboring places,
By reason of the clouds shall fall
    to war.
The lobsters, locusts, and gnats,
The fault of Geneva shall appear
    very naked,

The failure of the League of Nations and the advent of war are prophesied.

86

Par les deux testes & trois bras se-
    parez,
La cite grande par eau sera vexes,
Des grandes d'entr'aux par exil
    esgarez,
Par teste Perse, Bisance fort
    pressee.

Divided in two heads and parted
    in three arms,
The great city shall be troubled
    with waters,
Some great ones among them scat-
    tered by banishment,
By a Persian head, Turkey shall be
    much oppressed.

Paris surrenders to Nazi Germany on June 14, 1940, and is overrun (inundated) with Germans. French leaders scatter, and at the same time there is much unrest in the East (Russia) as Hitler attacks the Russians on June 22, 1940.

87

L'an que Saturne sera hors de serv-
age,
Au franc terroir sera d'eau inonde;
De sang Troyen sera son mariage,
Et sera seur d'Espagnol circonder.

In the year that Saturn out of servitude,
In the free country shall be
drowned by water,
With Trojan blood his marriage
shall be,
And he surely shall be surrounded
by Spaniards.

The term "Trojan blood" refers to the French Nation. The meaning
to be gathered from this stanza seems to be that, at the time of a great
flood in France, a notable marriage will be made which will endanger
French and Spanish relations.

88

Sur le sablon par un hydeux deluge,
Des autres mers trouve monstre
marin;
Proche du lieu sera fait un refuge,
Tenant Savone esclave de Turin.

Upon the sand through a hideous
deluge
Of other seas, shall be found a sea
monster,
Near to that place shall be made
a sanctuary,
Which shall make Savoy a slave to
Turin.

Warfare between two Italian political factions is here predicted.

89

Dedans Hongrie par Boheme, Na-
varre,
Et par bannieres feintes seditious;
Par fleurs de lys pays portant la
barre,
Contre Orleans fera esmotions.

In Hungaria, through Bohemia and
Navarre,
And by banners feigned seditious,
By Fleur de Lys, peace that carries
the bar,
Against Orleans shall make com-
motions.

The first two lines of this quatrain foretold the religious troubles that
were to happen in Hungaria, Bohemia and Navarre. The last two tell of
the Prince of Condé, whose coat of arms bears the flower and the bar, who
seized Orleans for the Protestant party.

90

Dans les Cyclades, en Corinthe, &
    Larisse,
Dedans Sparte tout le Peloponese;
Si grand famine, peste, par faux
    connisse,
Neuf mois tiendra & tout le cher-
    rouesse.

In the Cyclades, in Corinth and
    Larissa,
In Sparta, and all the Pelopon-
    nesus,
Shall be so great a famine and
    plague
To last nine months in the south-
    ern peninsula.

All the Greek regions mentioned shall be afflicted with famine and plague.

91

Au grand marche qu'on dit des
    mesongers,
De tout torrent & champ Athe-
    nien,
Seront surprins par les chevaux
    legers,
Par Albanois, Mars, Leo, Sat, au
    versien.

In the great market called of the
    liars,
Which is all torrent and Athe-
    nian field,
They shall be surprised by the light
    horses,
Of the Albanese, Mars in Leo, Sa-
    turn in Aquarius.

Athens shall be overrun by the Nordics, here called Albanese by Nostradamus, after albus, Latin for white or blond.

92

Apres le siege tenu dix sept ans,
Cinq changeront en tel revolu
    terme,
Puis sera l'un esleu de mesme
    temps,
Qui des Romains ne sera trop con-
    forme.

After the seat possessed seventeen
    years,
Five shall change in such a space
    of time,
After that, one shall be elected at
    the same time,
Who shall not be very conformable
    to the Romans.

France has had but one ruler who reigned for seventeen years and that was Louis Philippe (1831–1848) and he had five sons. His successor, Napoleon III, was "elected," as forecast by Nostradamus.

93

Sous le terroir de rond globe lu-
naire,
Lors que sera dominateur Mercure,
L'isle d'Escosse sera un luminaire,
Qui les Anglois mettra a deconfi-
ture.

Under the territory of the round
lunary globe,
When Mercury shall be lord of the
ascendant,
The Island of Scotland shall make
a luminary,
That shall put the English to a
revolution.

Out of Scotland shall come a great light that will bring about a revolution in England.

94

Translatera en la grand Germanie,
Brabant & Flandres, Gand, Bruges,
& Bologne;
La treue sainte le grand duc d'Ar-
menie.
Assaillira Vienne & la Cologne.

He shall translate into the Great
Germany,
Brabant, Flanders, Gand, Bruges
and Bullen,
The truce feigned, the great Duke
of Armenia,
Shall assault Vienna and Cologne.

Germany will attempt to assimilate Belgium and Holland, while a
feigned truce with the great Eastern Power will be broken, and the end
will be the destruction of Germany itself.

95

Nautique rame invitera les umbres
Du grand Empire, lors viendra con-
citer;
La mer Egee des lignes les en-
combres,
Empeschant l'onde Tyrrene de
floter.

The nautical branch shall invite
the shadows,
Of the great Empire, then it shall
come to stir,
The Aegean Sea, with lines of en-
cumbers,
Hindering the Tyrrenian Sea to
roll.

The navy of a great Empire shall take the lead in a rebellion centering
in the Mediterranean.

96

Sur le milieu du grand monde la rose,	In the middle of the great world shall be the rose,
Pour nouveaux faits sang public espandu,	For new deeds, blood shall be publicly spilt,
A dire vray on aura bouche close,	To say the truth, every one shall close his mouth,
Lors au besoin viendra tard l'attendu.	Then at the time will be the one long looked for.

Nostradamus predicts the coming of a great world leader and, by a simple play on words as expressed in the first line, we have his name: rose and world (*welt*, in German) combine to make Roosevelt.

97

Le nay difforme par horreur suffoque,	The deformed shall through horror be suffocated,
Dans la cite du grand Roy habitable,	In the habitable city of the great King.
L'edit severe des captifs rovoque,	The severe edict against the banished shall be revoked,
Gresle & tonnerre Condon inestimable.	Hail and thunder shall do inestimable harm at Condon.

Condon is a city in old France, the rest is obvious.

98

A quarante-huit degre climatterique,	At the climacterical degree of eight and forty,
Afin de Cancer si grande secheresse,	At the end of Cancer, shall be such a drought,
Poisson en mer, fleuve, lac cuit hectique,	That fish in the sea, river, and lake shall be boiled hectic,
Bearn, Bigorre par feu ciel en detresse.	Bearn and Bigorre by heavenly fire shall be in distress.

Nostradamus here foretells of a period of great heat and drought, mostly in provinces in France.

99

Milan, Ferrare, Turin & Aquillee,	Milan, Ferrara, Turin and Aquilia,
Capne, Brundis vexez par gent Cel-	Capne, Brundis, shall be vexed by
tique,	the French,
Par le Lyon a Phalange aquilee,	By the Lion and Troop of Aquelia,
Quand Rome aura le chef vieux	When Rome shall have as chief,
Britannique..	old Britannia.

England shall conquer Italy assisted by the French Army, and the military Governor of Rome shall be an Englishman.

100

Le boute-feu par son feu attrape,	The arsonist shall be overtaken by
De feu du ciel par Tarcas & Co-	his own fire,
minge,	Heavenly fire shall fall at Tartas
Foix, Aux, Mazeres, haut vieillard	and Cominge,
eschappe,	Foix, Auch, Mazere, a tall old man
Par ceux de Hasse, des Saxons &	shall escape,
Turinge.	By means of those of Hesse, Sax-
	ony, and Thuringia.

The ones who set the world on fire, shall be overtaken by stern justice. The Germans shall aid in the escape of one of the guilty ones.

A clear prophecy of the Eichman trial and indication that Hjalmar Schact the master mind and financial genius who master minded the Nazi fiasco shall escape the Nuremburg trials.

1

Au tour des Monts Pyrenees grand amas,	About the Pyrenean Mountain there shall be a great gathering
De gent estrange, secourir Roy nouveau;	Of strange nations to succour a new King,
Pres de Garonne du grand temple du Mas,	Near Garonne and the great temple of the Maas,
Un Romain chef le craindra dedans l'eau.	A Roman captain shall fear him in the water.

Assistance by a group of nations shall raise a new ruler to power near the Pyrenees Mountains. A Roman leader shall fear this new threat.

2

En l'an cinq cens octante plus & moins,	In the year five hundred eighty more or less,
On attend le siecle bien estrange;	There shall be a strange age,
En l'an sept cens & trois (cieus en tesmoins)	In the year seven hundred and three (witness heaven)
Que plusieurs regnes un a cinq feront change.	Many kingdoms, one to five shall be changed.

Nostradamus commences his count of time from A. D. 325, the date of the Council of Nicaea. In the above stanza, by using the figure 325 as a key, we find that (1)589 added to it, gives us the date 1914, one of the most important dates in the history of the world. Similarly, (1)703 added to 325 gives us 2028, in which year, Nostradamus tells us, there will be a complete change in the lineup of nations.

3

Fleuve qu'esprouve le nouveau nay Celtique,
Sera en grande de l'Empire discorde;
Le jeune prince par gent Ecclesiastique,
Ostera le sceptre coronal de concorde.

The river that makes trial of the new-born Celtic,
Shall be at great variance with the Empire,
The young prince shall be an Ecclesiastical person,
And have his sceptre taken off, and the crown of concord.

The Rhine River shall be the scene of trial for a new Prince of France.

4

Le Celtique fleuve changera de rivage,
Plus ne tiendra la cite d'Agripine;
Tout trasmue ormis le vieil langage,
Saturne, Leo, Mars, Cancer en rapine.

The river Rhine shall change her shores,
It shall touch no more the city of Cologne,
All shall be transformed, except the language,
Saturn, Leo, Mars, Cancer in rapine.

The borders of Germany shall change so as to no longer include Cologne. A complete upheaval will take place in Germany after a period of great unrest.

5

Si grand famine par une pestifere,
Par pluye longue le long du Pole Artique;
Samarobryn cent lieux de l'hemisphere,
Vivront sans loy, exempt de politique.

So great a famine with a plague,
Through a long rain shall come along the Arctic Pole,
Samarobryn a hundred leagues from the hemisphere,
Shall live without law, exempt from politics.

From the northern hemisphere shall come a devastating plague, followed by a period of anarchy throughout the affected countries.

6

Apparoistra vers le Septentrion,
Non loing de Cancer l'estoille che-
  velue;
Suse, Sienne, Boece, Eretrion,
Mourra de Rome grand, la nuit
  disperue.

Towards the North shall appear,
Not far from Cancer, a blazing star,
Suza, Sienna, Boetia, Eretrion,
There shall die at Rome a great
  man, the night being past.

A light in the sky will appear, and a powerful Italian, unable to live in its glare, shall die.

7

Norvege & Dace, & l'isle Britan-
  nique,
Par les unis freres seront vexees;
Le chef Romain issu du sang Gal-
  lique,
Et les copis aux forest repoulsees.

Norway and Dacia, and the British
  Island,
Shall be vexed by the brothers
  united,
The Roman Captain issued from
  French blood,
His forces shall be beaten back to
  the forest.

At last, a Pope whose origin is French will be chosen. Here Nostradamus forecasts a retrenchment of Catholicism. The first two lines speak of a conflict between NATO and the Warsaw Pact nations.

8

Ceux qui estoient en regne pour
  scavoir,
Au Royal change deviendront a
  pouvris,
Uns exilez sans appuy, or n'auoir,
Lettres & lettres ne seront a grand
  pris.

Those that were in esteem for their
  learning,
Upon the change of a King will
  become poor,
Some banished, without help, having no gold,
Learned and learning shall not be
  much valued.

A period of oppression against scholars and scientists shall arise.

9

Aux *temples saints seront faits grands scandales,*	To the holy temples shall be done much scandals,
Comptez *seront par honneur & louanges,*	That shall be accounted for honors and praises,
D'un *que l'on graue d'argent, d'or les medalles,*	By one, whose medals are graven in gold and silver,
La *fin sera en tourmens bien estranges.*	The end of it shall be in very strange torments.

As an adherent of the Roman Catholic Church, Nostradamus could only look with disapproval on the Protestant party under the leadership of the future Henry IV. As the King of Navarre, he had medals and money stamped with his image for use in the holy temples and cathedrals. The last line proved prophetic, when on St. Bartholomew's Day, August 24, 1572, the Protestant Massacre occurred.

10

Un *peu de temps les temples de couleurs,*	Within a little while the temples of the colours,
De *blanc & noir les deux entremeslee;*	White and black shall be intermixt,
Rouges *& jaunes leur embleront les leurs,*	Red and yellow shall take away their colours,
Sang, *terre, peste, faim, feu, d'eau affolce.*	Blood, earth, plague, famine, fire, water shall destroy them.

After a period of much travail all the races of the world shall lose their prejudices and be as one.

11

Des *sept rameaux a trois seront reduits,*	The seven branches shall be reduced to three,
Les *plus aisnez seront surprins par mort,*	The eldest shall be surprised by death,
Fratricider *les deux seront seduits,*	Two shall be said to kill their brothers,
Les *conjures en dormant seront morts.*	The conspirators shall be killed being asleep.

Seven brothers shall be reduced to three; of those one shall die suddenly and it will be suspected that he was killed by the other two. And they in turn shall meet violent deaths.

12

Dresser copies pour monter a l'Empire,	To raise an army, to ascend the Empire,
Du Vatican le sang Royal tiendra;	Of the Vatican, the Royal blood shall endeavor,
Flamans, Anglois, Espaigne aspire,	Flemings, English, Spain shall aspire,
Contre l'Italie & France contendre.	And shall contend against Italy and France.

There shall be a great commotion among the nations of Europe over the election of a Pope.

13

Un dubieux ne viendra loing du regne,	A doubtful man shall not come far from the reign,
La plus grand part le voudra soustenir,	The greatest part will uphold him,
Un captiole ne voudra point qu'il regne,	A capitol will not consent that he should reign,
Sa grande chaire ne pourra maintenir.	His great chair he shall not be able to maintain.

Napoleon, after great successes, was finally forced to abdicate.

14

Loing de sa terre roy perdra la bataille,	Far from his country the king shall lose a battle,
Prompt eschappe poursuivy suyuant prins,	Nimble, escaped, followed, following taken,
Ignare prins soubs la doree maille,	Ignorantly taken under the gilded coat of mail,
Soubs faint habit & l'ennemy surprins.	Under a feigned habit the enemy taken.

The Battle of Moscow was the turning point in the career of Napoleon; it was the beginning of the end.

15

Dessous la tombe sera trouve le prince,
Qu'aura le pris par dessus Nuremberg;
L'Espagnol Roy en Capricorn mince,
Feinct & trahy par le grand Vitemberg.

Under the tomb shall be found the prince,
That shall have a price above Nuremberg.
That Spanish King in Capricorn shall be thine,
Deceived and betrayed by the great Lutheran.

A prince shall commit suicide thus foiling the dictates of the Nuremberg judges. There will be a betrayal of a powerful Spaniard by a German ruler.

16

Ce que ravy sera du jeune Milve,
Par les Normans de France & Picardie;
Les noirs du temple du lieu Negrisilve,
Feront aux berg & feu de Lombardie.

That which shall be taken from the young Kite,
By the Normans of France and Picardy,
The black ones of the temple of the Black Forest,
Shall make a rendezvous and a fire in Lombardy.

The Normans shall succeed in overthrowing a young arrogant Prince, and to celebrate their victory they will build a temple in the Black Forest.

17

Apres les livres bruslez les asiniers,
Constraints seront changer habits divers;
Les Saturnins bruslez par les musniers,
Hors la plus part qui ne sera musniers.

After the books shall be burnt, the asses,
Shall be compelled several times to change their clothes,
The Saturnins shall be burnt by the millers,
Except the greater part, that shall not be discovered.

The millers (unlearned persons) shall attempt to annihilate the culture of the Saturnins (studious people) even to the wholesale burning of books. This prophecy was fulfilled in its entirety when the Nazis publicly banned and burned all books that were against their ideology.

18

Par les physiques le grand Roy delaisse,	The great King being forsaken by the physician,
Par fort non art ne l'Ebrieu est en vie;	Shall be kept alive by power, and not by the art of a Hebrew,
Luy & son genre au regne haut pousse,	He, and his kindred shall be put at the top of the kingdom,
Grace donne a gent qui Christ envie.	Grace shall be given to a people that envieth Christ.

A sick King, deserted by his physician, shall be cured by the help of a Jew, and as a token of the King's gratitude, the Jews of that nation will enjoy great privileges.

19

La vray flamme engloutira la dame,	The true flame shall swallow up the lady,
Que voudra mettre les innocens a feu,	That went about to burn the guiltless,
Pres de l'assaut l'excercite s'enflamme,	Before the assault the army shall be encouraged,
Quand dans Seville monstre en boeuf sera veu.	When in Seville, a monster like an ox shall be seen.

A monster shall be seen in Seville, similar to the ancient Minotaur who demanded a tribute of innocent children.

20

L'union feinte sera peu de duree,	The feigned union shall not last long,
Des uns changes reformez la pluspart,	Some shall be changed, others for the most part reformed,
Dans les caisseaux sera gent endures,	In the ships people shall be penned up,
Lors aura Rome un nouveau leopart.	Then shall Rome have a new leopard.

An unstable temporary union between Egypt and Israel. A new leader at Rome will be installed when the union dissolves.

21

Quand ceux de Pole Artique unis ensemble,
En Orient grand effrayeur & crainte,
Esleu nouveau soustenu le grand temple,
Rodes, Bisance de sang Barbare taints.

When those of the Arctic Pole shall be united together,
There shall be in the East, great fear and trembling,
One shall be newly elected, that shall bear the brunt,
Rhodes, Constantinople, shall be dyed with Barbarian blood.

The people of northern Europe shall unite against those of the East. The actual battle shall take place near Turkey.

22

Dedans la terre du grand temple celique,
Nepueu a Londres par paix faincte meurtry,
La barque alors deviendra scismatique,
Liberte faincte sera au corne & cry.

Within the ground of the great celestial temple,
A nephew at London by a feigned peace shall be murdered,
The boat at that time shall become schismatical,
A feigned liberty shall be with hue and cry.

In St. Paul's Cathedral, London, the murdered body of a famous person will be found. It will cause great dissension among the churchmen since one of them will be suspected of the crime.

23

D'esprit de Roy munisememens descriees,
Et seront peuples esmeus contre leur Roy,
Paix, fait nouveau, sainctes loix empirees.
Rapis onc fut en si tresdur arroy.

Despite the King, the coin will be brought lower,
The people shall rise against their King,
Peace being made, holy laws made worse,
Paris was never in such a great disorder.

This is a remarkable account of the French Revolution, in proper chronological order—collapse of the financial structure, rising of the people, abandonment of religion and Paris in disorder.

24

Mars & le Sceptre se trouvera con-
  jont,
Dessous Cancer calamiteuse guerre;
Un peu apres sera nouveau Roy
  oingt,
Qui par long temps pacifiera la
  terre.

Mars and the Sceptre, being con-
  joined together,
Under Cancer shall be a calamitous war,
A little while after a new King
  shall be anointed,
Who, for a long time, shall pacify
  the earth.

Nostradamus here speaks of a constellation called the Sceptre. Looking far into the future, he foretells of a time when this constellation shall be in conjunction with Mars, and the terrible war that will break out under this influence. And out of the debacle there will arise a new world leader and peace will reign for a long time afterward.

25

Par Mars constraire sera la Monarchie,
Du grand pescheur en trouble ruyneux;
Jeune, noire, rouge prendra la hier-
  archie,
Les prodieurs iront jour bruyneux.

By Mars contrary shall the monarchy.
Of the great fisherman, be brought
  into ruinous trouble,
A young, black red shall possess
  himself of the hierarchy,
The traitors shall undertake it on
  a misty day.

Nostradamus uses noire as an anagram for roi (seventeen different times) and here as roi-N (for NAPOLEON). The day that Napoleon overthrows the Directory, November 9, 1798, is known as the Eighteenth of Brumaire or "day of the fog."

26

Quartre ans le siege quelque peu
  bien tiendra,
Un surviendra libidineux de vie,
Ravenne & Pise, Veronne sou-
  stiendront,
Pour eslever la croix du Pape envie.

Four years he shall keep the Papal
  seat pretty well,
Then shall succeed one of a libidinous life,
Ravenna, Pisa, shall take Verona's
  part,
To raise up the Pope's cross to life.

A continuation of the preceding stanza, this predicts that the usurper will reign four years, being then succeeded by a notorious sensualist, whose main support shall come from those in the above-mentioned cities.

27

Dedans les isles de cinq fleuves a un,	In the islands from five rivers to one,
Par le croissant du grand Chyren Selin;	By the increase of the great emperor Henry,
Par les bruynes de l'air fureur de l'un,	By the frost of the air and the fury of one,
Six eschappez, cachez fardeaux de lyn.	Six shall escape, hidden within bundles of flax.

Again we have a play on words: Chyren meaning Henry, and Selin meaning King. Just what king or ruler Nostradamus refers to is not clear, and it is quite possible that he means by this obscurity to indicate some future world leader.

28

Le grand Celtique entrera dedans Rome,	The great Celtique shall enter into Rome,
Menant amas d'exilez & bannis;	Leading with him a great number of banished men,
Le grand pasteur mettra a mort tout homme	The great shepherd shall put to death every man,
Qui pour le Coq estoit aux Alpes unis.	That was united for the Cock, near the Alps.

The campaign of Napoleon, which culminated in the French victory over Italy, is foretold.

29

La vefue saincte entendant les nouvelles,	The holy widow hearing the news,
De ses rameaux mis en perplex & trouble,	Of her branches put in perplexity or trouble,
Qui sera duict appraiser les querelles,	That shall be skillful in appeasing of quarrels,
Par son pourchas des razes fera comble.	By his purchase shall make a heap of shaven heads.

Nostradamus here discusses a time of interregnum—the period after the death of a Pope until a new one is elected—and refers to the various parts of the Church in his usual obscure manner: by "the holy widow" he means the City of Rome; the "branches" are the clergymen; and the "shaven heads" refer to priests.

30

Par l'apparence de faincte sainctete,
Sera trahy aux ennemis le siege,
Nuict qu'on coidoit dormir en seu-
    rete,
Pres de Braban marcheront ceux du
    Liege.

By the appearance of a feigned
    holiness,
The siege shall be betrayed to the
    enemies,
In a night that everyone thought
    to be secure,
Near Brabant shall march those of
    Liege.

This appears to be a description of some trouble which occurred between the two regions mentioned.

31

Roy trouvera ce qu'il desiroit tant,
Quand le Prelat sera reprins a tort;
Responce au Duc le rendra mal
    content,
Qui dans Milan mettra plusieurs
    a mort.

A King shall find what he so much
    longed for,
When a Prelate shall be censured
    wrongfully,
His answer to the Duke will make
    him discontented,
Who in Milan shall put many to
    death.

Nostradamus discusses one of the many involved quarrels between the State and the Church.

32

Par trahisons de verges a mort
    battu,
Puis surmonte sera par son de-
    sordre;
Conseil frivole au grand captif
    sentu,
Nez par fureur quand Berich
    viendra mordre.

By treason one shall be beaten
    with rods to death,
Then the traitor shall be overcome
    by his disorder,
The great prisoner shall try a frivo-
    lous counsel,
When Berich shall bite another's
    nose through anger.

"When traitors fall out amongst themselves, honest men rejoice." Such is the sense of this stanza.

33

Sa main derniere par Alus sangui-
naire,
Ne se pourra plus la mer garentir;
Entre deux fleuves craindre main
militaire,
Le noir l'ireux le fera repentir.

His last hand bloody through all
U. S.
Shall not save him by sea,
Between two rivers he shall fear
the military hand,
The black and wrathful one shall
be repentant.

The rise of Black Power and riots in the U.S.

34

De feu volant la machination,
Viendra troubler au grand chef
assiegez;
Dedans sera telle sedition,
Qu'en desespoir seront les profli-
gez.

The contraption of flying fire,
Shall trouble so much the captain
of the besieged,
And within shall be so much riot-
ing,
That the besieged shall be in de-
spair.

Predicting flame-throwing tanks that besieged the countryside around Paris, leading to its downfall. The "contraption of flying fire" could be nothing less than a flame-throwing tank.

35

Pres de Rion & proche Blanche-
laine,
Aries, Taurus, Cancer, Leo, la Vi-
ergge,
Mars, Jupiter, les Sol ardra grand
plaine,
Bois & cites lettres cachez au cierge.

Near Rion and towards Blanche-
laine,
Aries, Taurus, Cancer, Leo, Virgo,
Mars, Jupiter, the Sun shall burn a
great plain,
Woods and cities, letters hidden in
a wax candle.

The first line of this verse is anagrammatic—the word "rion," spelled backwards, becomes noir, black; "blanche" contains the letters blanc, meaning white. Therefore, we must surmise that when the above-mentioned constellations are in conjunction there will be a fire of almost worldwide proportions, the aftermath of which will be a definite division in the world of "black" and "white."

36

Ne bien ne mal par bataille ter- restre,	Neither good nor evil by a loud fight,
Ne parviendra aux confins de Pe- rouse,	Shall reach to the borders of Pe- rusia,
Rebeller Pise, Florence voir mal estre,	Pisa shall rebel, Florence shall be in a bad way,
Roy nuict blesse sur mulet a noire housse.	A King being on his mule shall be wounded in the darkness.

All the cities named are in Italy; the balance should be easy to decipher.

37

L'oeuvre ancienne se parachevera,	The ancient work shall be finished,
Du toict cherra sur la grand mal ruyne,	From the house tops shall fall great misfortunes,
Innocent faict mort on accusera,	The innocent in fact, shall be ac- cused after his death,
Nocent cache, taillis a la bruyne.	The guilty shall be hidden in a wood in misty weather.

King Louis XVI attempted to escape from the rebels, but was appre-hended in a forest hiding-place.

38

Aux profilgez de paix les ennemis,	To the vanquished the enemies of peace,
Apres avoir l'Italie supperee;	After they shall have overcome Italy,
Noir sanguinaire, rouge sera com- mis,	A bloody Black One shall be com- mitted,
Feu sang verser, eau de sang col- oree.	Fire and blood shall be discharged, and water coloured with blood.

This is the prognostication of the rape of Italy by the Fascists under the leadership of Mussolini.

39

L'enfant du regne par paternelle prince,	The child of the kingdom through his father's imprisonment,
Expolie sera pour delivrer;	Shall be deprived of his kingdom for the delivering of his father,
Aupres du Lac Trasimen l'azur prinse,	Near the Lake Trasimene shall be taken in a tower,
La trope hostage pour trop fort s'enyurer.	The troop that was in hostage being drunk.

Lake Trasimene, where Hannibal fought a famous battle with the Romans, is the only clear expression in this otherwise obscurely worded quatrain.

40

Grand de Magonce pour grand soif estaindre,	The great one of Mayence to quench a great thirst,
Sera prive de la grand dignite;	Shall be deprived of his high dignity,
Ceux de Cologne si fort le viendront plaindre,	Those of Cologne shall mourn him so much,
Que le Grand Groppe au Ryn sera jette.	That the Great Groppe shall be thrown into the Rhine.

The German populace shall feel the loss of their great prestige, and shall mourn the loss of their leader, Schickel-GROPPE (Hitler), even to the point of making his name synonymous with the German National Symbol, the River Rhine.

41

Le second chef du regne Danne-marc,	The second head of the Kingdom of Denmark,
Par ceux de Frise & l'isle Britan-nique,	By those of Holland, and the British Isles,
Fera despendre plus de cent mille marc,	Shall cause to be spent over 100 thousand marks,
Vain exploiter voyage en Italique.	Vainly trying to find a way into Italy.

A signification that Danish, Dutch, and English forces will attempt a costly and ultimately futile invasion of Italy.

42

A l'Ogmyon sera laisse le regne,
Du grand Selin qui plus sera de
faict,
Par l'Italie estendra son enseigne,
Regne sera par prudent contrefait.

Unto l'Ogmion shall be left the
kingdom,
Of great Selyn, who shall do more
than the rest,
Through Italy he shall spread his
ensigns,
He shall govern by prudent for-
geries.

A King of France shall dictate to the Vatican and exert great influence
throughout Italy.

43

Long temps sera sans estre habitee,
Ou Seine & Marne autour vient
arrouser,
De la Tamise & martiaux tentee,
Deceus les gardes en evidant re-
pousser.

For a long time shall be unin-
habited
Where the Seine and Marne come
to water about,
From the Thames and martial
people, they shall attempt
To deceive the guards into thinking to resist.

Because of traitors within her gates ruin will fall upon Paris, and the
flight of the inhabitants will result in an almost deserted city.

44

De nuict par Nantes l'iris apparoistra,
Des Arcs Marins susciteront la
pluye,
Arabique Goulfre grand classe parfondra,
Un monstre en Saxe naistra d'ours
& truye.

By night in Nantes the rainbow
shall appear,
Arches of the Sea shall cause rain,
The Arabian Gulf shall drown a
great fleet,
A monster shall be in Saxony from
a bear and a sow.

Incendiary bombs shall light up the nights in France; and in Germany,
the British shall cause great destruction.

45

Le gouverneur du Regne bien sca-
vant,
Ne consentir voulant au fait Royal,
Mellile classe par le contraire vent,
Le remettra a son plus desloyal.

The governor of the Kingdom being wise,
Shall not consent to the King's
will
He shall ponder setting out a fleet
by the contrary wind,
Which he shall put into the hands
of the most disloyal.

After the Franco-German armistice in 1940, the French fleet remained in the hands of the Vichy government. By 1942 when the Allies invaded North Africa, the French fleet, stationed at Toulon, was about to be seized by the Germans but was scuttled and sabotaged, thus preventing the Germans from using this valuable asset.

46

Un juste sera en exil anvoye,
Par pestilence aux confins de Non
seggle,
Response au rouge le fera desvoyer,
Roy retirant a la Rane & l'Aigle.

A just person shall be banished,
By plague to the borders of Non-
Seggle,
The answer to the red one shall
make him deviate,
Retiring himself to the Frog and
the Eagle.

Russia, formerly allied against France, shall be privately assured that her best interests lie in deserting her partner and joining France and her allies.

47

Entre deux monts les deux grands
assemblees,
Delaiseront leur simulte secrette;
Bruxelles & Dolle par Langres ac-
cablees,
Pour a Malignes executer leu1
peste.

Between two mountains the two
great ones shall meet,
They shall forsake their secret en-
mity,
Brussels and Dolle shall be crushed
by Langres,
To put their plague in execution at
Maline.

The Mideast is in focus here. Nostradamus correctly anticipates the alliance between Anwar Sadat and Menachem Begin. Meeting in the Sinai ("between two mountains") they forsook their enmity.

48

La sainctete trop saincte & seductive,
Accompagnee d'une langue diserte;
La cite vieille & Palme trop has-
tive,
Florence & Sienne rendront plus
desertes.

The feigned and seducing holiness,
Accompanied with a fluent tongue,
Shall cause the old city and the too
hasty Parma,
Florence and Sienna to be more
desert.

The sanctimonious mouthings of a fluent demagogue shall influence
many people in Rome and other important Italian cities, and cause them
to abet him in his nefarious schemes.

49

De la partie de Mammer grand
pontife,
Subjuguera les confins du Danube,
Chasser les croix par fer raffe ne
riffe,
Captifs, or, bagues, plus de cent
mille rubles.

By the project of Mammon, high
priest,
They shall subjugate the borders
of the Danube,
They shall pursue crosses of iron,
topsy-turvy,
Slaves, gold, jewels, more than a
hundred thousand rubles.

The Swastika, crooked-cross emblem of the Nazis, is clearly foreseen
by Nostradamus; also the financial origin of their unholy crimes against
humanity.

50

Dedans le puits seront trouvez les
os,
Sera l'incest commis par la maras-
tre;
L'estat change, on querre bruit les
los,
Et aura Mars ascendant pour son
astre.

In the well shall be found the
bones,
Incest shall be committed by the
stepmother,
The state being changed, there
shall be a great stir about the
bones,
And she shall have Mars for her
ascending planet.

A stepmother shall have a child by her son-in-law, and will commit
infanticide, throwing the body in a well. When the bones are discovered
a great furor will take place.

51

Peuple assemble voir nouveau spectacle
Princes & Roys par plusieurs assistans,
Pilliers faillir, murs, mais comme miracle,
Le Roy sauve & trente des instans.

People assembled to see a new show,
Princes and Kings, with many assistants,
Pillars shall fail, walls also, but as a miracle,
The King saved, and thirty of the standers-by.

This pertains to the Congress of Vienna, which convened after the defeat of Napoleon and effected many changes among the nations of Europe.

52

En lieu du grand qui sera condamne,
De prison hors, son amy en sa place;
L'espoir Troyen en six mois joint mort nay,
Le Sol a l'Vurne seront prins fleuves en glace.

Instead of the great one that shall be condemned,
And put out of prison, his friend being in his place,
The Trojan hope in six months united, still-born,
The Sun in Aquarius, then rivers shall be frozen.

Richard Nixon resigns the presidency; his vice-president, Spiro Agnew (Greek descent), had also resigned but was kept out of jail.

53

Le grand Prelat Celtique a Roy suspect,
De nuict par cours sortira hors du regne,
Par Duc fertille a son grand Roy Bretagne,
Bisance a Cypres & Tunes insuspect.

The great Celtic Prelate suspected by his King,
Shall in haste by night go out of the government.
By means of a Duke, fruitful to his King, Great Britain,
Turkey to Cyprus, and Tunis shall be unsuspected.

A Prelate of Celtic origin shall be removed from power by his King. Great Britain shall be the gainer.

54

Au poinct du jour second chant du coq,
Ceux de Tunes, de Fez, & le Bugie,
Par les Arabes captif le Roy Maroq,
L'an mil six cens & sept de Liturgie.

At the break of day, at the second crowing of the cock,
Those of Tunis, and Fez and Bugia,
By means of the Arabians, shall take prisoner the King of Morocco
In the year 1607 by liturgy.

Here again we have recourse to Nostradamus' key figure (as noted in quatrain 2, Century VI). By using this number, 325, and adding to it the figure 1607 referred to above, we get 1932. In this instance, the date is approximate, since the inference gathered from the quatrain clearly applies to conditions leading up to the Spanish Civil War which began in 1936.

55

Au Chelme Duc, en arrachant l'esponce,
Voille Arabesque voir, subit descouverte;
Tripolis, Chio, & ceux de Trapesonce,
Duc Prins, Marnegro, & sa cite deserte.

The Chelme Duke, on throwing the sponge,
Shall see Arabian Sails suddenly discovered,
Tripoli, Chios, and those of Trapesan,
The Duke shall be taken, Marnegro, and the city shall be deserted.

The regions mentioned are near or in Turkey. Chelme is a German word signifying a rogue. The meaning here seems to be that there shall be conflict between this wicked Duke and the rulers of these various cities.

56

La crainte armee de l'ennemy Narbon,
Effrayera si fort les Hesperiques;
Parpignan vuide par L'aveugle d'-Arbon,
Lors Barcelon par mer donra les piques.

The feared army of the enemy Narbonne
Shall so much terrify the Spaniards,
That Parpignan shall be left empty by the blind d'Arbon,
Then Barcelona by sea shall give the weapons.

Parpignon, a border town between France and Spain, shall be captured by the French. Barcelona shall come to the rescue by way of the sea

57

Celuy qu'estoit bien avant dans le regne,	He that was a great way in the kingdom,
Ayant chef rouge proche la hierarchie;	Having a red head and near the hierarchy,
Aspre & cruel, & se fera tant craindre,	Harsh and cruel, shall make himself so dreadful,
Succedera a Sacree Monarchie.	That he shall succeed to the Sacred Monarchy.

A Cardinal of great power—backed by much influence—shall make himself so indispensable to the Vatican, that he will be awarded the Papacy.

58

Entre les deux monarques eslongnez,	Between the two monarchs that live far from each other.
Lors que Sol par Selin cler perdue;	When the Sun shall be eclipsed by Selene,
Simulte grande entre deux indignez,	Great enmity shall be between the two,
Qu'aux Isles & Sienne la liberte rendue.	So that liberty will be restored to the Isles and Sienna.

When the Sun is eclipsed by the Moon, Sienna shall have its liberty restored.

59

Dame en fureur par rage d'adultere,	A lady in fury by rage of an adultery,
Viendra a son prince conjurer non de dire,	Shall come to her prince and conjure him to say nothing,
Mais bref cogneu sera le vitupere,	But soon shall the shameful thing be known,
Que seront mis dixsept a martyre.	So that seventeen shall be put to death.

An explicit statement that should be clear to all.

60

Le prince hors de son terroir Celtique,
Sera trahy, deceu par interprete;
Rouan, Rochelle, par ceux d'Armorique,
Au Port de Blaye deceus par moine
& prestre.

The Prince being out of his Celtic
country,
Shall be betrayed and deceived by
an interpreter.
Rouen, Rochelle, by those of Gascony,
At the Port of Bordeaux shall be
deceived by a monk and priest.

A false interpretation of a political message shall cause an uproar
throughout France.

61

Le grand tapis plie ne monstrera,
Fors qu'a demy la pluspart de l'his-
torie;
Chasse du regne loing aspre apparoistra.
Qu'au fait bellique chacun le viendra eroire.

The great carpet folded shall not
show,
But by half the greatest part of the
history,
The exiles of the kingdom shall
appear sharp afar off.
In warlike matters everyone shall
believe.

The true historical facts concerning an exiled leader, who maintained
his powerful influence even during his banishment, shall be forever concealed from posterity.

62

Trop tard tous deux, les fleurs seront perdues,
Contre la loy serpent ne voudra
faire;
Des ligueurs forces par gallops con-
fondues,
Savone, Albigne, par Monech
grand martyre.

Both the flowers shall be lost too
late,
Against the law the serpent shall
do nothing,
The forces of the leaguers, by gallops, shall be confounded,
Savoy, Albigne, by Monaco shall
suffer great martyrdom.

Nostradamus here expresses his hatred for heretics by referring to them
as serpents. By "gallops" he means horsemen, and the meaning to be drawn
from this stanza is that the heretics of the above-named towns shall be
persecuted and driven out.

63

La dame seule au regne demeuree,	The lady shall be left to reign alone,
L'unique estaint premier au lict d'- honneur,	The unique one being extinguished, first in the bed of honour,
Sept ans sera de douleur exploree,	Seven years she shall weep for grief,
Quis longue vie au regne par grand heur.	After that she shall live long in the reign by grandeur.

Catherine de Medici outlived her husband, Henry II of France, by many years. After his death she went into deep mourning for seven years.

64

On ne tiendra pache aucun arreste,	No binding agreement shall be kept,
Tous recevans iront par tromperie;	Those that admit of it deal in trumpery,
De paix & trefue, terre & mer pro- teste;	There shall be no protestations by land and sea,
Par Barcelone classe prins d'indus- trie.	Barcelona shall take a fleet by ingenuity.

An armed truce with trickery on all sides shall beset the nations, and Spain shall be the gainer.

65

Gris & bureau, demie ouverte guerre,	Between the grays and the bureaus shall be half open war,
De nuict seront assailliz & pillez;	By night they shall be assaulted and plundered,
Le bureau prins passera par la serre,	The government being taken shall put in custody,
Son temple ouvert, deux aux plas- tres grillez.	His temple shall be opened, two shall be put in the grate.

Conflict between lower classes and bureaucrats is foreshadowed ending with the overthrow of a government.

66

Au fondement de la nouvelle secte,	At the founding of a new sect,
Seront les os du grand Romain trouvez,	The bones of the great Roman shall be found,
Sepulchre en marbre apparoistra converte.	The Sepulchre shall appear covered with marble,
Terra trembler en Avril, mal enfovez.	The earth shall quake in April, they shall be ill-buried.

The order (sect) founded by St. Francis, for whom San Francisco is named. A major earthquake will occur in April as it once already did in 1906.

67

Au grand Empire par viendra tout un autre,	To the great Empire quite another shall come,
Bonte distant plus de felicite;	Being distant from goodness and happiness,
Regi par un issu non loing du peautre,	Governed by one of base parentage,
Corruer Regnes grande infelicite.	The Kingdom shall fall, a great unhappiness.

The rise and dominance of Communism will progress toward the subjugation of the Western democracies and cause great unhappiness.

68

Lors que soldats fureur seditieuse,	When the seditious fury of the soldiers,
Contre leur chef feront de nuict fer livre,	Against their chief shall make the iron shine by night,
Ennemy d'Albe soit par main furieuse,	The enemy d'Albe shall by a furious hand,
Lors vexer Rome & principaux seduire.	Then vex Rome and seduce the principal one.

The Duke of Alba, commander of the Spanish Army in the war against the Roman forces of the Pope, unmercifully forced the war to a successful conclusion for his master, Emperor Charles V.

69

La grand pitie sera sans long tarder,
Ceux qui donoient seront con-
    traints de prendre,
Nuds affamez de froid, soif, soy
    bander,
Passer les monts en faisant grand
    esclandre.

What a great pity will it be before
    long,
Those that did give, shall be con-
    strained to receive,
Naked, famished with cold, to mu-
    tiny,
To go over the mountains making
    great disorders.

A land of plenty shall soon be in want and the people will revolt.

70

Un chef du monde le grand Chy-
    ren sera;
Plus outre, apres ayme, craint, re-
    doute;
Son bruit & los les cieux sur pas-
    sera,
Et du seul titre Victeur, fort con-
    tent.

A chief of the world, the great
    Henry shall be,
At first, beloved, afterwards feared,
    dreaded,
His fame and praise shall go be-
    yond the heavens,
And shall be contented with the
    title of Victor.

The nations will organize a super-government covering the entire
world. The president will be named Henry.
    "Chyren" by transposition of letters is an anagram for "Henryc," the
then current form of Henry.

71

Quand on viendra le grand Roy
    parenter,
Avant qu'il ait du tout l'ame ren-
    due,
On le verra bien tost apparenter,
D'Aigles, Lions, Crois, Couronne
    vendue.

When they shall come to celebrate
    the obsequies of the great King,
A day before he be quite dead,
He shall be seen presently to be
    allied,
With Eagles, Lions, Crosses,
    Crowns of Rue.

A continuation of the previous stanza; at the end of Henry's reign,
he shall be exposed as being allied with predatory interests, bringing
much sorrow and suffering to mankind.

72

Par fureur faincte d'esmotion divine,
Sera la femme du grand fort violee;
Judges voulants damner telle doctrine,
Victime au peuple ignorant immo-
   lee.

By a feigned fury of divine inspiration,
The wife of the great one shall be
   ravished,
Judges willing to condemn such a
   doctrine,
A victim shall be sacrificed to the
   ignorant people.

Marie Antoinette, wife of Louis XVI of France, was condemned to death by the judges of the revolution and guillotined in the presence of a howling mob.

73

En cite grand un moyne & artisan,
Pres de la porte logez & aux murail-
   les;
Contre modene secret, cave disant,
Trahis pour faire sous couleur d'es-
   pousailles.

In a great city a monk and an
   artisan
Dwelling near the gate and walls,
Against woman secrets, beware
   further,
A treason shall be plotted under
   pretense of marriage.

The life and history of the Reverend Daniel Berrigan is here portrayed. He leaves the ministry and marries, but not before much protest and plotting.

74

La dechassee au regne tournera,
Ses ennemis trouvez des conjurez;
Plus que jamais son temps triom-
   phera,
Trois & septante a mort trop asse-
   urez.

The expelled shall come again to
   the kingdom,
Her enemies shall be found to be
   conspirators,
More than ever his time shall triumph,
Three and seventy appointed by
   death.

Napoleon I and his Empire were removed but later restored under Napoleon III. He triumphed but eventually met death from surgery in 1873 in England.

75

Le grand Pilot sera par Roy mande,
Laisser la classe, pour plus haut lieu
    attaindre;
Sept ans apres sera contrebande,
Barbare armee viendra Venise
    craindre.

The great Pilot shall be sent for
    by Royal mandate,
To leave the fleet, and be preferred
    to a higher place,
Seven years after he shall be coun-
    termanded,
A barbarian army shall put Venice
    to fear.

A great leader, long absent from public life, shall be recalled to pilot
his country's destiny during a time of great stress. The latter part of the
stanza indicates his final fall from grace in the face of overwhelming
public opposition.

76

La cite antique d'Antenoree forge,
Plus ne pouvant le tyran supporter;
Le manche fainct au temple couper
    gorge,
Les siens le peuple a mort viendra
    bouter.

The ancient city founded by An-
    tenor,
Not being able to bear the tyrant
    any longer.
The feigned handle in the temple
    cut a throat,
The people will come to put his
    servants to death.

The city founded by Antenor, who came to Italy with Aeneas, is Padua.
Being a university city, it will not be able to stand the antics of a
tyrant any longer. He shall have his throat cut, and his companions will
also be put to death.

77

Par la victoire du deceu fraudu-
    lente,
Deux classes une, la revolte Ger-
    mains,
Le chef meurtry & son fils dans la
    tente,
Florence, Imole pourchassez dans
    Romaine.

By the deceitful victory of the de-
    ceived,
One of the two fleets shall revolt to
    the Germans,
The chief and his son murdered
    in their tent,
Florence, Imole, persecuted in
    Romania.

The Germans shall be deceived into thinking that they have won a
victory. Trouble in Italy shall hasten their disillusionment and contribute
to their final defeat.

78

Crier victoire du grand Selin crois-
    sant,
Par les Romains sera l'Aigle clame,
Ticcin, Milan & Gennes ny con-
    sent,
Puis par eux mesmes Basil grand
    reclame.

They shall cry at the victory of the
    great Selin's crescent,
By the Romans the Eagle shall be
    claimed,
Ticin, Milan and Genoa consent
    not,
Then by themselves the great Basil
    shall be claimed.

The Romans, defeated in a battle with the Turks, will request aid from
other Italian cities. Being refused by them, they will then appeal to the
great King (Basil from the Greek word *Basileus*).

79

Pres de Tesin les habitants de
    Logre,
Garonne & Saone, Siene, Tar &
    Gironde,
Outre les monts dresseront pro-
    montoire,
Conflict donne, Pau granci, sub-
    merge onde.

Near the Tesin the inhabitants of
    Logre,
Garonne and Saone, Siene, Tar
    and Gironde,
Shall erect a promontory beyond
    the mountains,
Conflict given, the Po passed over,
    some shall be drowned.

The Italians shall attempt to build an empire beyond their own borders.
Eventually they will be defeated in this purpose, and shall suffer great losses.

80

De Fez le Regne parviendra a ceux
    d'Europe,
Feu leur cite, & lame trenchera;
Le grand d'Asie terre & mer a
    grand troupe,
Que bleux, pars, croix a mort de-
    chassera.

The Kingdom of Fez shall come to
    those of Europe,
Fire and sword shall destroy their
    city,
The great one of Asia, by land and
    sea with a great army,
So that blues, greens, crosses to
    death he shall drive.

"A strange prophecy if it prove true," said a 17th century disciple of
Nostradamus. And time so proves it—that this is the prediction of the
Spanish Civil War, of the uprisings which began in Morocco and spread
to Spain; and even indicates the aid that was given the Loyalists by Russia
and Franco by Germany.

81

Pleurs, cris, & plaincts, hurlemens, effrayeurs,	Tears, cries and complaints, howlings, fear,
Coeur inhuman, cruel, noir, & transy.	An inhuman heart, cruel black and astonished,
Leman, les Isles, de Gennes les majeurs,	Geneva, the Islands of the great ones of Genoa,
Sang espancher, tochsain, a nul mercy.	Shall spill blood, the bell shall ring and no mercy given.

During the course of a war that shall involve most of the earth's surface, a battle of great importance will be fought with the Dodecanese Islands as the prize.

82

Par les deserts de lieu, libre, & farouche,	Through the deserts of a place free and ragged,
Viendra errer nepueu du grand Pontife;	The nephew of the Pope shall come to wander,
Assomme a sept avec ques lourde souche,	Knocked in the head by seven with a heavy club,
Par ceux qu'apres occuperont le cyphe.	By those who after shall obtain the cipher.

A nephew of the Pope shall be exiled to a desert, where he shall be attacked by seven men, one of which will afterwards gain the Papacy.

83

Celuy qu'aura tant d'honneur & carresses,	He that shall have had so many honors and welcomes,
A son entree en la Gaule Belgique,	At his going into French Belgium,
Un temps apres fera tant de rudesses,	A while after shall commit so many rudenesses,
Et sera contre a la fleur tant bellique.	And shall be against the warlike flower.

This concerns the Duke of Alencon who was sent into the Low Countries as Governor for Henry III, King of France. So entranced was he by the beauty and riches of Antwerp, that he attempted to seize the city, but he was overcome by the citizens and most of his followers were destroyed.

84

Celuy qu'en Sparte Claude ne veut
regner,
Il fera tant par voye seductive;
Que de court, long, le fera araigner,
Que contre Roy fera sa perspective.

He that Claudius will not have to
reign in Sparta,
The same shall do so much by a
deceitful way,
That he shall cause him to be ar-
raigned short and long,
As if he had made his prospect
upon the King.

One shall be hindered from reigning, by the machinations of another.

85

La grand cite de Tharse par Gau-
lois,
Sera destruite, captifs tous a Tur-
ban,
Secours par mer, du grand Portu-
galois,
Premier d'este le jour de sacre
Urban.

The great city of Tharse taken by
the French,
All who wore the turban shall be
made slaves,
Help by sea from the great Portuguese,
The first day of summer and the
installation of Urban.

What is meant by the taking of Tarsus, the birthplace of the Apostle
Paul, is not clear to me. The rest of the stanza refers to the persecution
and enslavement of non-Christians during the reigns of various early
Popes (indicated by "Urban," the name taken by eight different Popes,
the last of whom held the office from 1623 to 1644).

86

Le grand Prelat un jour apres son
songe
Interprete au rebours de son sens;
De la Gascongne luy surviendra un
monge,
Qui fera eslire le grand Prelat de
Sens.

The great Prelate the next day
after his dream,
Interpreted contrary to his sense,
From Gascony shall come to him
a monk,
That shall cause the great Prelate
of Sens to be elected.

A lowly monk shall come to a princely churchman, and, following his
advice, the Prelate will be elected to a high office.

87

L'election faicte dans Francfort,
N'aura nul lieu, Milan s'opposera;
Le sien plus proche semblera si
  grand fort,
Qu'outre le Rhin es mareschs chas-
  sera.

The election made at Frankfort,
Shall be void, Milan shall oppose
  it;
He of the Milan party shall be so
  strong,
As to drive the other beyond the
  marshes of the Rhine.

At Frankfort in Germany, the ancient German rulers were elected.
Milan is the place where the Italian Fascist leaders first became powerful.
The rest is plain.

88

Un regne grand demourra desole,
Aupres del Hebrose seront assem-
  blees;
Mont Pyrenees le rendront console,
Lors que dans May seront terres
  tremblees.

A great king shall be left desolate,
Near the River Hebrus an assembly
  shall be made,
The Pyrenean Mountains shall
  comfort him,
When in May shall be an earthquake.

A reference to an ancient incident, this concerns a King who, after
being defeated in battle near the River Hebrus (the ancient name for
the River Maritza), loses his kingdom and is forced to flee to the shelter
of the Pyrenees Mountains.

89

Entre deux cymbles pieds & mains
  estachez,
De miel face oingt, & de laict sub-
  stante;
Geuspes & mouches seront amour
  fachez,
Poccilateurs faucer, cyphe tente.

Between two boats one shall be
  tied hand and foot,
His face anointed with honey, and
  be nourished with milk,
Wasps and bees shall make much
  of him mad,
For being treacherous cup bearers,
  and poisoning the cup.

A description of a form of ancient torture meted out to poisoners—put
between two troughs called boats, their bodies were daubed with honey,
so that wasps and bees could torment them to death.

90

L'honnissement puant abominable,
Apres le faict sera felicite;
Grand excuse, pour n'estre favor-
    able,
Qu'a paix Neptune ne sera incite.

The stinking and abominable de-
    filing,
After the deed shall be successful,
The great one excused for not be-
    ing favorable,
That Neptune might be persuaded
    to peace.

This refers to an infamous pact, agreed upon by several nations, ostensibly for the preservation of peace. The Munich Pact and the temporary acclamation of the role played by Chamberlain are clearly indicated.

91

Le conducteur de la Guerre Navale,
Rouge effrene, severe, horrible
    grippe,
Captif eschappe de l'aisne dans la
    baste;
Quand il naistra du grand un fils
    Agrippe.

The leader of the Naval War,
Red, rash, severe, horrible execu-
    tioner.
Being slave, shall escape, hidden
    among the harness,
When shall be born to the great
    one, a son named Agrippa.

Cornelius Agrippa, 1486–1535, a German soldier, philosopher and alchemist, is here alluded to.

92

Prince de beaute tant venuste,
Au chef menee, le second faict
    trahy;
La cite au glaive de poudre face
    aduste,
Par trop grand meurtre le chef du
    Roy hay.

A Prince of an exquisite beauty,
Shall be brought to the chief, the
    second fact betrayed,
The city shall be given to fire and
    sword,
By too great a murder, the chief
    man of the King shall be hated.

Louis XVI, a prince of beauty, was beheaded by the guillotine (glaive/single-edged blade).

93

Prelat avare, d'ambition trompe,
Rien ne fera que trop cuider
viendra,
Ses messagers, & luy bien attrape,
Tout au rebours voir qui le bois
fendra.

A covetous Prelate, deceived by
ambition,
Shall do nothing but covet too
much,
His messengers and he shall be
trapped,
When they shall see one cleave the
the wood the contrary way.

There will be a counter-religious movement downgrading the radio
and video-evangelist preachers.

94

Un Roy ire sera aux sedifragues,
Quand interdicts seront hernois de
guerre,
La poison taincte au succre par les
fragues,
Par eaux meurtris, morts disant
serre serre.

A King shall be irate against the
treaty breakers,
When the warlike armour shall be
forbidden,
The poison with sugar shall be put
in the strawberries,
They shall be killed and die, saying, "close, close."

After a trial, held against the treaty breakers, they shall be executed saying, "We came very close."

95

Par detracteur calomnie a puis nay;
Quand istront faict enormes &
martiaux;
La moindre part dubieuse a l'aisne,
Et tost au regne seront faicts par-
tiaux.

The youngest son shall be slan-
dered by a detractor,
When enormous and martial deeds
shall be done,
The least part shall be doubtful to
the eldest,
And soon after they shall both be
equal in the government.

Nostradamus here predicts that Ted Kennedy will become president.
He is (1) "youngest son," (2) "martial deeds" have been done (Vietnam),
(3) John Kennedy, already assassinated, is, of course, unaware of the
new development, and (4) the equality in government reveals that Ted
Kennedy will be president.

96

Grand cite a soldats abandonnee,
Onc ny eut mortel tumult si
    proche,
O qu'elle hideuse calamite s'ap-
    proche,
Fors une offense n'y sera pardon-
    nee.

A great city shall be abandoned to
    the soldiers,
There never was a mortal tumult
    so near,
Oh! what a hideous calamity ap-
    proaches,
Except one offense, nothing shall
    be pardoned.

A great city shall be pillaged by a barbarian horde; the only ones
spared shall be those of the same race.

97

Cinq & quarante degrez ciel bru-
    slera,
Feu approcher de la grand cite
    neuve,
Instant grand flamme esparse sau-
    tera,
Quand on voudra des Normans
    faire preuve.

The heaven shall burn at five and
    forty degrees,
The fire shall come near the great
    new city,
In an instant a great flame dis-
    persed shall burst out,
When they shall make a trial of
    the Normans.

A cataclysmic fire shall engulf the greatest and newest of the world's
big cities, particularly at the level of the 45th parallel, i.e., New York,
Chicago, Minneappolis, San Francisco, Bucharest, Belgrade, Rome, Paris,
and Madrid.

98

Ruyne aux Volsques de peur si fort
    terribles,
Leur grand cite taincte, faict pesti-
    lent;
Piller sol, lune, & violer leurs
    temples;
Et les deux fleuves rougir de sang
    coulant.

Ruin shall happen to the Vandals
    that will be terrible,
Their great city shall be tainted, a
    pestilent deed;
They shall plunder sun and moon,
    and violate their temples,
And two rivers shall be red with
    running blood.

The atomic bombing of Hiroshima is foretold by Nostradamus. Its
location, between two rivers, is given, as well as the mention of the temples
of the Japanese.

99

L'ennemy docte se tournera confus,
Grand camp malade, & de faict par
embusches,
Mont Pyrenees & Pernus luy seront faict refus,
Proche du fleuve descouvrant antiques ruches.

The learned enemy shall go back
confounded,
A great camp shall be sick and in
effect through ambush,
The Pyrenean Mountains shall
refuse him,
Near the river discovering the
ancient hives.

An educated yet barbarous nation shall be defeated in its attempt to
foist its culture on other peoples, and its leaders shall be refused sanctuary
wherever they try to flee.

100

Fille de l'Aure, asyle du mal sain,
Ou jusqu'au ciel se void l'ampthi-
teatre;
Prodige veu, ton mal est fort prochain,
Seras captive, & des fois plus de
quatre.

Daughter of Laura, sanctuary of
the sick,
Where to the heavens is seen the
amphitheatre;
A prodigy being seen, the danger
is near,
Thou shalt be taken captive above
four times.

An ingenious stanza, it contains many things. The reference to "Daughter of Laura" concerns the city of Nismes in Languedoc, famous for its
amphitheatre and for being the birthplace of Laura, mistress of the poet
Petrarch. The last two lines contain a warning of approaching civil war
in France, clearly an indication of the far-in-the-future French Revolution.

LEGIS CAUTIO CONTRA INEPTOS CRITICOS

Qui legent hos versus, mature censunto;
Prophanum vulgus & inscium ne attrectato.
Omnesque Astrologi, Blenni, Barbari procul sunto,
Qui aliter faxit, is rite sacer esto.

INVOCATION OF THE LAW AGAINST INEPT CRITICS

Those who read these verses, let them consider with mature mind,

Let not the profane, vulgar and ignorant be attracted to their study.

All Astrologers, Fools and Barbarians draw not near,

He who acts otherwise, is cursed according to rite.

[Various quatrains within the following Century were found to duplicate those occurring in the previous Centuries, and therefore have been deleted. The numbering of the quatrains has been maintained according to the original sequence.]

1

L'arc du thresor par Achilles deceu,
Aux procrees sceu la quadrangulaire;
Au faict Royal le comment sera sceu,
Corps veu pendu au veu du populaire.

The arch of the treasure by Achilles deceived,
Shall show to posterity the quadrangle,
In the royal deed the comment shall be known,
The body seen hung in full view of the people.

Marshal d'Ancre, Treasurer of France, and favorite of the Queen Regent, Marie de Medici, was exposed by Achilles de Harlay, President of Paris, and convicted for the mishandling of funds. By order of Louis XIII, he was killed in the quadrangle of the Louvre and his body was later hanged in a public place.

2

Par Mars ouvert Arles ne donra guerre,
De nuict seront les soldats estonnez;
Noir, blanc, a l'Inde dissimule en terre,
Sous la saincte ombre traistre verrez & sonnez.

Arles shall not proceed by open war,
By night the soldiers shall be astonished,
Black, white, and blue dissembled on the ground,
Under the feigned shadow will be proclaimed traitors.

Nostradamus anticipates the use of laser beams in warfare. "Arles" is an anagram of laser, which is particularly useful in night combat. The use of a laser beam focused upon the ground from an orbiting satellite is yet to occur but it is predicted for the near future.

3

Apres de France la victoire navale,
Les Barchinons, Sallinons, les Phocens,
Lierre d'or, l'enclume serre dedans
  la balle,
Ceux de Toulon au fraud seront
  consents.

After the naval victory of the
  French,
Upon those of Tunis, Salle, and
  the Phocens,
Keg of gold, the anvil shut up in
  a ball,
Those of Toulon to the fraud shall
  consent.

A naval victory of the French over those of the Barbary Coast shall
be attained by means of a novel weapon, an anvil and a ball, shut up in
a keg of gold.

4

Le Duc de Langres assiege dedans
  Dole,
Accompagne d'Ostin & Lyonnois;
Geneve, Auspourg, joinct ceux de
  Mirandole,
Passer les monts conter les Ancon-
  nois.

The Duke of Langres shall be be-
  sieged in Dole,
Being in company with those of
  Autun and Lion,
Geneva, Augsburg, those of Miran-
  dola,
Shall go over the mountains against
  those of Ancona.

France, Italy, Switzerland, and Germany shall be involved in a military
expedition.

5

Vin sur la table en sera respandu,
Le tiers n'aura celle qu'il preten-
  doit;
Deux fois du noir de Parme des-
  cendu,
Perouse a Pise ce qu'il cuidoit.

Wine shall be spilt upon the table,
By reason that a third person shall
  not have her,
Twice, the black one, descended
  from Parma,
Shall do to Perugia and Pisa what
  he intended.

The all-powerful Black One in Italy shall dominate and ravage Italian
centers of culture at will.

6

Naples, Palerme, & tout la Sicile,	Naples, Palermo and all Sicily,
Par main barbare sera inhabitee,	By barbarous hands shall be depopulated,
Corsique, Salerne & de Sardeigne, l'Isle,	Corsica, Salerno and the Island of Sardinia,
Faim, peste guerre, fin de maux intemptee.	In them shall be famine, plague, war and endless evils.

A picture, as foreseen by Nostradamus, of conditions in Italy in the closing years of World War II.

7

Sur le combat des grands chevaus legers,	At the fight of the great light horsemen,
On criera le grand croissant confond,	They shall cry out, confound the great crescent,
De nuict tuer moutons, habits de bergers,	By night they shall kill sheep dressed as shepherds,
Abismes rouges dans le fosse profond.	Red abysms shall be in the deep ditch.

East-West conflict here. "Confounding the great crescent" is meant to include the Soviet (sickle). Defeat of the Reds is forecast in line 4.

8

Flora, fuis, fuis le plus proche Romain,	Flora, fly, fly from the nearest Roman,
Au Fesulan sera conflict donne;	In the Fesulan shall be the fight,
Sang espandu, les plus grands prins a main,	Blood shall be spilt, the greatest shall be taken,
Temple ne sexe ne sera pardonne.	Neither temple nor sex shall be spared.

When the Nazis retreated from Florence they blew up the bridges across the Arno. However, rather than destroy the famous Ponte Vecchio, they blew up the buildings on either side of the bridge, thereby making it impassable.

9

Dame a l'abscence de son grand
  capitaine,
Sera priee d'amour du Viceroy,
Faincte promesse & mal'heureuse
  estraine,
Entre les mains du grand Prince
  Barroys.

A lady in the absence of her great
  captain,
Shall be entreated of love by the
  Viceroy,
A pretended promise and unhappy
  New Year's gift,
In the hand of the great Prince of
  Bar.

Bar was a principality adjoining Lorraine, which Henry IV gave as a
marriage gift to his sister Catherine, when she married the Duke of Lorraine's son. The rest of this quatrain indicates some unhappiness connected with this match.

10

Par le grand Prince limitrophe du
  Mans,
Preux & vaillant chef de grand ex-
  ercite;
Par mer & terre de Gallois & Nor-
  mans,
Caspre passer Barcelonne pille Isle.

The great Prince dwelling near Le
  Mans,
Stout and valiant, general of a
  great army,
Of Britons and Normans by sea
  and land,
Ravaging Cape Barcelona and
  plunder the Island.

Charles de Gaulle epitomized the gallantry of French royalty with his
military bearing and statesmanlike posture.

11

L'enfant Royal contemnera la
  mere,
Oeil, pieds blessez, rude, inobeis-
  sant,
Nouvelle a dame estrange & bien
  amere,
Seront tuez des siens plus de cinq
  cens.

The Royal Infant shall despise his
  mother,
Eye, feet wounded, rude, disobedi-
  ent,
News to a lady very strange and
  bitter,
There shall be killed about five
  hundred.

In 1615, when Louis XIII, King of France, was about fifteen years of
age, he was persuaded to make war against his own mother, Marie de
Medici, then Regent of the Kingdom. In the ensuing battle about five
hundred of the Queen's soldiers were slain.

12

Le grand puisnay fera fin de guerre,
Aux dieux assemble les excusez,
Cahors, Moissac iront long de la serre,
Rusec, Lectore, les Agenoise rasez.

The great young brother shall make an end of the war,
In two places he shall gather the excused,
Cahors, Moissac, shall go out of his clutches,
Russec, Lectore and those of Agen shall be cut off.

When Ted Kennedy is president ("the great young brother") he shall end a war the United States is engaged in. The two places where he shall gather the excused will be revealed later.

13

De la cite marine & tributaire,
La teste raze prendra la satrapie;
Chasser sordide qui puis sera contraire,
Par quatorze ans tiendra la tyrannie.

Of the maritime city and tributary,
The shaven head shall take the government,
He shall turn out a vile man who shall oppose him,
During fourteen years he will keep away the tyranny.

Napoleon was known to his soldiers as "le petit tondu" (the little crop-head). He made his mark early in the siege of the maritime city of Toulon and enjoyed absolute power for fourteen years, from 1799 to 1814.

14

Faux exposer viendra topographie,
Seront les cruches des monuments ouvertes;
Pulluler secte, sainte philosophie,
Pour blanches, noires, & pour antiques vertes.

They shall show topography falsely,
The urns of the monuments shall be open,
Sects shall multiply and holy philosophy,
Shall give black for white, and green for gold.

A corrupt period in history is foretold, when too many sects will spring up, creating great conflict in the church.

15

Devant cite de l'insubre countree,
Sept ans sera le siege devant mis;
Le tres grand Roy y fera son entree,
Cite puis libre hors de ses ennemis.

Before a city of the lower country,
Seven years of siege shall be laid,
The most great King shall make
  his entry into it,
Then the city shall be full being
  out of the enemies' hands.

A city in the Low Country will be under siege for seven years, after which it will be liberated and the former inhabitants, who had fled from their enemy, will return to enjoy the new freedom.

16

Entree profonde par la grand
  Royne faicte;
Rendra le lieu puissant inacces-
  sible;
L'armee des trois Lyons sera def-
  faicte,
Faisant dedans cas hideux & ter-
  rible.

The deep trench made by the
  Queen,
Shall make the place powerful and
  inaccessible,
The army of the three lions shall
  be defeated,
Doing within a hideous and ter-
  rible thing.

An army, owing allegiance to an alliance of three predatory monarchs, shall be defeated but not before committing hideous crimes against captured civilians.

17

Le Prince rare en pitie & clemence,
Apres avoir la paix aux siens baille,
Viendra changer par mort grand
  cognoissance,
Par grand repos le regne travaille.

The Prince, rare in pity and clem-
  ency,
After he shall have given peace to
  his subjects,
Shall by death change his great
  knowledge,
After great rest the kingdom shall
  be troubled.

This concerns Henry IV, peace-loving King of France, who was assassi-nated on May 14, 1610, by Ravaillac. After his death there was much trouble in the Kingdom caused by the dissension among the Princes.

18

Les assiegez couleront leurs paches,
Sept jours apres feront cruelle issue,
Dans repoulez, feu sang, sept mis
    a l'hache,
Dame captive qu'avoit la paix issue.

The besieged shall color their ar-
    ticles,
Seven days after they shall make a
    cruel issue,
They shall be beaten back, fire,
    blood, seven put to the axe,
The lady shall be prisoner who
    tried to make peace.

The political dissidents, later known as the "Chicago Seven," tried to
upset a Democratic National Convention and were eventually brought to
trial.

19

Le fort Nicene ne sera combatu,
Vaincu sera par rutilant metal,
Son faict sera un long temps de-
    batu,
Au citadins estrange espouvantal.

The Nicene fort shall not be fought
    against,
By shining metal it shall be over-
    come,
The doing of it shall a long time
    be debated,
It shall be a strange fearful thing
    to the citizens.

Monte Carlo (Monaco) is adjacent to Nice and has long dominated
it through its revenues from gambling ("shining metal"—gold!).

20

Ambassadeurs de la Toscane lan-
    gue,
Avril & May Alpes & mer passer,
Celuy de veau exposera l'harangue,
Vie Gauloise en voulant effacer.

The ambassadors of the Tuscan
    tongue,
In April and May, shall go over the
    Alps and the sea,
One like a calf, shall make a speech,
Attempting to defame French cus-
    toms.

On May 7, 1938, Mussolini, in a mutual admiration session with the
Fuehrer, in Berlin, flamboyantly stated, "Germany and Italy have left
behind them the Utopias to which Europe has entrusted her destiny. It
is this law which Nazi Germany and Fascist Italy has obeyed obeys, and
will obey."

21

Par pestilente inimitie Volsique,
Dissimulee chassera le tyran;
Au pont de Sorgues se fera la traf-
   fique,
De mettre a mort luy & son adher-
   ent.

By a pestilent Italian enmity,
The dissembler shall expel the
   tyrant,
The bargains shall be made at Sorgues bridge,
To put him and his adherent to
   death.

Premier Pierre Laval, cohort of Mussolini, was eventually expelled,
captured and executed, thus fulfilling the prophecy.

22

Les Citoyens de Mesopotamie,
Irez encontre amis de Tarraconne,
Jeux, Ris, banquets, toute gent en-
   dormie,
Vicaire au Rhosne, prins cite, ceux
   d'Ausone.

The citizens of Mesopotamia,
Being angry with the friends of
   Tarrogona,
Sport, laughter, banquets, every-
   body being asleep,
The vicar being in Rhone, the city
   taken by those of Bordeaux.

This concerns a region of France which lies between two rivers, and
its long since forgotten quarrel with the citizens of Bordeaux.

23

Le Royal Sceptre sera contrainct de
   prendre,
Ce que ses predecesseurs voint en-
   gage;
Puis que l'aigneau on fera mal entendre,
Lors qu'on viendra le palais sacca-
   ger.

The Royal Sceptre shall be con-
   strained to take
What his predecessors had mortgaged,
After that they shall misinform the
   lamb,
When they shall come to plunder
   the palace.

Clearly, this refers to the plunder of the royal palace in Iran when the
Shah abdicated in 1979. The assets of the Pahlavi dynasty were mortgaged
for armaments, planes, and sophisticated military hardware.

24

L'ensevely sortira du tombeau,	The buried shall come out of his grave,
Fera de chaines lier le fort du pont,	The fort of the bridge shall be tied with chains,
Empoisonne avec oeufs de Barbeau,	Poisoned with the roe of a Barbel,
Grand de Lorraine par le Marquis du Pont,	Shall a great one of Lorraine be, by the Marquis Dupont.

The first part of this verse has no importance or relationship to the prophecy, which concerns the poisoning of the Duke of Lorrain by the Marquis Du Pont.

25

Par guerre longue tout l'exercite espuiser,	By a long war, all the army drained dry,
Que pour soldats ne trouveront pecune,	So that to raise soldiers, they shall find no money,
Lieu d'or, d'argent, cuir on viendra cuser,	Instead of gold and silver, they shall stamp leather,
Gaulois aerain, signe croissant de Lune.	The French copper, marked with the signs of the crescent moon.

Before the discovery of the West Indies, and the consequent expansion and exploitation of the colonies, many European countries were forced to use substitutes for the usual gold and silver coins.

26

Fustes galees autour de sept navires,	Flying boats and galleys round about seven ships,
Sera livree une mortelle guerre;	Shall be in the livery of deadly war,
Chef de Madrid, recevra coup de vires,	The chief of Madrid shall receive blows of oars,
Deux eschapees, & cinq menees a terre.	Two shall escape, and five carried to land.

The concept of "flying boats" could forecast the original Howard Hughes "Spruce Goose" and the initial Pan American Airways Clipper which landed on water. And further, the multiple nuclear warheads of the Trident missile class fired from underwater by submarines is foretold in lines 1 and 2.

27

Au coin de vast la grand cavalerie,
Proche a Ferrare empeshce au ba-
gage,
Pompe a Turin feront tel volerie,
Que dans le fort raviront leur hos-
tage.

In a corner of the wasted, the great
cavalry,
Near Ferrara, shall be busy about
the baggage,
Pomp at Turin, they shall make
such a robbery,
That in the fort they shall ravish
their hostage.

During a war the people of the country will sustain great losses and suffer greatly, while their leaders will lead lives of luxury in a fortified city.

28

Le captaine conduira grande proye,
Sur la montagne des ennemis plus
proche,
Environne, par feu fera telle voye.
Tous eschappez, or trente mis en
broche.

The captain shall lead a great prey,
Upon the mountain, that shall be
nearest to the enemies,
Being encompassed with fire, he
shall make such a way,
All shall escape, except thirty that
shall be spitted.

A leader, surrounded by enemy soldiers, shall contrive to lead his men out of danger, except thirty who will be taken and tortured by their captors.

29

Le grand duc d'Albe se viendra rebeller,
A ses grands peres fera le tradi-
ment;
Le grand de Guise le viendra de-
beller,
Captif mene & dresse monument.

The great Duke of Alba shall rebel,
To his grandfathers he shall make
the plot,
The great Guise shall vanquish
him,
Led prisoner, and a monument
erected.

The Duke of Alba was sent to Rome by Charles V of Spain, to lend his aid to others of the Spanish Party in that city.

30

Le sac s'approche, feu, grand sang
  espandu,
Pau, grand fleuve, aux bouvirs l'entreprinse,
De Gennes, Nice, apres long attendu,
Foussan, Turin, a Savillan la prinse.

The sack draws near, fire, abundance of blood spilt,
Pau, a great river, an enterprise by
  churls,
Of Genoa, Nice after they shall
  have stayed long,
Fossan, Turin, the prize shall be
  at Savillan.

For four years, 1555-59, there was constant fighting among various
cities in Italy, especially those near the River Pau (Po).

31

De Langeudoc, & Guienne plus de
  dix,
Mille voudront les Alpes repasser;
Grans Allobroges marcher contre
  Brundis,
Aquin & Bresse les viendront re-
  casser.

From Languedoc and Guienne
  more than 10,000
Would be glad to repass the Alps,
Great Allobroges shall march
  against Brundis,
Aquin and Bresse shall beat them
  back.

A French army passing over the Alps into Italy will regret this maneuver.

32

Du Mont Royal naistra d'une ca-
  sane,
Qui duc, & compte viendra tyran-
  niser,
Dresser copie de la marche Mil-
  lane,
Favence, Florence d'or & gens es-
  puiser.

Out of Montreal shall be born in a
  cottage,
One that shall tyrannize over duke
  and earl,
He shall raise an army in the land
  of the rebellion,
He shall empty Favence and Florence of their gold.

Pierre Elliot Trudeau was born in Montreal in 1919 and served as
the Canadian Prime Minister from 1968–1979 and again in 1981. The
rebellion referred to is between the French- and English-speaking Ca-
nadians.

33

Par fraude, regne, forces expolier,
La classe obsesse, passages a l'es-
pie;
Deux faicnts amis se viendront
t'allier,
Esueiller haine de long temps assoupie.

By fraud a kingdom and army shall
be despoiled,
The fleet shall be possessed, passages shall be made to spies,
Two feigned friends shall agree
together,
They shall raise up a hatred that
had long been dormant.

The alliance between Hitler and Mussolini is predicted. The infiltration
by propaganda, the rousing of Anti-Semitism and their "divide and conquer" technique are described.

34

En grand regret sera la gent Gauloise,
Coeur vain, leger croira temerite;
Pain, sel, ne vin, eau, venin ne cer-
voise,
Plus grand captif, faim, froid, ne-
cessite.

In great regret shall the French
nation be,
Their vain and light heart shall believe rashly,
They shall have neither bread, salt,
wine nor beer,
Moreover, they shall be prisoners
and shall suffer hunger, cold and
need.

This continuation of the preceding stanza tells of conditions in France
under the heel of the Axis invader.

35

Le grand poche viendra plaindre,
pleurer,
D'avoir esleu, trompez seront en
l'aage,
Guiere avec eux ne voudra demeu-
rer;
Deceu sera par ceux de son langage.

The great pouch shall bewail and
bemoan,
Having elected one, they shall be
deceived,
His age shall not stay long with
them,
He shall be deceived by those of
his own language.

This continues the previous prediction of conditions in France, under
Hitlerism; and goes on to outline the sabotaging, by the French underground movement, of the Vichy regime under Marshal Petain.

36

Dieu, le ciel tout le divin verbe a
  l'onde,
Porte par rouges sept razes a Bizance,
Contre les oingts trois cens de Tre-
  bisonde,
Deux loix mettront, & horreur,
  pluis credence.

God, Heaven all the divine world
  in water,
Carried by red ones, seven shaved
  heads at Stamboul,
Against the anointed, three hundred of Trebizond,
They shall put two laws, and horror, and afterwards believe.

A great disputation is to take place in Constantinople, seven priests
against three hundred unbelievers.

37

Dix envoyez, chef de nef mettre a
  mort,
D'un adverty, en classe guerre ouverte;
Confusion chef, l'un se picque &
  mord,
Le ryn, stecades nefs, cap dedans
  la nerte.

Ten shall be sent to put the captain of the ship to death,
He shall have notice by one, the
  fleet shall be in open war,
Great confusion shall be, by pricks
  and bites,
The Rhine, dung boats, within the
  north cape.

A mutiny shall take place within the German Navy.

38

L'aisne Royal sur coursier volti-
  geant,
Picquer viendra si rudement courir;
Cueulle, lipee, pied dans l'estrain
  pliegnant,
Traine, tire, horriblement mourir.

The eldest Royal, prancing upon a
  horse,
Shall spur, and run fiercely,
Open mouth, the foot in stirrup,
  complaining,
Drawn, pulled, die horribly.

The eldest son of a King shall die a horrible death as the result of
being thrown from a horse.

39

Le conducteur de l'armee Francoise,
Cuidant perdre le principale phalange;
Par sus pave de l'Avaigne & d'ardoise,
Soy parfondra par Gennes gent estrange.

The leader of the French army,
Hoping to rout the principal phalanx,
Upon the pavement of Avaigne and slate,
Shall sink in the ground by Genoa, a strange nation.

A French General shall meet with disaster in his attempt to attack the strongest flank of the enemy. The land being strange to him, he shall lead his men into swampy territory and they shall flounder and sink into the ground, and thus be routed.

40

Dedans tonneaux hors oingts d'huile & gresse,
Seront vingt un devant le port fermez,
Au second guet par mort feront prouesse,
Gaigner les portes, & du guet assommez.

In empty tuns slippery with oil and grease,
Before the harbor, one and twenty shall be shut,
At the second watch by death they shall do great feats of arms,
To win the gates, and be killed by the watch.

By a stratagem, twenty-one men shall attempt to sneak through the gates of an enemy harbor but shall fail and be killed.

41

Les os des pieds & des mains enserrez,
Par bruit maison long temps inhabitee,
Seront par songes concavant deterrez,
Maison salubre & sans bruit habitee.

The bones of the feet and hands in shackles,
By a noise a house shall be a long time deserted,
By a dream the buried shall be taken out of the ground,
The house shall be salubrious, and inhabited without noise.

A ghost shall inhabit a house, wherein a skeleton is shackled. After decent burial of the remains the house shall again be at rest.

42

Quand Innocent tiendra le lieu de Pierre,	When Innocent shall hold the place of Peter,
Le Nizaram Sicilian se verra,	The Sicilian Nizaram shall see himself,
En grands honneurs, mais apres il cherra,	In great honors, but after that he shall fall,
Dans le bourbier d'une civil guerre.	Into the dirt of a civil war.

This prognostication is remarkable for its clarity of wording and the exactness of its fulfillment. Setting the period of time, our first reference is to Innocent X who was elected Pope in 1644. His noted contemporary, the French Cardinal Mazarin (anagrammatically referred to here as Nizaram) was of Italian origin. Under the sponsorship of Richelieu he became a citizen of France and eventually the successor of the great Cardinal. He was one of the most powerful figures of his time and led the fortunes of France during the closing years of the Thirty Years' War.

43

Lutece en Mars, Senateurs en credit,	Lutetia in Mars, Senators shall be in credit,
Por une unit Gaule sera troublee,	In a night France shall be troubled,
Du grand Croesus l'Horoscope predit,	The Horoscope of the Great Croesus predicts,
Par Saturnus, sa puissance exilee.	That by Saturn his power shall be put down.

Lutetia is the Latin word for Paris. After the death of Henry IV, King of France, the Parliament of Paris began to check on the activities of various noblemen, among them the Marquis d'Ancre. His fate is described in Quatrain 1, Century VII.

44

Deux de poison saisis nouveaux Venus,	Two by poison provided by the new Venus,
Dans la cuisine du grand Prince verser;	To pour in the kitchen of the great Prince,
Par le souillard tous deux au faict cogneus,	By the scullion the fact shall be known,
Prins qui cuidoit de mort l'aisne vexer.	And be taken, that thought by death to vex the elder.

A woman shall provide poison, in a plot to do away with a great Prince. A cook's boy shall discover the plot when tasting the King's dish.

73

Renfort de sieges manubis & man-
  iples,
Changez le sacre & passe sur le
  Pronsne,
Prins & captifs n'arreste les priz
  triples,
Plus par fonds mis, esleve, mis au
  trosne.

Recruit of sieges, spoils and prizes,
Holy day shall be changed and
  passed over the Pronsne,
Taken, made captive and not held
  in the triple field,
Moreover, one from the bottom
  shall be raised to the throne.

A period of military unrest will take place, resulting in the raising of
a little Corporal to the throne.

80

L'Occident libres les Isles Britan-
  niques,
Le recogneu passer le bas, puis
  haut,
Ne content trist Rebel, corff, Esco-
  tiques,
Puis rebeller par plui & par nuict
  chaut.

The West shall be free, and the
  British Isles,
The discovered shall pass low, then
  high,
Scotch Pirates shall be, who shall
  rebel,
In a rainy and hot night.

John Paul Jones, called by the British "the Scotch Pirate and Rebel,"
is here referred to by Nostradamus, as is the fact that the West (America)
shall be free.

82

La stratageme simulte sera rare,
La mort en voye rebelle par con-
  tree,
Par le retour du voyage Barbare,
Exalteront la protestante entree.

The simulated stratagem shall be
  scarce,
Death shall be in a rebellious way
  through the country,
By the return from the Barbarian
  voyage,
They shall exalt the Protestant entrance.

A political stratagem shall result in the triumph of the Protestants.

83

Vent chaut, conseil, pleurs, timidite,
De nuict au lit assailly sans les armes,
D'oppression grande calamite,
L'Epithalame converty pleurs & larmes.

Hot wind, counsel, tears, fearfulness,
He shall be assaulted in his bed by night without arms,
From that oppression shall be raised a great calamity,
The Epithalamium shall be converted into tears.

The Epithalamium, a nuptial song or poem in praise of the bride or bridegroom, is referred to here. The connected event can be gathered from the text of the stanza.

EPISTLE TO HENRY II

To the most invincible, most high, and most Christian King of France, Henry the Second: Michael Nostradamus, his most obedient servant and subject, wishes victory and happiness.

By reason of that singular observation, O most Christian and victorious King, my face, which had been cloudy a great while, did present itself before your immeasurable Majesty. I have been ever since perpetually dazzled, continually honoring and worshipping that day, in which I presented myself before it, as before a singular and humane Majesty. Now seeking after some occasion whereby I might make appear the goodness and sincerity of my heart and extend my acquaintance toward your most excellent Majesty, and seeing that it was impossible for me to declare it by effects, as well as because of the darkness and obscurity of my mind, even for the enlightening it did receive from the face of the greatest Monarch in the world. It was a great while before I could resolve to whom I should dedicate these three last Centuries of my Prophecies, which make the complete thousand. After I had a long time considered, I have with a great temerity made my address to your Majesty, being no way daunted by it, as the great author Plutarch related in the Life of Lycurgus, that, seeing the offerings and gifts that were sacrificed in the temples of their heathen gods, many came no more, lest the people should wonder at the expense.

Notwithstanding, seeing your royal splendor joined with an incomparable humanity, I have made my address to it, not as to the Kings of Persia, of

---

This dedicatory letter was used by Nostradamus as the preface to his second edition which contained new prophecies.

The following notation appeared, on the page preceding the above epistle, in the 1672 edition of *The Prophecies or Prognostications of Michael Nostradamus*, translated and annotated by Theophilus de Garencieres.

Friendly Reader,

Before you read the following epistle, I would have you be warned of a few things: One is, that according to my opinion, it is very obscure and intelligible (sic) in most places, being without any just connection, and besides the obscurity of the sense, the crabbedness of the expression is such, that had not the importunity of the Bookseller prevailed, I would have left it out, but considering the respect due to Antiquity, the satisfaction we owe to curious persons, who would perhaps have thought the Book imperfect without it, we let it go, trusting to your candor and ingenuity.

whom to come near it was forbidden, but as to a most prudent and wise prince. I have dedicated my nocturnal and prophetical calculations, written rather by a natural instinct and poetical furor than by any rules of poetry; and the most part of it written and agreeing with the years, months and weeks, of the regions, countries and most of the towns and cities in Europe; touching also something of Africa, and of a part of Asia, by the change of regions that come near to those climates, and compounded in a natural fashion. But some may answer (who hath need to blow his nose) that the rhyme is as easy to be understood, as the sense is hard to get at. Therefore, O most humane King, most of the prophetical stanzas are so difficult, that there is no way to be found for the interpretation of them. Nevertheless, being in hope of setting down the towns, cities, and regions, wherein most of those shall happen, especially in the year 1585, and in the year 1606, beginning from this present time, which is the 14th of March, 1557.

Going further to the fulfilling of those things, which shall be in the beginning of the seventh millenary, according to my astronomical calculation and other learning which I could reach (at which time the adversaries of Christ and of His Church shall begin to multiply), all has been composed and calculated in days and hours of election, and well disposed, and all as accurately as was possible for me to do. And the whole *"Minerva libera et non invita,"* * calculating almost as much of the time that is come, as of that which is past, comprehending it in the present time, and what by the course of the said time shall be known to happen in all regions punctually as it is here written, adding nothing superfluous, although it be said *"Quod de futuris non est determinata omnino veritas."* ** It is very true, Sir, that by my natural instinct given me by my progenitors, I did think I could foretell anything; but having made an agreement between this said instinct of mine, and a long calculation of art, and by a great tranquility and repose of mind, by emptying my soul of all care, I have foretold most part of these *ex tripode œneo* (by the brass tripod), though there be many who attribute to me some things that are no more mine than what is nothing at all. Only the eternal God, who is the searcher of men's hearts, being pious, just, and merciful, is the true Judge of it; Him I beseech to defend me from the calumny of wicked men, who would as willingly question how all your ancient progenitors, the Kings of France, have healed the disease called the Kings-evil; how some other nations have cured the biting of venomous beasts; others have had a certain instinct to foretell things that are to come, and of others too tedious to be here inserted. Notwithstanding those in

---

* "When Minerva was free and favorable."
** "There can be no truth entirely determined for certain which concerns the future."

whom the malignancy of the wicked spirit shall not be suppressed by
length of time, I hope that after my decease my work shall be in more
esteem than when I was alive.

However, if I should fail in the calculation of times, or should not
please some, may it please your most imperial Majesty to forgive me,
protesting before God and His Saints, that I do not intend to insert
anything in writing in this present Epistle that may be contrary to the true
Catholic faith, while consulting the astronomical calculations, according
to my learning. For the space of times of our fathers that have been before
us are such, submitting myself to the correction of the most learned, that
the first man Adam was before Noah, about one thousand two hundred
and forty-two years, not computing the time according to the Gentile
records, as Varro did, but only according to the Sacred Scriptures, taking
them as a guide to my astronomical calculations, and to the best of my
understanding. After Noah and the universal flood, about a thousand
and fourscore years, came Abraham, who was a supreme astrologer, according to most men's opinion, and did first invent the Chaldean letters; after
that came Moses, some five hundred and fifteen or sixteen years after.
And between the time of David and Moses there passed about five hundred and seventy years. After which, between the time of David and that
of our Saviour and Redeemer Jesus Christ, born of the Virgin Mary, there
passed (according to some chronographers) a thousand three hundred and
fifty years.

Some may object, that this calculation is not true; because it differs
from that of Eusebius. And from the time of human redemption, to that
of the execrable seduction of the Saracens, have passed six hundred and
four and twenty years or thereabouts. From that time hitherto, it is
easy to gather what times are past. If my computations be not good among
all nations, however, all has been calculated by the course of the celestial
bodies joined with emotion infused in me at certain loose hours, the
emotion which has been handed down to me by my ancient progenitors.
But the danger at this time (most excellent King) requires that such
secret events should not be manifested except by an enigmatical sentence,
having but one sense and only one intelligence, without having mixed
with it any ambiguous or amphibological calculation. But rather under
a cloudy obscurity, through a natural infusion, coming near to the sentence
of one of the thousand and two Prophets, that have been since the Creation
of the world, according to the calculation and Punic Chronicle of Joel:
"Effundum spiritum meum super omnem carnem, et prophetabunt filii
vestri, et filiae vestrae." * But such a prophecy did proceed from the mouth
of the Holy Spirit, who was the supreme and eternal power, which being

---

* See Joel ii.28.

come with that of the celestial bodies, has caused some of them to predict great and wonderful things.

For my part I challenge no such thing in this place, God forbid. I confess truly, that all comes from God, for which I give Him thanks, honor, and praise, without having mixed anything of that divination which proceeds à fato, but à Deo, à natura (which proceeds from fate, but from God, and nature). And most of it is joined with the motion and course of the celestial bodies, much as if seeing in a lens, and through a cloudy vision, the great and sad events, the prodigious and calamitous accidents that shall befall the worshippers. First upon the temples of God, and secondly upon those who draw their support from earth, this draws near, with a thousand other calamitous accidents, which shall be known in the course of time.

For God will take notice of the long barrenness of the great Dame, who afterwards shall conceive two principal children. But, being in danger, she will give birth with risk at her age of death in the eighteenth year, and not able to go beyond thirty-six, shall leave behind her three males and one female, and he will have two who never had any of the same father. The differences between the three brothers shall be such, though united and agreed, that the three and four parts of Europe will tremble. By the lesser in years shall the Christian monarchy be upheld and augmented; sects shall rise and presently be put down again; the Arabians shall be put back; kingdoms shall be united and new laws made. Concerning the other children, the first shall possess the furious crowned Lions, holding their paws upon the escutcheons. The second, well attended by the Latins, will go so deep among the Lions, that a second trembling and furious descent will be made, to get upon the Pyrenees Mountains. The ancient monarchy shall not be transferred, and the third inundation of human blood shall happen; also for a good while Mars shall not be in Lent.

The daughter shall be given for the preservation of the Church, the dominator of it falling into the Pagan sect of the new unbelievers, and she will have two children, one from faithfulness, and the other from unfaithfulness, by the confirmation of the Catholic Church. The other, who to his confusion and late repentance, shall go about to ruin her, shall have three regions over a wide extent of leagues, that is to say, the Roman, the German, and the Spanish, and it will take a military hand to adequately take care of the area stretching from the 50th to the 52nd degree of latitude. And all those remote regions north above the 48th degree, who by vain fright shall quake, and then those of the west, south and east shall tremble because of their power, and the power of that what shall be done cannot be undone by warlike power. They shall be equal in nature, but much different in faith.

After this the barren Dame, of a greater power than the second, shall be admitted by two people, by the first made obstinate by him that had power over the others; by the second, and by the third, that shall extend his circuit to the east of Europe; there his forces will stop and be overcome, but by sea he will make his excursions into Trinacria and the Adriatic with his myrmidons. Germany shall fall, and the Barbarian Sect shall be wholly driven from among the Latins. Then the great Empire of Antichrist shall begin in the Attila, and Xerxes come down with an innumerable multitude of people, so that the coming of the Holy Ghost, proceeding from the 48th degree, shall transmigrate, driving away the abomination of the Antichrist, who made war against the royal person of the great vicar of Jesus Christ and against His Church, and His Kingdom, and reign per tempus, et in occasione temporis (for a time, and to the end of time). And before this shall precede a solar eclipse, the most dark and obscure that was since the creation of the world, till the death and passion of Jesus Christ, and from Him until now. There shall be in the month of October, a great revolution made, such that everybody will think that the earth has lost its natural motion and has gone down into perpetual darkness. In the spring before and after this, shall happen extraordinary changes, reversals of kingdoms, and great earthquakes; all this accompanied with the procreation of the New Babylon, a miserable prostitute large with the abomination of the first holocaust. And this shall last only seventy-three years and seven months.

Then from that stock that has been so long time barren, proceeding from the 50th degree, one will issue who will renovate all the Christian Church. Then shall be a great peace, union and concord, between some of the children of races long wandering and separated by diverse kingdoms; and such peace shall be made that the instigator and promoter of military function by diversity of religions, shall be tied to the bottom of the deep, and united to the kingdom of the furious who shall counterfeit the wise. The countries, towns, cities and provinces that had deserted their first ways to free themselves, captivating themselves more deeply, shall be secretly angry at their liberty and religion lost, and shall begin to strike from the left, to return once more to the right.

Then restoring the holiness, so long beaten down with their former writings, afterwards will come the great dog, the irresistible mastiff (war) who shall destroy all that was done before. Churches shall be built up again as before, the clergy shall be restored to its former state, until it falls back again into whoredom and luxury, and commits a thousand crimes. And being near to another desolation, when she shall be in her higher and more sublime dignity, there shall rise powers and military hands, who shall take away from her the two swords, and leave only the resemblance, after which, tired of the crookedness that is about them, the people will cause these things to straighten. Not willing to submit unto them by the end opposite to the sharp hand that touches the ground they shall provoke. To the branch long barren, will proceed one who shall deliver the people of the world from that meek and voluntary slavery; putting themselves under the protection of Mars, depriving Jupiter of all his honors and dignities, for the free city established and seated in another little Mesopotamia. And the chief governor shall be thrust out of the middle, and set in the high place of the air, being ignorant of the conspiracy of the conspirators, with the second Thrasibulus, who long before did prepare for this thing. Then shall the impurities and abominations be objected with great shame, and made manifest to the darkness of the veiled light, and shall cease toward the end of the change of his kingdom, and the chief men of the Church shall be put back from the love of God and many of them shall apostatize from the true faith.

Of the three sects (Lutheran, Catholic, and Mahometan), that which is middlemost, by the actions of its worshippers, shall be thrown into ruins. The first, wholly in all Europe, and the most part of Africa undone by the third, by means of the poor in spirit, who by madness elevated shall, through libidinous luxury, commit adultery. The people will rise and maintain it, and shall drive away those that did adhere to the legislators, and it shall seem, from the kingdoms spoiled by the Eastern men, that God the Creator has loosed Satan from his infernal prison, to cause to be born the great Dog and Dohan (Gog and Magog), who shall make so great and abominable a breach in the Churches, that neither the reds nor the whites, who are without eyes and without arms, shall not judge of it, and their power shall be taken away from them.

Then shall there be a greater persecution against the Church than ever was, and in the meantime shall be so great a plague, that two parts of three in the world shall fail, so much so that no one shall be able to know the true owners of fields and houses, and there shall happen a total desolation to the clergy, and martial men shall usurp what shall come from the City of the Sun, and from Malta, and from the Islands of Hières, and the great chain of the port shall be open which takes its name from a sea ox (Bosphorus).

A new incursion shall be made from the sea coasts, willing to deliver the Castulan Leap from the first Mahometan taking, and the assaulting shall not altogether be in vain, and that place where the habitation of Abraham was, shall be assaulted by those who shall have reverence for the Jovials. The great eastern city of Achem shall be encompassed and assaulted on all sides by a great power of armed men. Their sea forces shall be weakened by the western men, and to that kingdom shall happen great desolation, and the great cities shall be depopulated, and those that shall come in shall be comprehended within the vengeance of the wrath of God. The Holy Sepulchre, held in great veneration for so long a time, shall remain a great while open to the universal aspect of the heavens, sun and moon. The sacred place shall be converted into a stable for cattle small and large, and put to profane uses. O what a calamitous time shall be then for women with child! For then the principal Eastern Ruler, being for the most part moved by the Northern and Western men, shall be vanquished and put to death, beaten, and all the rest put to flight, and the children he had by many women put in prison. Then shall be fulfilled the prophecy of the Royal Prophet. *"Ut audiret gemitus compeditorum, et solveret filios interemptorum."* *

What great oppression shall be made then upon the princes and governors of kingdoms, and especially on those that shall live eastward and near the sea, their languages intermixed with all nations. The language of the Latin nations mixed with Arabic and North African communication. All the Eastern kings shall be driven away, beaten and brought to nothing, not altogether by means of the strength of the kings of the North, and the drawing near of our age, but by means of three secretly united, seeking for death by ambushes one against another. The renewing of the triumvirate shall last seven years, while the fame of such a sect shall be spread all the world over, and the sacrifice of the holy and immaculate host shall be upheld. And then shall the lords be two in number, victorious in the North against the Eastern ones, and there shall be such a great noise and warlike tumult that all the East shall quake for fear of those two brothers of the North who are yet not brothers. And because, Sir, by this discourse, I put all things confusedly in these predictions as to the time concerning the event of them; for the account of the time which follows, very little is conformable, if at all, to that I have done before, being by astronomic rule and according to the Sacred Scriptures, in which I cannot err.

I could have set down in every quatrain the exact time in which they shall happen, but it would not please everybody, and much less the interpretation of them, till, Sir, your Majesty has granted me full power so to do, that my calumniators may have nothing to say against me. Nevertheless, reckoning the years since the creation of the world to the birth of Noah, there passed 1506 years, and from the birth of Noah to the building of the ark at the time of the universal flood, 600 years passed (whether solar years, or lunar, or mixed), for my part according to the Scriptures, I hold that they were solar. And at the end of those 600 years Noah entered into the ark to save himself from the flood, which flood was universal upon the earth and lasted a year and two months; and from the end of the flood to the birth of Abraham did pass 295 years; and from the birth of Abraham to that of Isaac did pass 100 years;

---

* "Let the sighing of the prisoner come before thee, to release the children of death" (Ps. lxxviii. 11).

from Isaac to Jacob, sixty years; and from the time he went into Egypt until he came out of it, did pass 130 years; and from the time that Jacob went into Egypt until his posterity came out of it did pass 430 years; and from the coming out of Egypt to the building of Solomon's Temple in the fortieth year of his reign did pass 480 years; and from the building of the Temple to Jesus Christ, according to the computation, of the chronographers, did pass 490 years. And thus by this calculation, which I have gathered out of the Holy Scriptures, the whole comes to about 4173 years and eight months more or less. But since the time of Jesus Christ hitherto, I leave it because of the diversity of opinion. Having calculated these present prophecies in accordance to the order of the chain which contains the revolution, and all by astronomical rule, and according to my natural instinct; after some time, and including in it the time Saturn takes to turn to come in on the 7th of the month of April until the 25th of August; Jupiter from the 14th of June to the 7th of October; Mars from the 27th of April till the 22nd of June; Venus from the 9th of April to the 22nd of May; Mercury from the 3rd of February to the 24th of the same; afterwards from the 1st of June to the 24th of the same; and from the 25th of September to the 16th of October, Saturn in Capricorn, Jupiter in Aquarius, Mars in Scorpio, Venus in Pisces, Mercury within a month in Capricorn, Aquarius in Pisces, the moon in Aquarius, the Dragon's head in Libra, the tail opposite to her sign. Following a conjunction of Jupiter and Mercury, with a quadrin aspect of Mars to Mercury, and the head of the Dragon shall be with a conjunction of Sol and Jupiter; the year shall be peaceful without eclipse.

Then the beginning of that year shall see a greater persecution against the Christian Church than ever was in Africa, and it shall be in the year 1792,* at which time everyone will think it a renovation of the age. After that the Roman people shall begin to stand upright again, and to put away the obscure darkness, receiving some of its former light, but now without great divisions and continual changes. Venice, after that, with great strength and power will lift up her wings so high that she will not be much inferior to the strength of ancient Rome. And at that time great Byzantine sails, joined with the Italians by the help and power of the North, shall hinder them so that those of Crete shall not keep their faith. The ships built by the ancient martial men will keep company with them under the waves of Neptune. In the Adriatic there shall be a great discord, what was united shall be put asunder, and what was before a great city shall become a house, including the Pampotan and Mesopotamia of Europe, in (19)45, and others to 41, 42, and 47. And

---

* Date of French Revolution.

in that time and those countries the infernal power shall rise against the Church of Jesus Christ. This shall be the second Antichrist, which shall persecute the said church and its true vicar by the means of the power of temporal kings, who through their ignorance shall be seduced by tongues more sharp than any sword in the hands of a madman.

The said reign of Antichrist shall not last but till the ending of him who was born of Age, and of the other in the city of Plancus (Lyons), accompanied by the elect of Modena, Fulcy by Ferrara, maintained by the Adriatic, Liguriens, and the proximity of the great Trinacria (Sicily). Afterwards the Gallic Ogmion shall pass the Mount Jovis (Barcelona), followed with such a number that even from afar off the Empire shall be presented with its grand law, and then and for some time after, shall be profusely spilled the blood of the innocents by the guilty raised on high. Then by great floods the memory of those things contained in such instruments, shall receive incalculable loss, even to the letters themselves. This will happen to the Northerns. By the Divine Will Satan will be bound once more, and universal peace shall be among men, and the Church of Jesus Christ shall be free from all tribulation, although the Azostains (debauchees) would desire to mix with the honey their pestilent seduction. This shall happen about the seventh millenary, when the sanctuary of Jesus Christ shall no more be trodden down by the unbelievers that shall come from the North. The world will then be near its great conflagration, although by the calculations of my prophecies, the course of time goes much further.

In the epistle that some years ago I dedicated to my son Caesar Nostradamus, I have openly enough declared some things without prognosticating. But here, Sir, are comprehended many great and wonderful events, which those that come after us shall see. And during the said astrological computation, in harmony with the Sacred Scriptures, the persecution of the clergy shall have its beginning in the power of the Northern Kings joined by the Eastern ones. And that persecution shall last eleven years, or a little less, at which time the chief Northern king shall fail, which years being ended, shall come in his stead a united Southern one, who shall yet more violently persecute the clergy of the Church for the space of three years by the apostolical seduction of one that shall have absolute power over the militant Church of God. The holy people of God and keepers of His law, and all order of religion, shall be grievously persecuted and afflicted, so much that the blood of the true ecclesiastical men shall flow all over. One of these horrid kings shall be praised by his followers for having spilt more human blood of the innocent clergymen than anybody has done to wine. The said king shall commit incredible crimes against the Church; human blood shall run through public streets and Churches, as water coming from an impetuous

rain. Next, rivers shall be red with blood. In a sea fight the sea shall
be red, so that one king will say to another, "*Bellis rubuit navalibus
aequor.*" * After that in the same year, and those following, shall happen
the most horrible pestilence, caused by the famine preceding, and so great
tribulations as ever did happen since the first foundation of the Christian
Church throughout all the Latin regions, some marks remaining in some
countries under Spain.

Then the third Northern king (Russia?), hearing the complaint of
the people of his principal title, shall raise up so great an army, shall go
through the limits of his last ancestors and progenitors, that they will
all be set up again in their first state. The great Vicar of the Cope shall
be restored in his former estate, but desolate and altogether forsaken,
shall then go back to the sanctuary that was destroyed by Paganism, when
the Old and New Testament will be thrust out and burnt. After that
shall the Antichrist be the infernal prince. And in this last era all the
kingdoms of Christianity and also of the unbelievers shall quake for the
space of years, and there shall be more grievous wars and battles; towns,
cities, castles and other buildings shall be burnt, desolated and destroyed
with a great effusion of vestal blood, married women and widows ravished,
sucking children dashed against the walls of towns, and so many evils
shall be committed by the means of the infernal prince, Satan, that almost
the entire world shall be undone and desolate.

Before these events many unusual birds shall cry through the air,
crying, "Huy, huy." ("Now, now.") A little while after they shall
vanish. After this shall have lasted a good while, there shall be renewed
a reign of Saturn and a golden age. God the Creator shall say, hearing
the affliction of His people, Satan shall be put and tied in the bottom
of the deep, and there shall begin an age of universal peace between
God and man. The ecclesiastical power shall return in force and Satan
shall be bound for the space of a thousand years, and then shall be
loosed again.

All these figures are justly fitted by the Sacred Scriptures to the
celestial things, that is to say, Saturn, Jupiter and Mars, and others joined
with them, as may be seen more at large in some of my quatrains. I would
have calculated it more deeply, and coordinated one with the other, but
seeing, O most excellent King, that some stand ready to censure me, I
shall now withdraw my pen to its nocturnal repose.

"*Multa etiam, O Rex potentissime proeclara, et sane in brevi ventura,
sed omnia in hac tua Epistola, innectere non possumus, nec volumus, sed
ad intellegenda quoedam facta, horrida fata pauca libanda sunt, quamvis
tanta sit in omnes tua amplitudo et humanitas homines, deosque pietas, ut*

---

* "The sea blushed red with the blood of naval fights."

solos amplissimo et Christianissimo Regis nomine, et ad quem summa totius religionis auctoritas deferatur dignus esse videare." * But I shall only beseech you, O most merciful King, by your singular and prudent goodness, to understand rather the desire of my heart, and the earnest desire I have to obey your most excellent Majesty, ever since my eyes were so near to your royal splendor, than the greatness of my word can attain to or deserve.

Faciebat   Michael Nostradamus
Solonoe Petrae Provincae

From Salon this 27th June, 1558

---

* "So many things, O most potent King of all, of the most remarkable kind are to happen soon, that I neither would nor could incorporate them all into this epistle; but in order to intelligently comprehend certain facts, a few horrible fated events must be set down in extract, although your amplitude and humanity toward mankind is so great, as is your piety to God, that you alone seem worthy of the great title of the most Christian King, and to whom the highest authority in all religion should be deferred."

1

Pau, nay, loron plus feu qu'a sang
sera,
Laude nager, fuir grand aux surrez,
Les aggassas entree refusera,
Pampon, Durance, les tiendra en-
serrez.

Pau, nay, loron, more in fire their
blood shall be,
Seen to swim, great ones shall run
to their surreys,
The aggassas shall refuse the entry,
Pampon, Durance shall keep them
enclosed.

This seemingly obscure and unintelligible quatrain conceals a complex play on words by means of which Nostradamus predicts the advent of Napoleon, viz., nay-pau-loron, a man of fire (gunfire?). Also the dispatch of the pre–French-Revolution nobility in flight in their surreys. Aggassas in French is magpie or pie or pius, whom Napoleon held hostage (Pius VI and Pius VII).

2

Condon & Aux & autour de Mi-
rande,
Je voy du ciel feu qui les environne,
Sol, Mars, conjoint au Lion, puis
Marmande,
Foudre, grand guerre, mur tombe
dans Garonne.

Condon and Aux, and about Mirande,
I see a fire from heaven that sur-
rounds them,
Sol, Mars, in conjunction with the
lion, and then Marmande
Lightning, great war, wall falls into
the Garonne.

Fire from heaven suggests extra-terrestrial spacecraft landing amid a great war on earth.

3

Au fort chasteau de Vigilanne &
    Resviers,
Sera serre le puisnay de Nancy;
Dedans Turin seront ards les pre-
    miers,
Lors que de dueil Lyon sera transy.

In the strong castle of Vigilanne
    and Resviers,
Shall be kept close the youngest
    son of Nancy,
Within Turin, the first shall be
    burnt up,
When Lyons shall be overwhelmed
    with sorrow.

Contemporary politics, that loomed large at the time but which have since lost their significance, are here recorded.

4

Dedans Monech le Coq sera receu,
Le Cardinal de France apparoistra,
Par Logarion Romain sera deceu,
Foiblesse a l'Aigle, & force au Coq
    naistra.

Within Monaco the Cock shall be
    received,
The Cardinal of France shall ap-
    pear,
By Logarion Roman shall be de-
    ceived,
Weakness to the Eagle, and
    strength to the Cock shall grow.

Monaco, then an Italian possession, admitted the French for the first time, persuaded by the policy of Cardinal Richelieu, the Gallic Cock being the gainer thereby.

5

Apparoistra temple luisant orne,
La lampe & cierge a Borne & Bre-
    tueil,
Pour la Lucerne le canton des-
    torne,
Quand on verra le grand Coq cer-
    cueil.

A brilliantly adorned temple shall
    appear,
The lamp and wax candle of Borne
    and Bretueil,
For Lucerne the canton is turned,
When the great Cock shall be seen
    in his coffin.

After the death of a French King the glory of France will be at its zenith.

6

Charte fulgure a Lyon apparente
Luysant, print Malte, subit sera
    estrainte,
Sardon, Mauris traitera decevante,
Geneve a Londres a Coq trahison
    fainte.

A thundering light at Lyons ap-
    pearing,
Brightly, Malta instantly shall be
    put out,
Sardon shall treat Mauris deceit-
    fully,
From Geneva to London, the Cock
    a pretended treason.

Tremendous aerial bombardments shall devastate France and extend
even to Malta and Sardinia. The French shall pretend to be unfaithful
to Geneva and London.

7

Verceil, Milan donra intelligence,
Dedans Tycin sera fait la paye,
Courir par Seine eau, sang feu par
    Florence,
Unique choir d'haut en bas faisant
    maye.

Verceil, Milan shall give intelli-
    gence,
In the Ticin shall the peace be
    made,
Run through Seine water, blood,
    fire through Florence,
Only one shall fall from top to
    bottom making friends.

Italian cities in northern Italy shall make peace with the French;
only one person shall suffer by this act.

8

Pres de Linterne dans de tonnes
    fermez,
Chivaz fera pour l'Aigle la menee,
L'esleu casse, luy ses gens enfermez,
Dedans Turin rapt espouse em-
    menee.

Near Linterne, enclosed within the
    farms,
Chivas shall drive the plot for the
    Eagle,
The elect dismissed, he and his
    men shut up,
Within Turin, the bride raped
    and carried away.

Linterne and Chivas are small towns in Italy. In a plot to gain power,
the local government will be overcome and the prize seized.

9

Pendant que l'Aigle & le Coq a
Savone
Seront unis, Mer, Levant & Hon-
grie,
L'armee a Naples, Palerme, Mar-
que d'Ancone,
Rome, Venise, par barbe horrible
crie.

While the Eagle and Cock at Sa-
vonna
Shall be united, Sea, Levant and
Hungary,
The army at Naples, Palermo,
Mark of Ancona,
Rome, Venice, cry because of a
horrid barb.

The American Eagle and the French Cock shall be in a united campaign against the Italians, Hungarians, etc., and the Italian armies shall
be in great distress because of a new and punishing weapon used against
them.

10

Puanteur grande sortira de Lausanne,
Qu'on ne scaura l'origine du fait,
L'on mettra hors tout la gent loing-
taine,
Feu veu au ciel, peuple estranger
deffait.

A great stink shall come forth from
Lausanne,
So that no one shall know the ori-
gin of it,
They shall put out all the foreign-
ers,
Fire seen in heaven, a strange peo-
ple defeated.

The presages contained in this quatrain are now *faits accomplis*, written
with a bloody pen on the pages of History. The Conference of Lausanne
is predicted and the signing of many diplomatic instruments, including
the Treaty of Peace itself. Cynically Nostradamus refers to the "stink that
shall come forth from Lausanne," indicating the cynicism of the partici-
pants; he even shows the blind faith with which these documents were
accepted by the people of the world. He foretells that the "peace" shall
be short-lived; that minorities shall be persecuted; that the fires of war
shall be rekindled and again sweep over the earth.

11

Peuple infiny paroistra a Vicence,
Sans force feu brusler la basilique,
Pres de Lunage deffait grande de
Valence,
Lors que Venise par mort prendra
pique.

Infinite number of people shall appear at Vincenza,
Without force, fire shall burn in
the basilick,
Near Lunage the great one of Va-
lencia shall be defeated,
When Venice by death shall be
piqued.

Basilick is the name of an old Italian fort which was heavily fortified
by cannon. The sense of this verse then is that Italy will be engaged in
a war.

12

Apparoistra aupres de Buffalore
L'haut & procere entre dedans Mi-
lan,
L'Abbe de Foix avec ceux de Sainct
Maure,
Feront la forbe habillez en vilain.

Near the Bufalore shall appear
The high and tall, come into Mi-
lan,
The Abbot of Foix with those of
Saint Maure,
Shall make the deceit, being
clothed like a villain.

Foix and St. Mauve are towns in France. This concerns a debate
among the clergymen of these communities.

13

Le croise frere par amour effrenee,
Fera par Praytus Bellerophon
mourir,
Classe a mil ans la femme forcenee,
Beu le bruvage, tous deux apres
perrir.

The crossed brother through un-
bridled love,
Shall cause Bellerophon to be killed
by Praytus,
Fleet to thousand years, the women
frantic,
The drink being drunk, both after
that shall perish.

Bellerophon was a hero of Greek mythology. He fell from his steed
Pegasus and perished, while attempting to fly to heaven.

14

Le grand credit, d'or, d'argent,
l'abundance,
Aveuglera par libide l'honneur;
Cogneu sera d'adultere l'offense,
Qui parviendra a son grand des-
honneur.

The great credit, of gold, of silver,
great abundance,
Shall blind honor by lust,
The offense of the adulterer shall
be known,
Which shall come to his great dis-
honor.

Most appropriately, the economic plight of the twentieth century in-
cludes soaring inflation and currency devaluation, alongside universal
laxity in morals and lust rampant with little social restraint.

15

Vers Aquilon grands efforts par hommasse
Presque l'Europe & l'univers vexer,
Les deux eclipses mettre en telle chasse,
Et aux Pannons vie & mort renforcer.

Towards the North great endeavours by a masculine woman,
To trouble Europe, and almost all the world,
The two eclipses shall be put to flight,
And shall reinforce life, and death to the Poles.

Catherine the Great, 1729–96, Empress of Russia, is here indicated. She was a disciple and friend of the Encyclopaedists, especially of Voltaire, and although she started out with the intention of following their principles in the matters of domestic reform, it was short-lived and completely shattered by the advent of the French Revolution. During her reign she engineered the shameless partitions of Poland, to the great detriment of that nation.

16

Au lieu que Jieson feit sa nef fabriquer,
Si grand deluge sera & si subite,
Qu'on n'aura lieu ne terres s'ataquer,
L'onde monter Fesulan Olympique.

In the place where Jason carried his ship to be built,
So great a flood shall be and so sudden,
That there shall be neither place nor land to save themselves,
The waves shall climb upon the Olympic Fesulan.

Mount Olympus, the mythical home of the gods, is where Jason built his ship, for the Argonauts' voyage. The sense of this stanza is that an inexorable movement shall engulf all those in authority and a new order be created.

17

Les bien aisez subit seront desmis,
Le monde mis par les trois freres en trouble,
Cite marine saisiront ennemis,
Faim, feu, sang, peste, & de tous maux le double.

Those that were at ease shall be put down,
The world shall be put in trouble by three brothers,
The maritime city shall be seized by its enemies,
Hunger, fire, blood, plague, and double of all evils.

Social conditions are to change; world wide repercussions with an abundance of misfortunes shall beset all, due to the machinations of three brothers.

18

De Flore issue de sa mort sera cause,
Un temps devant par jeusne & vielle bueyre,
Car les trois lys luy feront telle pause,
Par son fruit sauve comme chair crue mueyre.

Issued from Flora, shall be the cause of her death,
A time before, by fasting and stale drink,
For the three lilies, shall make her such a pause,
Saved by her fruit, as raw flesh dead.

The three lilies represent the Fleur de Lys, symbol of France. After a period of want and suffering France will be succored by the sacrifices of her patriots.

19

A soustenir la grand cappe troublee,
Pour l'esclaireir les rouges marcheront,
De mort famille sera presque accablee,
Les rouges rouges, le rouge assommeront.

To maintain up the great troubled cloak,
The red ones shall march to clear it,
A family shall be almost crushed to death,
The red reds, shall knock down the red one.

Nostradamus predicts great peril for the Pope. The red ones (cardinals) surround and protect him from the red reds (Communists, terrorists), who in their turn do kill a cardinal and simultaneously, in a crowd panic, almost crush a family of observers.

20

Le faux message par election feinte,
Courir par urban rompue pache arreste,
Voix aceptees, de sang chapelle tainte,
Et a un autre l'empire contraincte.

The false message, by a fraudulent election,
Shall be stopped from going about the town,
Voices shall be bought, and a chapel tinted with blood,
By another, who contests the rule.

By bribery a fraudulent rumor shall be perpetrated, and a bloody struggle will arise in the church.

21

Au port de Agde trois fustes entre-ront,	In the Port of Agda, three ships shall enter,
Portant infection avec foy & pesti-lence,	Carrying with them infection and pestilence,
Passant le pont mil milles emble-ront,	Going beyond the bridge, they shall carry away thousands.
Et le pont rompre a tierce resist-ance.	At the third resistance the bridge shall be broken.

Agda, a city in France, shall be the entering point for foreign propaganda, eventually conquering the country thereby.

22

Gorsan, Narbonne, par le sel ad-vertir,	Gorsan, Narbonne, by the salt shall give notice,
Tucham, la grace Parpignan trahie,	To Tucham, the grace Perpignan betrayed,
La ville rouge n'y voudra consentir,	The red city will not give consent to it,
Par haulte Voldrap gris vie faillie.	By high Voldrap, gray life ended.

French cities are named; by an edict from the "red city" (Rome) help will be given to their inhabitants.

23

Lettres trouvees de la Royne les coffres,	Letters found in the Queen's coffers,
Point de subscrit sans aucun nom d'autheur,	No superscription, no name of author,
Par la police seront cachez les of-fres,	By the police shall be concealed the offers,
Qu'on ne scaura qui sera l'amateur.	So that no one shall know who shall be the lover.

The affair of The Diamond Necklace, involving Cagliostro, the master swindler, Cardinal Rohan, and the Queen of France, is here indicated.

24

Lieutenant a l'entree de l'huys
Assommera la grand de Perpignan,
En se cuidant sauver a Montper-
tuis,
Sera deceu bastard de Lusignan.

The lieutenant shall at the entrance
of the door,
Knock down the great one of Perpignan,
Thinking to save himself at the
mountain straits,
And the bastard of Lusignan shall
be deceived.

Perpignan, at the frontier between Spain and France, shall be the scene of many disgraceful events.

25

Coeur de l'amant ouvert d'amour
furtive,
Dans le ruisseau fera ravir la Dame,
Le demy mal contrefera lascive,
Le pere a deux privera corps de
l'ame.

The lover's heart, being by a furtive love
Shall cause the lady to be ravished
in the brook,
The lascivious shall counterfeit
half a discontent.
The father shall deprive them both
of their souls.

A father, discovering his mistress and his son in a compromising situa-tion, shall kill both of them.

26

De Carones trouvez en Barcelonne,
Mys descouvers, lieu terrouers &
ruyne,
Le grand qui tient ne voudra Pam-
plonne,
Par l'abbaye de Montferrat bruyne.

From Carons found in Barcelona,
Found discovered, in place of soil
and ruin,
The great that hold, will not Pam-
pelone,
By the abbey of Montserrat, a fine
rain.

This evidently refers to the discovery of some sort of plant, which eventually becomes one of the staple foods of the poor people of Europe.

27

La voye Auxelle l'un sur l'autre
    fornix,
Du muy de ser hor mis brave &
    genest,
L'escript d'Empereur le Phoenix,
Veu en celuy ce qu'a nul autre
    n'est.

The way Auxelle, one arch upon
    another,
Being brave and gallant put out the
    iron vessel,
The writing of the Emperor, the
    Phoenix,
In it shall be seen, what nowhere
    else is.

The return of Napoleon from Elba is here compared to the rising of
the phoenix from its ashes.

28

Les simulachres d'or et d'argent
    enflez,
Qu'apres le rapt, lac au feu furent
    jettez,
Au descouvert estaincts tous &
    troublez,
Au marbre escripts, perscripts in-
    teriettez.

The idols swollen with gold and
    silver,
Which after the rape were thrown
    into the lake and fire,
Being discovered after the putting
    out of the fire,
Shall be written in marble, pre-
    cepts being inserted.

An incident of antiquity is described here: the stealing of gold and
silver idols from a temple, their desecration by fire and water, and the
subsequent erection of a marble monument inscribed in their honor.

29

Au quart pilier l'on sacre a Saturne,
Par tremblant terre & deluge
    fendu,
Sous l'edifice Saturin trouves urne,
D'or Capion, ravy & puis rendu.

At the fourth pillar where they
    sacrifice to Saturn,
Shaken by an earthquake and a
    flood,
A funeral urn shall be found under
    that Saturnin edifice,
Full of gold, stolen, and then re-
    turned.

A funeral urn, in which the ancient Romans kept the ashes of their great
ones, shall be uncovered by an upheaval, but gold will be found in it
instead.

30

Dedans *Tholose* non *loing de Belu-*
zer,
Faisant un puis loing, palais d'es-
pectacle
Thresor trouve un chacun ira vexer,
Et en deux locs tout & pres des
vesacle.

Within Toulouse not far from Be-
luzer,
Digging a well, for the palace of
spectacle,
A treasure found that shall vex
everyone,
In two parcels and near the Basacle.

In Toulouse, in the industrial part of the city called the Basacle, a Pandora's box will be found.

31

Premier grand fruict le Prince de
Pesquiere;
Mais puis viendra bien & cruel
malin,
Dedans Venise perdra sa gloire
fiere,
Et mis a mal par plus joyue Celin.

The first great fruit the Prince of
Pescaire,
But he shall become very cruel and
malicious,
He shall lose his fierce pride in
Venice,
And shall be put to evil by the
young Turks.

Pescaire, a town near Naples, will be the birthplace of a statesman. Rising to power at an early age, he will become arrogant and over-confident. At the height of his career he will be killed in a duel with a Turk.

32

Garde toy roy Gaulois de ton ne-
pveu,
Qui fera tant que ton unique fils,
Sera meurtry a Venus faisant voeu,
Accompagne denuict que trois &
six.

Take heed, O French King, of thy
nephew,
Who shall cause that thine only
son,
Shall be murdered making a vow
to Venus,
Accompanied with three and six.

Napoleon III, nephew of Napoleon Bonaparte, is referred to here; the significance being the complete disintegration of Napoleonic prestige under his reign.

33

Le grand naistra de Veronne & Vincense,	The great one of Verona and Vincenza shall be born,
Qui portera un surnon bien indigne,	Who shall bear a very unworthy name,
Qui a Venise voudra faire vengeance,	Who shall endeavor at Venice to avenge himself,
Luy mesme prins homme du guet & signe.	But he shall be taken by a policeman.

Another reference to Mussolini, this retells the sordid details of his ignoble fate.

34

Apres victoire du Lion au Lion,	After the victory of the Lion against the Lion,
Sur la montagne de Jura Secatombe,	Upon the mountain of Jura, Hecatombe,
Delues, & brodes septiesme million,	Of them decorated, the seventh million,
Lyon, Ulme a Mausol mort & tombe.	Lyons, Ulme fall dead at Mausol.

The mention of places in Switzerland, France, Germany, and the word "lion" taken as meaning Great Britain, we believe that these things in connection with the phrases "seventh million" and "fall dead" refer to the world wars and their casualties.

35

Dedans l'entree de Garonne & Blaye,	Within the entrance of Garonne and Blaye,
Et la forest non loing de Damazan,	And the forest not far from Damazan,
Du Marsaves gelees, puis gresle & bize,	Of Marsaves frosts, then hail and north wind,
Dordonnois gelle par erreur de Mezan.	Dordonois frozen by the error of Mezan.

This describes an unusually bad winter in Europe—rivers frozen solid, terrible winds and hailstorms raging throughout the land.

36

Sera commis contre Oinde a Duche,	The Duche shall be committed against Oinde,
Se Saulne, & sainct Aubin & Beloeuvre,	Of Saulne and Saint Aubin and Beloeuvre,
Paver de marbre, de tous loing espluche,	To have with marble and of towers well picked,
Non Bleteran resister & chef d'oeuvre.	Not Bleteran to resist, and master stroke.

In these latter-day prophecies, we find a few obscure and unintelligible verses. This quite apparently is one of them.

37

Le forteresse aupres de la Thamise,	The fortress near the Thames,
Cherra par lors, le Roy dedans serre,	Shall fall, then the King that was kept within
Aupres du pont sera veu en chemisee,	Shall be seen near the bridge in his shirt,
Un devant mort, puis dans le fort barre.	One dead before, then in the fort kept close.

Charles was brought to Windsor Castle, overlooking the Thames, after his defeat on December 23, 1648. On January 30, dressed in a white shirt, he was taken out and beheaded.

38

Le Roy de Bloys dans Avignon regner,	The King of Blois in Avignon shall reign,
Un autre fois le peuple emonopole,	Another time the people do murmur,
Dedans le Rhosne par murs fera baigner,	He shall cause in the Rhone to be bathed through the walls,
Jusques a cinq, le dernier pres de Nolle.	As many as five, the last shall be near Nole.

A King of France shall occupy Avignon, a city in France belonging to a Pope. Some of the inhabitants, objecting to this seizure, shall be thrown over the city walls into the river.

39

Qu'aura este par prince Bizantin,
Sera tollu par prince de Tholose,
Lay foy de Foix, par le chef Tho-
lentin,
Luy faillira ne refusant l'espouse.

What shall have been by a Byzantine prince,
Shall be taken away by the prince
of Tholose,
The faith of Foix by the chief Tho-
lentin,
Shall fail him, not refusing the
spouse.

The French shall occupy territory in the Near East, formerly ruled by the Mohammedans.

40

Le sang du juste par Taur & la
Dorade,
Pour se venger contre les Saturnins
Au nouveau lac plongeront la
Mainade,
Puis marcheront contre les Alba-
nins.

The blood of the just by Taur and
Dorade,
To avenge themselves against the
Saturnins,
In the new lake shall plunge the
Mainade,
Then shall march against the Al-
banins.

The Byzantine and Arab influence in Algiers and its civil war with France in the late 1950s, ending in 1961, under Charles de Gaulle's leadership is predicted here. De Gaulle, the "prince" of Toulouse, grants independence to Algeria.

41

Esleu sera Renard ne sonnant mot,
Faisant le saint public, vivant pain
d'orge,
Tyrannizer apres tant a un cop,
Mettant la pied des plus grands
sur la gorge.

A fox shall be elected that said
nothing,
Making a public saint, living with
barley bread,
Shall tyrannize after upon a sudden
And put his foot upon the throat
of the greatest.

Nostradamus anticipates the appearance of a puritan ("barley bread") in the guise of a fox. (Robespierre, Napoleon III, or Premier Paul Reynaud, who was elected in 1940 at the time of the Nazi occupation.)

42

Par avarice, par force & violence,
Viendra vexer les siens chefs
    d'Orleans,
Pres Sainct Memire assault & re-
    sistance,
Mort dans sa tente, diront qu'il
    dort leans.

By avarice, and force and violence,
Shall come to vex his own chief of
    Orleans,
Near St. Memire, assault and re-
    sistance,
Dead in his tent, they shall say, he
    sleepeth there.

At St. Memire, a French town, a mutiny against the tyrannical local government chiefs shall result in the murder of one of them. To protect the murderer, the inhabitants shall, for a long time, attempt to conceal the body from the authorities.

43

Par le decide de deux choses bas-
    tars,
Nepveu du sang occupera le regne,
Dedans lectoure seront les coups de
    dards,
Nepveu par pleira l'enseigne.

By the decision of two things, bas-
    tards,
Nephew of the blood shall occupy
    the government,
Within Lectore shall be blows of
    darts,
Nephew through fear shall fold up
    his ensigns.

The nephew here foretold is Napoleon III, who became president of France in 1848 and soon began to pursue his absolutist policies as Emperor in 1852. However, he was defeated in the 1870 Franco-Prussian war and folded his insignia. After his release as a prisoner he retired to England to end his days.

44

Le procree naturel l'Ogmion,
De sept a neuf du chemin de-
    storner,
A roy de longue & amy au my
    hom,
Doit a Navarre fort de Pau pros-
    terner.

The natural begotten of Ogmion,
From seven to nine shall be put
    out of the way,
To king of long, and friend to
    half man,
Ought to Navarre prostrate the
    fort of Pau.

An illegitimate son of a great monarch shall attempt to murder the king.

45

La main escharpe & la jambe bandee,
Louis puisne de palais partira,
Au mot du guet la mort sera tardee,
Puis dans le temple a Pasques saignera.

The hand on a scarf and the leg bandaged,
The younger Louis shall depart from the palace,
At the watchword his death shall be protracted,
Then afterwards at Easter he shall bleed in the temple.

A remarkable prediction. The younger Louis here refers to the Dauphin, son of Louis XVI and Marie Antoinette, who died in prison. He had been named Louis XVII by the loyalists.

46

Pol Mensolee mourra trois lieues du Rhone,
Fuis les deux prochains Tarare destrois;
Car Mars fera le plus horrible throsne,
De coq & d'aigle, de France freres trois.

Paul Mensolee shall die leagues from the Rhone,
Avoid the two straits near the Tarara,
For Mars shall keep such a horrible throne,
Of cock and eagle, of France three brothers.

Paul Mensolee is warned to avoid the roads to Mt. Tarare, as they are infested with thieves and murderers.

47

Lac Trasmenian portera tesmoignage,
Des conjurez sarez dedans Perouse,
Un despolle contrefera le sage,
Tuant Tedesq de Sterne & Minuse.

Trasmenian Lake shall bear witness,
Of the conspirators shut up in Perugia,
A Des Polle shall simulate the prudent,
Killing Germans of Sterne and Minuse.

A reference to the victory of Hannibal at Lake Trasimenus near the town of Perugia, Italy.

48

Saturne en Cancer, Jupiter avec Mars,
Dedans Fevrier, Caldondon, salva-terre,
Sault, Castallon, assailly de trois pars,
Fres de Verbiesque, conflit mortelle guerre.

Saturn in Cancer, Jupiter with Mars,
In February Caldondon, ground saved,
The Republic assaulted on three sides,
Near Verbiesque, fight and mortal war.

The oft-repeated warning of a great war is here contained.

49

Satur au beuf, Jove en l'eau, Mars en fleiche,
Six de Fevrier mortalite donra,
Ceux de Tardaigne a Bruge si grand breche,
Qu'a Ponterose chef Barbarin mourra.

Saturn in bull, Jupiter in water, Mars in arrow,
The sixth of February shall give mortality,
Those of Tardaigne shall make in Bruges so great a breach,
That the chief Barbarin shall die at Ponterose.

The event indicated shall occur under the influence of these planets, when Saturn is in Taurus, Jupiter in Aquarius, and Mars in Sagittarius. By the death of the chief Barbarin is meant the death of Pope Urban VIII.

50

La pestilence l'entour de Capadille.
Une aurte faim pres de Sagone s'appreste
Le chevalier bastard de bon senille,
Au grand de Thunes fera tranche la teste.

The plague shall be round about Capadillo,
Another famine cometh near to that of Sagunce,
The knight bastard of the good old man,
Shall cause the great one of Tunis to be beheaded.

Drought, famine, and disease plague West Africa from 1975 on. The great one of Tunis is Habib Bourguiba. He was re-elected to his fourth five-year term in 1974, and then in 1975 was elected president for life. However, Nostradamus predicts his death by violent means.

51

Le Bizantin faisant oblation,	The Byzantin, making an offering,
Apres avoir Cordube a soy reprinse;	After he hath taken Cordova to himself again,
Son chemin long, repos pampla-tion,	His road long, rest, contemplation,
Mer passant proy par la Cologne prinse.	Crossing the sea hath a prey by Cologne.

The reference here is to the abdication of Charles V, King of Spain. He retired to a small house on the grounds of a monastery and spent the last years of his life in study and contemplation.

52

Le roy de Bloys Avignon regner,	The King of Blois shall reign in Avignon,
D'Amboise & seme viendra le long de Lyndre,	He shall come from Amboise and Seme, along the Linden,
Ongle a Poitiers sainctes aisles ruyner	A nail at Poitiers shall ruin his holy wing,
Devant Bony.	Before Bony.

One must delve deeply into this quatrain to gather its full meaning. It depicts the phenomenal rise of Napoleon, and even refers to the unprecedented procedure of the Pope's journey to Paris to crown Napoleon as Emperor.

53

Dedans Bologne voudra laver ses fautes,	Within Boulogne, he shall want to wash himself of his faults,
Il ne pourra au temple du soleil,	In the church of the sun, but he shall not be able,
Il volera faisant chose si hautes,	He shall fly, doing things too high,
En hierarchie n'en fut oneq un pareil.	That in the hierarchy was never the like.

This predicts that Cardinal Richelieu, who attained greater secular heights than any other man of the church, shall wish to go on a holy pilgrimage, but shall defer it too long and shall be prevented from doing so by his death.

54

Soubs la couleur de traicte mariage,
Fait magnanime par grand Chyren
Selin,
Quintin, Arras recouvrez au voy-
age,
D'Espagnols fait second banc
Macelin.

Under the pretense of a treaty of
marriage,
A magnanimous act shall be done
by Henry the Great,
St. Quentin and Arras, recovered
in the journey,
Of Spaniards shall be made a
second Macelin bench.

A King of France, Henry the Great, through a pretended treaty of
marriage, shall acquire new territories. The word Macelin is from the
Latin word Macellum which means shambles. And the meaning here is
that there will be a war and subsequent havoc in Spain.

55

Entre deux fleuves se verra enserre,
Tonneaux a caques unis a passer
outre,
Huict ponts rompus chef a tant
enferre,
Enfans parfaicts sont jugulez en
coultre.

Between two rivers he shall find
himself shut up,
Tuns and casks put together to
pass over,
Eight bridges broken, the chief at
last in prison,
Perfect children shall have their
throats cut.

A commander of an army, about to launch an attack, shall be tem-
porarily stopped by the destruction of all bridges across the river near
which the enemy is encamped. Causing a pontoon bridge to be built,
he and his men will cross over and by a surprise attack will overcome
and capture the enemy.

56

La bande foible le terre occupera,
Ceux du haut lieu feront horribles
cris,
Le gros troupeau d'estre coin
troublera,
Tombe pres D. nebro descouvert
les escrits.

The weak party shall occupy the
ground,
Those of the high places shall make
horrible cries,
It shall trouble the great flock in
the right corner,
He falleth near D. nebro discov-
ereth the writings.

The continuing struggles between "left" and "right" political parties
are here predicted. The obscurely worded last line leads us to believe
that Nostradamus purposely wished to withhold his views as to the ultimate outcome.

57

De souldat simple parveindre en empire,
De robe courte parviendra a la longue,
Vaillant aux armes, en eglise ou plus pire,
Vexer les prestres comme l'eau faict l'esponge.

From a simple soldier, he shall come to have supreme command,
From a short gown he shall come to a long one,
Valiant in arms, no worse man in the church,
He shall vex the priests, as water does a sponge.

A perfect picture of Oliver Cromwell: From a simple soldier he rose to be Lord Protector; from a student in the university he became a graduate of Oxford; and as for vexing the clergy, there was no one of his day who caused them more trouble.

58

Regne en querelle aux freres divise,
Prendre les armes & le nom Britannique,
Tiltre d'Anglican sera tard advise,
Surprins de nuict, mener a l'air Gallique.

A kingdom in dispute and divided between the brothers,
To take the arms and the Britannic name,
And the English title, he shall advise himself late.
Surprised in the night and carried into the French air.

This predicts the abdication of King Edward VIII, and the accession to the throne of his brother, Duke of York, who became George VI.

59

Par deux fois haut, par deux fois mis a bas,
L'Orient aussi l'Occident foiblira,
Son adversaire apres plusieurs combats,
Par mer chasse au besoing faillira.

Twice set up high, and twice brought down,
The East also the West shall weaken,
His adversary after many fights,
Expelled by sea, shall fail in need.

The role of Germany in World Wars I and II is predicted. Both times the goal of that country was world domination, and both times she was defeated by the combined efforts of East and West.

60

Premier an Gaule, premier en Romanie,	The first in France, the first in Romania,
Par mer & terre aux Anglois & Paris,	By sea and land to the English and Paris,
Merveilleux faits par celle grand mesnie,	Wonderful deeds by that great company,
Violant, Terax perdra le Norlaris.	By ravishing, Terax shall ruin Norlaris.

The rapidity of the Nazi expansion (the "blitz" technique) both East and West during the dark days of World War II, the wonderful yet vain resistance of the conquered peoples, the ravishing of the countries—all is here prognosticated.

61

Jamais par le decouvrement du jour	Never by the discovering of the day
Ne parviendra au signe sceptrifere	He shall attain to the scepter bearing sign,
Que tous ses siege ne soient en sejour,	Till all his martial trials be settled,
Portant au coq don du Tag amisere.	Carrying to the cock, a gift from Der Tag of misery.

Three factors in this verse—the use of the alien word "Tag," the warning of war, and the reference to the "Cock" (France)—lead us to believe that here is a prognostication of the now infamous words "Der Tag," which was Germany's rallying cry for the day of vengeance and hoped-for triumph over the democracies.

62

Lors qu'on verra expiler le sainct temple,	When one shall see spoiled the holy temple,
Plus grand du Rhosne & sacres prophaner,	The greatest of the Rhone, and sacred things profaned,
Par eux naistra pestilence si ample,	From them shall come so great a pestilence,
Roy faict injuste ne fera condamner.	That the King being unjust shall not condemn them.

When the city of Lyons, the greatest on the Rhone River, is invaded and pillaged, a pestilence will descend upon the city, destroying both inhabitants and invaders.

63

Quand l'adultere blesse sans coup
aura
Meurdry la femme & le fils par
despit,
Famme assoumes l'enfant estrang-
lera;
Huict captifs prins s'estouffer sans
respit.

When the adulterer wounded without a blow,
Shall have murdered the wife and
son by spite,
The woman knocked down, shall
strangle the child,
Eight taken prisoners, and stifled
without tarrying.

A tragic story is told here, of an adulterer who, through his philander-
ing, contracts a contagious disease and in turn infects his wife and child.
Being upbraided by his wife, he attempts to murder her and his son and
then flees from the scene. She, dying, strangles her child. Without attempting to investigate the facts of the case, eight innocent persons are
hanged for these two murders.

64

Dedans les Isles les enfans trans-
portez,
Les deux de sept seront en desespoir;
Ceux du terrouer en seront sup-
portez,
Nom pelle prins, des ligues fuy
l'espoir.

In the Islands the children shall be
transported,
The two of seven shall be in de-
spair,
Those of the company shall be
supported by
Nompelle taken, avoid the hope of
the league.

As usual, during wartime the children of the British Isles are to be
evacuated from London and other major cities to the countryside.

65

Le vieux frustre du principal espoir,
Il parviendra au chef de son empire;
Vingt mois tiendra le regne a grand,
pouvoir,
Tiran, cruel en delaissant un pire.

The old man frustrated of his chief
hope,
He shall attain to the head of the
empire,
Twenty months he shall keep the
kingdom with great power,
Tyrant, cruel, and leaving a worse
one.

Ayatollah Khomeini returns from exile in France to lead the Islamic
revolution in Iran. However, he is destined to die in the 1980s and leave
Iran in chaos.

66

Quand l'escriture D. M. trouvee,
Et cave antique a lamp descou-
    verte,
Loy, Roy & Prinse Ulpian esprou-
    vee,
Pavillon Royne & Duc sous la
    couverte.

When the writing D. M. shall be
    found,
And an ancient cave discovered
    with a lamp.
Law, King, and Prince Ulpian tried,
Tent, Queen and Duke under the
    cover.

Nostradamus here predicts the event of the re-discovery of his writings
and the great new meanings that will be found contained in them.

67

Par. Car. Nersas, a ruine grand dis-
    corde,
Ne l'un ne l'autre n'aura election,
Nersas du peuple aura amour &
    concorde,
Ferrare, Collone grand protection.

Par. Car. Nersas, to ruin great dis-
    cord
Neither one nor the other shall be
    elected,
Nersas shall have of the people love
    and concord,
Ferrara, Colonna shall have great
    protection.

A great variance of opinion shall lead to strife over the election of a
Pope, and as a result the two leading candidates will be defeated and a
hitherto unknown will gain that high honor. This, in fact, did occur in
1978 when John Paul II from Wadowice, Poland, was elected.

68

Vieux Cardinal par le jeune deceu,
Hors de sa charge se verra desarme,
Arles ne monstres double soit
    aperceu,
Et l'Aqueduct & le Prince em-
    baume.

An old Cardinal, by a young one
    shall be deceived,
And shall see himself out of his
    position,
Arles do not show, a double
    strength perceived,
And the Aqueduct, and the em-
    balmed Prince.

This prophesies the rivalry between (old) Cardinal Richelieu and his
young successor, twenty-two-year-old Cinq-Mars. Richelieu died on December 4, 1642, and was embalmed.

69

Aupres du jeune se vieux Ange
    baisser,
Et le viendra sur monter a la fin;
Dix ans esgaux aux plus vieux
    rabaisser,
De trois deux l'un huictiesme Sera-
    phin.

Near the young one the old angel
    shall bow,
And shall at last overcome him,
Ten years equal, to make the old
    one stoop,
Of three, two, one, the eighth a
    Seraphin.

An old man (referred to as an angel) shall humbly defer to a young man, even through he is aware that he is being cheated. After ten years the old one shall turn upon and overcome the young villain. (The mythical allusions in the last line seem to have no particular meaning.)

70

Il entrera vilain, meschant, infame
Tyrannisant la Mesopotamie
Tous amis faict d'adulterine dame,
Terre horrible noir de physiogno-
    mie.

He shall come in villain, wicked,
    infamous,
To tyrannize Mesopotamia,
He maketh all friends by an adul-
    terous lady,
Foul, horrid, black, in his physi-
    ognomy.

The country near Babylon shall be terrorized by a person of the Negro race.

71

Croistra le nombre si grand des
    Astronomes,
Chassez, bannis & livres censurez,
L'an mil six cens & sept par sacre
    glomes,
Que nul aux sacres ne seront as-
    seurez.

The number of Astronomers shall
    grow so great,
Driven away, banished, books cen-
    sured,
The year one thousand six hundred
    and seven years by Glomes,
That none shall be secure in sacred
    places.

Nostradamus dates all events from A. D. 325 (Council of Nicaea); thus 1607 plus 325 equals 1932. On January 30, 1933 Hitler became Chancellor of Germany, ushering in the era of the burning of books, the banishment of men of science, religion and art, the crushing of all culture that did not concur with Nazi doctrines.

72

Champ Perusin O l'enorme deffaite
Et le conflict tout aupres de
Ravenne,
Passage sacre lors qu'on fera la
feste,
Vainqueur vaincu, cheval manger
l'avenne.

Perugian field, O the enormous defeat,
And the fight about Ravenna,
Sacred passage when the feast shall
be celebrated,
The victorious vanquished, the
horse to eat up his oats.

Perugia and Ravenna are cities in Italy, where a decisive battle will be fought on a holiday.

73

Soldat barbare le grand roy frappera,
In justement non eslongne de
mort,
L'avare mere du faict cause sera,
Conjurateur & regne en grand
remort.

A barbarous soldier shall strike the
king,
Unjustly, not far from death,
The covetous mother shall be the
cause of it,
The conspirator and kingdom in
great remorse.

Mussolini ruled Italy from 1922 until 1945. He was hanged on April 28, 1945. Later, King Victor Emmanuel III abdicated and installed his son, King Humbert II, only to have him sent into exile with the establishment of the Republic.

74

En terre neuve bien avant Roy
entre,
Pendant subges luy viendront faire
acueil,
Sa perfidie aura tel recontre,
Qu'aux citadins lieu de feste &
receuil.

In a new land, well after a King
enters,
Whilst his subjects shall come to
welcome him,
His perfidy shall find such an accident,
To the citizens it shall be received
instead of feasts.

An unpopular ruler shall die while on tour in a conquered land. The citizens shall be joyful thereat.

75

Le pere & fils seront meurdris ensemble,	The father and son shall be murdered together,
Le prefecteur dedans son pavillon	The governor shall be so in his tent,
La mere a Tours du fils ventre aura enfle,	At Tours the mother shall be got with child by her son,
Cache verdure de fueilles papillon.	Conceal the greenness with butterfly leaves.

This depicts murder, violence and incest in the city of Tours—and the fruit of the incest shall be strangled at birth and secretly buried, the small grave covered with grass and leaves and left forever unmarked.

76

Plus Macelin que Roy en Angleterre,	More Macelin than King in England,
Lieu obscur nay par force aura l'empire,	Born in obscure place, by force shall rule the empire,
Lasche, sans foy, sans loy, seignera terre,	Of loose morals, without faith, without law, the ground shall bleed.
Son temps s'approche si pres que je souspire.	His time is drawing so near that I sigh.

Macelin is from the Latin word *Macellum*, meaning shambles. A ruler of England is to come, who will be one of the world's worst tyrants and will bring about the near ruin of his country.

77

L'Antechrist trois bien trois annichilez,	By Anti-Christ, three shall be brought to nothing,
Vingt & sept ans sang durera sa guerre,	His war shall last seven and twenty years,
Les heretiques morts; captifs exilez,	The heretics dead, prisoners exiled, exiled,
Son corps humain eau rougie, gresler terre.	Blood, human body, water made red, earth shrunk.

In 1918, defeated Germany (Anti-Christ) laid the foundations for her dream of world conquest, which came to an end exactly as Nostradamus predicted, twenty-seven years later in 1945.

78

Un Bragamas avec la langue torte	A Bragamas with his harmful tongue,
Viendra des dieux rompre le sanc-tuaire,	Shall come and break the God's sanctuary,
Aux heretiques il ouvrira la porte,	He shall open the gates to heretics,
En suscitant l'eglise militaire.	By raising the militant church.

The word "Bragamas" denotes a braggard, and the meaning of the verse is that he shall cause great harm to God's sanctuary (the Roman Catholic Church) by his boastful and false claims of great power.

79

Qui par fer pere perdra, nay de Nonnaire,	He who by iron shall destroy his father, born in Nonnaire,
De gorgon sur la fera sang per-fetant,	Shall in the end carry the blood of the gorgon,
En terre estrange fera si tout de taire,	Shall in a strange country make all so silent,
Qui bruslera luy mesme & son entante.	That he shall burn himself, and his double talk.

Adolf Hitler, born in Austria, ruled Germany, and in the end perished in a bomb cellar in Berlin, probably burned to death.

80

Des innocens le sang de vefue & vierge,	The blood of the innocent widow and virgin,
Tant de maux faicts par moyen de grand Roge,	Much evil committed by the means of that great rogue,
Saints simulachres trempez en ar-dant cierge,	Holy images, dipped in burning wax candles,
De frayeur crainte ne verra nul que boge.	For fear, nobody shall be seen to stir.

A band of marauders shall roam the countryside, despoiling the innocent. Church property shall be unsafe and the populace shall be in great fear.

81

Le neur empire en desolation	The new empire in desolation,
Sera change du pole aquilonaire,	Shall be changed from the Northern Pole,
De la Sicile viendra l'emotion,	The commotion shall come from Italy,
Troubler l'emprise a Philip, tributaire.	To trouble the undertaking, tributary to Phillip.

The empire of Germany shall be laid waste by invaders from both the north and south. Spain, her spiritual ally, shall be troubled at the same time.

82

Ronge long, sec, faisant du bon vallet,	Long devourer, dry, cringing and fawning,
A la parfin n'aura que son congie.	In conclusion shall have nothing, but leave to be gone,
Poignant poyson, lettres au collet,	Piercing poison and letters in his collar,
Sera saisi, eschappe, en dangie.	Shall be seized, escape and in danger.

This depicts the downfall, capture and escape of a tyrant, before whom people had cringed in fear for many years. Although he is never apprehended, he lives out his years in constant fear and danger and dies a miserable death.

83

Le plus grand voile hors du port de Zara,	The greatest sail out of the port of Zara,
Pres de Bisance fera son entreprise,	Near Turkey shall make his undertaking,
D'ennemy perte & l'amy ne fera,	There shall be no loss of foes or friends,
Le tiers a deux fera grand pille & prise.	The third shall make a great pillage upon the two.

The Venetians (Zara) shall take the Island of Tenedos, near Constantinople, without loss of life on either side.

84

Paterne aura de la Sicile crie,
Tous les aprests due Goulphre de Trieste,
Qui s'entendra jusques a la Trina-cria,
De tant de voïes, fuy, fuy, l'horrible peste.

Paterno shall have out of Sicily screaming,
All the preparations of the Gulf of Trieste,
That shall be heard as far as Trina-cria,
Of so many sails, fly, fly, the horrible plague.

There seems to be a misspelling here in the word Paterno. We believe it refers to Palermo, and warns of a plague that shall strike around that vicinity.

85

Entre Bayonne & a Saincte Jean de Lux,
Sera pose de Mars le promottoire;
Aux Hanix d'Aquilon, Nanar hostera Lux,
Puis suffoque au lict sans adjutoire.

Between Bayonne and St. Jean of Lux,
Shall be put down the promoting of Mars,
From the Hunix of the North, Nanar shall take away Lux,
Then shall be suffocated in bed without help.

After many years of war between France and Spain, peace was declared and a marriage arranged between the King of France and the Infanta of Spain. The last two lines have no significance and we believe they were put in merely to make up the rhyme.

86

Par Arnani, Tholose, Ville Fran-que,
Bande infinie par le Mont Adrian,
Passe riviere, hutin par pont la planque,
Bayonne entrer tous Bichoro criant.

By Arnani, Toulouse and Ville-franche,
An infinite number of people by Mont Adrian,
Cross rivers, noise upon the bridges and planks,
Come all into Bayonne crying Bichoro.

"Bichoro" is an old French word for Victory. Bayonne, on the border of Spain, shall be successfully invaded by the French.

87

Mort conspiree viendra en plein effect,
Charge donnee & voyage de mort,
Esleu, cree, receu, par siens deffaict,
Sang d'innocence devant soy par remort.

A conspired death shall come to an effect,
Charge given, and a journey of death,
Elected, created, received, by his own defeated,
Blood of innocence before him by remorse.

A conspiracy against an elected one is here foreshadowed.

88

Dans le Sardaigne un noble Roy viendra,
Qui ne tiendra que trois ans le Royaume,
Plusieurs couleurs avec soy conjoindra,
Luy mesme apres soin matriscome.

Into Sardinia shall come a noble King,
Who shall hold the Kingdom only three years,
He shall join many colors to his own,
Himself afterwards, care, sleep, repentance come.

The Kingdom of Sardinia was created in 1720, more than 150 years after Nostradamus predicted this occurrence.

89

Pour ne tomber entre mains de son oncle,
Qui les enfans par regner trucidez,
Orant au peuple mettant pied sur Peloncle,
Morts & traisne entre chevaux barbez.

That he might not fall into the hands of his uncle,
That had murdered his children for to rule,
Taking away from the people, and putting his foot on the bald-headed one,
Killed and drawn among horses.

A bald-headed tyrant shall be killed in a dishonorable manner after having misruled the country.

90

Quand des croisez un trouve de
  sens trouble,
En lieu du sacre verra boeuf
  cornu,
Par vierge porc son lieu lors sera
  double
Par Roy plus ordre ne sera soustenu.

When of the crossed, one of a
  troubled mind,
In a sacred place, shall see a horny
  ox,
By virgin swine then shall his place
  be double,
By King henceforth, order shall not
  be sustained.

A madman, whose symbol is a strange cross, shall be aided in his
schemes of conquest by unmitigated scoundrels (pure swine), but his
power will be short-lived.

91

Parmy les champs de Rodanes en-
  trees,
Ou les croisez seront presque unis,
Les deuz Brassiers en Pisces ren-
  contrees,
Et un grand nombre par deluge
  punis.

Through the fields where the
  Rhone meanders,
Where the crossed shall be almost
  united,
The two Brassiers met in Pisces,
And a great number punished by
  a flood.

This quatrain continues from the preceding one, indicating the near-
success of the plots of the "madman" and his cohorts and predicting their
final overthrow.

92

Loin hors du regne mis en hazard
  voyage,
Grand ost duyra, pour soy l'occupera,
Le Roy tiendra les siens captif,
  ostage,
A son retour tour pays pillera.

Far from the kingdom a hazardous
  journey undertaken,
He shall lead a great army, which
  he shall make his own,
The King shall keep his prisoners
  and pledges,
At his return he shall plunder all
  the country.

A General shall mutiny against a King. In retaliation, the King shall
hold his relatives hostage; but on the General's return he shall pillage
the country.

93

Sept mois sans plus obtiendra pre-lature	Seven months and no more he shall obtain the prelacy,
Par son decez grand scisme fera naistre,	By his decease he shall cause a great schism,
Sept mois tiendra un aurte la pre-ture,	Another shall be seven months governor,
Pres de Venise paix union renaistre.	Near Venice peace and union shall grow again.

A sharp division of opinion will occur on the death of a Pope after only seven months in office. It will be further aggravated by the death of a governor who also held office for only seven months. When both offices are again filled, to the satisfaction of the dissenting parties, peace will reign once more.

94

Devant le lac ou plus cher fut gette,	Before the lake, wherein most dear was thrown,
De sept mois, & son ost desconfit,	Of seven months and his army discomfited,
Seront Hispans par Albannois gastez,	Spaniards shall be spoiled by Albanians,
Par delay perte en donnant le conflit.	By delaying, loss in giving the battle.

The League of Nations at Lake Geneva is meant here. Spain shall delay giving battle to the English and be the loser thereby.

95

Le seducteur sera mis dans la fosse,	The deceiver shall be put into the dungeon,
Et estache jusques a quelque temps,	And bound fast for a while,
Le clerc uny, le chef avec sa crosse,	The clergy united, the chief with his cross emblem,
Pycante droite attraira les contens.	Pointing upright, shall draw in the contented.

Those of the party of the Cross shall be supported by the rich. Dissenters shall be thrown into jail in order to keep them from spreading their doctrines of heresy.

96

La Synagogue sterile sans nul fruit,
Sera receue entre les infideles,
De Babylon la fille du persuit,
Misere & triest luy trenchera les
   aisles.

The Synagogue barren, without
   fruit,
Shall be received among the in-
   fidels,
In Babylon, the daughter of the
   persecuted,
Miserable and sad shall cut her
   wings.

There will be a period of great persecution of the Jews, and their Synagogues will become empty and desolate because of it.

97

Aux fine du var changer le pem-
   potans,
Pres du rivage, le trois beaux enfans
   naistre,
Ruyne au peuple par aage com-
   petans
Regne au pays charger plus croistre.

At the finish of the war, to change
   the glory,
Near the shore shall three fair children be born,
Ruin to the people, by competent
   age,
To change that country's Kingdom
   and see it grow no more.

Truly a fantastic prediction of the three Kennedy brothers involved in the affairs of government. The recessions of 1970 and 1982 are also forecast.

98

Des gens d'Eglise sang sera
   espanche,
Comme de l'eau en si grand abon-
   dance
Et d'un long temps ne sera
   restranche,
Veue au clerc ruine & doleance.

The blood of churchmen shall be
   spilt,
As water in such great abundance,
And for a long time shall not be
   stayed,
Ruin and grievance shall be seen
   to the clergy.

The persecution of the clergy in Soviet-dominated countries is here anticipated.

99

Par la puissance de trois Roys temporels,	By the power of three temporal Kings,
En autre lieu sera mis le Saint Siege;	The Holy See shall be put in another place,
Ou la substance de l'esprit corporel,	Where the substance of the corporeal spirit,
Sera remis & receu pour vray siege.	Shall be restored, and admitted for a true seat.

A coalition of three temporal rulers shall attempt to change the location of the Holy City.

100

Pour l'abundance de l'arme respandue,	Through the abundance of the army scattered,
Du haut en bas, par le bas au plus haut,	High will be low, low will be high,
Trop grande foy par jeu vie perdue,	Too great a faith, a life lost in jesting,
De soif mourir par abondant deffaut.	To die by thirst, through abundance of want.

Nations will increase their military might and great armies will be scattered throughout the world. The people, burdened with the increased taxes for the maintenance of these armies, will finally rebel, and world-wide revolution will follow.

Automation and the discovery of new sources of energy will make it possible to reduce all of our power requirements to a point where Labor will not have to be employed more than twelve hours per week. This will eliminate the chief cause of the wars of agression that have plagued the world since the industrial revolution for the diminishing natural resources but will also create a new and powerful Politico-Labor group that will hold the balance of power.

In the United States this shall manifest itself in a new third party built on the foundations of the Union Labor movement.

1*

Seront confus plusieurs de leurs attente,	Many shall be confounded in their expectation,
Aux habitants ne sera pardonne,	The people shall not be pardoned,
Qui bien pensoient perseverer l'attente,	Who thought to persevere in their resolution,
Mais grand loisir ne leur sera donne.	But there shall not be given them a great leisure for it.

The collaborationists shall not escape; they shall be sought out and prosecuted.

2

Plusieurs viendront, & parleront de paix,	Many shall come and talk of peace,
Entre Monarques & Seigneurs bien puissans,	Between Monarchs and Lords very powerful,
Mais ne sera accorde de si pres,	But it shall not be agreed to it so soon,
Que ne se rendent, plus qu'autres obeissans.	If they do not show themselves more obedient than others.

We are just on the verge of the fulfillment of this prophecy; relations between powerful industrialists and leaders of the labor organizations shall not be settled soon, unless a greater spirit of cooperation develops.

3

Las quelle fureur, helas quelle pitie,	See! what fury, alas what pity,
Il y aura entre beaucoup de gens!	There shall be betwixt many people,
On ne vit onc une telle amitie,	There never was seen such a friendship,
Qu'auront les loups a courir diligens.	As the wolves shall have in being diligent to run.

Under the guise of political organizational activity, various elements of society shall be set at each other's throats.

* These six stanzas have heretofore been included with Century VIII.

4

Beaucoup de gens viendront parle-
menter,
Aux grands seigneurs qui leur
feront la guerre,
On ne voudra en rien les escouter,
Helas! si Dieu n'enuoye paix en
terre.

Many peoples shall come to speak,
To great lords that shall make war
against them,
They shall not be admitted to a
hearing,
Alas! If God does not send peace
upon earth.

The United Nations debates peace among warlike nations but fails to prevent or stop war.

5

Plusieurs secours viendront de tous
costez,
De gens loingtains qui voudront
resister;
Ils seront tout a coup bien hastez,
Mais ne pourront pour celte heure
assister.

Many helps shall come on all sides,
Of peoples far off, that would want
to resist,
They shall be upon a sudden all
very hasty,
But for the present they shall not
be able to assist.

At a time of need, when a great emergency threatens, the nations of the world will promise to aid the needy, but will not be in a position to give immediate help.

6

Las quel plaisir ont Princes estrang-
ers!
Garde toy bien qu'en ton pays ne
vienne,
Il y auroit de terribles dangers,
En maints contrees, mesme en la
Vienne.

Ha! Pleasure take foreign Princes,
Guard thyself lest any should come
into thy country,
There should be terrible dangers,
In several countries, and chiefly in
Vienna.

A clear warning to the nations of the world to profit by the example of Austria, and to arm themselves against subversive foreign propaganda.

1

Dans la maison du traducteur de Boure,
Seront les lettres trouvees sur la table,
Borgne, roux blanc, chenu tiendra de cours,
Qui changera au nouveau Connestable.

In the house of the translator of Boure,
The letters shall be found upon the table,
Blind of one eye, red, white, hoary, shall keep its course,
Which shall change at the coming of the new constable.

A disseminator of subversive propaganda will be exposed upon the election of a new local governor.

2

Du haut du Mont Aventin voix ouye,
Vuides, vuidez de tous les deux costez,
Du sang des rouges sera l'ire assomie,
D'Arimin, Prato, Columna debotez.

From the top of Mount Aventine, a voice was heard,
Get you gone, get you gone on all sides,
With the blood of the red one, the passions shall be glutted,
From Arimini and Prato, the Colonnas shall be driven away.

Mt. Aventine is one of seven hills of Rome. A fratricidal struggle shall take place in Italy resulting in the ruin of the Colonna family.

3

La magna vaqua a Ravenne grand
  trouble,
Conduicts par quinze enserrez a
  Fornase;
A Rome naistra deux monstres a
  teste double,
Sang, feu, deluge, les plus grands
  l'espase.

The magna vaqua great trouble at
  Ravenna,
Conducted by fifteen, shut up at
  Fornase,
At Rome, shall be born two mon-
  sters with a double head,
Blood, fire, flood, the greater ones
  astonished.

The expression "magna vaqua" is a derisive term, meaning a great
nothing. The significance of the quatrain lies in the prediction of the monstrous Rome-Berlin Axis, and the indication of its short but bloody period
of existence.

4

L'an ensuyvant descouverts par
  deluge,
Deux chefs esleuz, le premier ne
  tiendra,
De fuyr ombre a l'un d'eux le refuge,
Saccagee case qui premier main-
  tiendra.

The year following being discovered by a flood,
Two chiefs elected, the first shall
  not hold,
To fly from shade, to one shall be a
  refuge
That house shall be plundered
  which shall maintain the first.

A follow-up of the preceding stanza, this predicts the flight of Mussolini
to Germany, after the crumbling of his power, and the eventual ruin of
both him and Hitler.

5

Tiere doibt du pied au premier
  semblera
A un nouveau Monarque de bas
  haut
Qui Pise & Luiques tyran occupera,
Du precedent corriger le deffault.

The third toe shall be like the first,
To a new high monarch come from
  a low estate,
Who being a tyrant shall occupy
  Pisa and Lucca,
To correct the faults of him that
  preceded him.

One of low estate, pretending to improve conditions in Italy, shall seize
power and become a dictator.

6

Par la Guyenne infinite d'Anglois	There shall be in Guyenne an in-
Occuperont par nom d'Angle Aquitaine,	finite number of English,
Du Languedoc, I, palme Bour- delois,	Who shall occupy it by the name of Aquitanian England,
Qu'ils nommeront apres Barboxi- taine.	On Languedoc, near the land of Bordeaux,
	Which afterwards they shall call Barboxitain.

The prediction here is that the English will invade and occupy the west coast of France near Bordeaux. This was fulfilled in the twelfth, thirteenth fourteenth, fifteenth, and twentieth centuries.

7

Qui ouvrira le monument trouve,	He that shall open the found sepulchre,
Et ne viendra le serrer prompte- ment,	And shall not close it again promptly,
Mal luy viendra, & ne pourra prouve,	Evil will befall him, and he shall not be able to prove
Si mieux doit estre Roy Breton ou Normand.	Whether is best, a British or Nor- man King.

The discovery and opening of the tomb of Tutankhamen brought sudden and mysterious death to the discoverer and to members of his family.

8

Puisnay Roy fait son pere mettre a mort,	A Younger King causeth his father to be put
Apres conflict de mort tres in hon- este;	To a dishonest death, after a battle,
Escrit trouve soupcon, donra remort,	Writing being found shall give sus- picion and remorse,
Quand loup chasse pose sur la couchette.	When a hunted wolf shall pose on the cot.

A young prince, during the action of a battle, shall turn and, unseen by others, shall kill his father. However, after a short time, documents will turn up in which his murderous intentions are clearly outlined, and he shall be overthrown.

9

Quand lampe ardente de feu inex-
  tinguible
Sera trouvee au Temple des Vestales,
Enfant trouve, feu, eau passant par
  crible;
Nismes eau perir, Tholose cheoir
  les hales.

When a lamp burning with an unquenchable fire,
Shall be found in the Temple of
  the Vestals,
A child shall be found, water running through a sieve,
Nismes to perish by water, the city
  hall shall fall at Toulouse.

There was a custom among the Vestal Virgins of ancient Rome, pertaining to the punishment of those among them who had forreited their
honor. They were buried alive in a cave, with some bread and water and
a lamp with an infinitesimal amount of oil. Beyond this reference, this
quatrain holds no greater meaning.

10

Moine, Moinesse d'enfant mort expose,
Mourir par ourse ravy par verrier,
Par Foix & Panniers le camp sera
  pose,
Contre Tholose, Carcas, dresser
  sorrier.

Monk and Nun having exposed a
  dead child,
To be killed by a bear and be carried away by a glazier,
The camp shall be pitched at Foix
  and Panniers,
Against Toulouse, Carcassone shall
  be against them.

Neglect of the teaching of spiritual values shall cause innocent children
to fall prey to false doctrines.

11

Le just a tort a mort l'on viendra
  mettre
Publiquement, & du milieu estaint;
Si grand peste en ce lieu viendra
  naistre,
Que les jugeans fouyr seront contraints.

The just shall be put to death
  wrongfully,
Publicly, and being taken out of
  the midst,
So great a plague, shall break into
  that place,
That the judges shall be compelled
  to run away.

Charles I was executed in 1649 in England, and the great plague occurred in 1665–1666.

12

Le tant d'argent de Diane & Mercure,	The so much silver of Diana and Mercury,
Les simulachres au lac seront trouvez;	The statues shall be found in the lake,
Le figulier cherchant argille neuve,	The potter seeking for a new clay,
Luy & les siens, d'or seront abbreuvez.	He and his, shall be filied with gold.

A smooth-tongued demagogue, ever seeking new victims under the pretense of reform, shall be shown to have betrayed and looted all.

13

Les exilez autour de la Solongne	The exiles in the tower of Sologne,
Conduicts de nuict pour marcher en l'Auxois,	Being conducted by night to go into Auxois,
Deux de Modene truculent de Bologne,	Two of Modena, the cruel of Bologna,
Mis, descouverts par feu de Burancois.	Shall be discovered by the fire of Burancois.

Pertaining to a local incident of Nostradamus' time, this merely describes the escape and eventual capture of some criminals.

14

Mis en planure chauderon d'infecteurs,	On the plain shall be put a great dyers vat,
Vin, miel, & huyle, & bastis sur fourneaux,	Filled with wine, honey and oil and built on a furnace,
Seront plongez, sans mal dit malfacteurs,	In it shall be plunged without evil, those called malefactors,
Sept, fum, extaint au canon des Bordeaux.	Seven, summoned, at the law of Bordeaux.

Boiling in oil, a favorite punishment reserved for counterfeiters in ancient France, shall be meted out to seven persons at Bordeaux.

15

Pres de Parpan les rouges detenus,
Ceux du milieu parfondrez menez
   loing;
Trois mis en pieces, & cinq mal
   soustenus,
Pour le Seigneur & Prelat de Bour-
   boing.

Near unto Parpan, the red ones
   detained,
Those of the middle sunk and carried far away,
Three cut in pieces and five ill sustained,
For the Lord and Prelate of Bur-
   going.

One of the many feuds among the cardinals and lesser clergymen is
herein described.

16

De Castel Franco sortira l'assemblee,
L'ambassadeur non plaisant fera
   scisme;
Ceux de Riviere seront en la
   meslee,
Et au grand goulphre desnier ont
   l'entree.

From Spanish Franco shall come
   the assembly,
The Ambassador not pleased, shall
   make a separation,
Those of the Riviera, shall be in
   the melee,
And shall deny entry into the great
   gulf.

This quatrain is remarkable in that it exactly names the protagonist
involved. The reference is, of course, to Franco, the Spanish Civil War and
its repercussions. It also refers to the Axis powers who, after consultation
with Franco, were denied domination of Gibraltar and entrance into the
("great gulf") Mediterranean.

17

Le tiers premier, pis que ne fit
   Neron,
Vuidez vaillant que sang humain
   respandre,
R'edificer fera le Forneron,
Siecle d'or, mort, nouveau Roy
   grand esclandre.

The third first, worse than ever did
   Nero,
Go out of the valiant, he shall
   spill much human blood,
He shall cause the Forneron to be
   rebuilt,
Golden age dead, new King great
   troubles.

"The third first"—the Third Reich (Nazi Germany), worse than Nero
with massacres of Central European Jews and political dissidents.

COMPLETE PROPHECIES OF NOSTRADAMUS

18

Le lys Dauffois portera dans Nancy,
Jusques en Flandres Electeur de
l'Empire,
Neufve obturee au grand Montmorency,
Hors lieux prouvez delivre a clere
peyne.

The Dauphin shall carry the lily
into Nancy,
As far as Flanders the Elector of
the Empire,
New hindrance to great Montmorency,
Out of proved places, delivered to
a clear pain.

An incident in the reign of Louis XIII when Nancy was conquered by
the Dauphin. The events forecast occurred some ninety years after Nostradamus wrote this quatrain. Montmorency was charged with rebellion
against Louis XIII and was subsequently beheaded.

19

Dans le milieu de la Forest May-
enne,
Sol au Lyon la fourdre tombera,
Le grand bastard issu du grand du
Maine,
Ce jour Fougere pointe en sang en-
trera.

In the middle of the Forest of
Mayenne,
Sol being in Leo, the lightning shall
tumble,
The great bastard, begat by the
great du Main,
That day Fougeres shall enter its
point into blood.

An incident pertaining to one of the noble families of ancient France,
this needs no further interpretation.

20

De nuict viendra par la forest de
Reines,
Deux pars Voltorte Herne, la pierre
blanche,
Le moine noir en gris dedans
Varennes,
Esleu cap. cause tempeste, feu,
sang tranche.

By night shall come through the
forest of Reines,
Two parts Voltorte Herne, the
white stone,
The black monk in gray within
Varennes,
Elected captain, causeth tempest,
fire, blood running.

At Varennes, Louis XVI, disguised in a monk's cloak, was intercepted
as he attempted to escape from the Revolutionists.

21

Au temple haut de Bloys sacre
  Salonne,
Nuict pont de Loyre, Prelat, Roy
  pernicant;
Cuiseur victoire aux marests de la
  Lone,
D'ou Prelature de blancs abor-
  meant.

At the high temple of Blois sacred
  Salon,
In the night the bridge of Loire,
  Prelate, King pernicious,
A poignant victory in the marshes
  of Lone,
Whence Prelature of white shall
  be abortive.

During the course of one night, both a Prelate and a King will meet
their deaths on a bridge, much to the rejoicing of the lesser clergy of the
region.

22

Roy & sa court au lieu de langue
  halbe,
Dedans le temple vis a vis du palais,
Dans le jardin Duc de Mantor &
  d'Albe,
Albe & Mantor, poignard, langue
  & palais.

King and his court in the place of
  half language,
Within the church, near the palace,
In the garden, Duke of Mantor
  and of Alba,
Alba and Mantor, dagger, tongue
  in the palace.

This continues the story of the previous quatrain, describing the intrigue and scandal that prevailed in both the church and the palace.

23

Puisnay jouant au fresch dessous la
  tonne,
Le haut du toit du millieu sur la
  teste,
Le pere Roy au temple sainct
  Salonne,
Sacrifiant sacrera fum de feste.

The youngest son playing under
  the tun,
The top of the house shall fall on
  his head,
The king, his father, in the temple
  of Saint Soulaine,
Sacrificing shall make festival
  smoke.

A young prince shall be injured by the cave-in of a house. No greater
significance can be gathered from this obscure verse.

24

Sur le palais au rocher des fenestres
Seront ravis les deux petits royaux,
Passer Aurelle, Lutece, Denis clois-
tres,
Nonnain,   Mallods   avalle   verts
noyaux.

Upon the palace at the rock of the
windows,
Shall be carried the two little royal
ones,
To pass Aurele, Lutece, Denis
cloisters,
Nonnain, Mollods to swallow green
kernels of fruit.

The journey of two children of a royal household is herein described.

25

Passant les Ponts, venir pres des
rosiers,
Tard arrive plustost qu'il cuydera,
Viendront les noves Espagnols a
Besiers,
Qui icelle chasse emprinse cassera.

Going over the bridge, to come
near the rose-trees,
Arriving late, much sooner than he
thought,
Shall come the news of Spaniards
to Beziers,
Who shall chase this hunting undertaking.

In this particular section Nostradamus seems concerned merely with
trivial events of his day; this quatrain continues in that vein, describing
an incident in a hunting expedition.

26

Nice sortie sur nim des lettres
aspres,
La grand cappe fera present non
sien;
Proche de vultry aux murs de vertes
capres
Apres Plombin le vent a bon
escient.

A foolish going out, caused by
sharp letters,
The great cap shall give what is
not his,
Near Vultry by the walls of green
capers,
About Piombino the wind shall be
in good earnest.

The Pope is here referred to as "the great cap," and the meaning is
that he shall be the arbitrator in a dispute between the Italian cities of
Velitrum and Piombino.

27

De bois la garde, vent clos rond pont sera,	The fence being of wood, close wind, bridge shall be broken,
Haut le receu frappera de Dauphin,	He that is received high, shall strike at the Dauphin,
Le vieux Teccon bois unis passera,	The old Teccon shall pass over smooth wood,
Passant plus outre du Duc le droict confin.	Going to the right on the side of the Duke.

Malcontents shall attempt to form a conspiracy against the government, but it shall be put down almost immediately due to the leaders betraying their cause and going over to the side of the Duke.

28

Voille Symacle, Port Massiliolique,	Symaclian Sail, Massillion port,
Dans Venise port marcher aux Pannons,	In Venice to march towards the Hungarians,
Partir du goulfre & Synus Illyrique,	To go away from the Gulf and Illyrian Straits,
Vast a Sicille, Ligurs coups de canons.	Towards Sicily, the Genoese, with cannon shots.

A great expedition from Marseilles, arriving at Venice, shall march towards the Hungarians. The Genoese will be driven from Sicily by cannon shots.

29

Lors que celuy qu'a nul ne donne lieu,	When he that giveth place to nobody,
Abandonner voudra lieu prins non pris;	Shall forsake the place taken and not taken,
Feu, nef, par saignes, bitument a Charlieu,	Fire, ship, by bloody bitumen at Charlieu,
Seront Quintin, Balez reprins.	Then St. Quentin and Calais shall be taken.

The powerful dictator shall retreat from northern France, and Calais shall be retaken from him.

30

Au port de Puola & de Saincte
Nicolas,
Perir Normandie au Goulfre Phan-
atique,
Cap de Bizance rues crier helas!
Secors de Gaddes & du grand
Philippique.

At the harbor of Puola and St.
Nicolas,
A Norman ship shall perish in the
Fanatic Gulf,
At the Cape of Byzantia, the streets
shall cry "Alas!"
Help from Cadiz and from the
Spanish King.

The reference here is to the port of Malta, which was besieged by the
Turks. Philip II, King of Spain, sent an army to relieve it, which caused
a great commotion among the people of Constantinople.

31

Le tremblement de terre a Mortars,
Cassich, Sainct Georges a demy
perfondrez,
Paix assoupie, la guerre esueillera,
Dans temple a Pasques abysmes
enfondrez.

There shall be an earthquake by
mortars,
Cassich, St. George shall be half
swallowed up,
The war shall awake the sleeping
peace,
On Easter Day, shall be a great
hole sunk in the temple.

Terrific artillery fire shall shake the earth; England (St. George) shall
be almost defeated; the war shall spread to the ends of the earth. This
refers to the bombing of the Cathedral at Coventry at Eastertime in 1941.
An extremely accurate prediction.

32

De fin porphire profond collon
trouvee
Dessous la laze escripts capitolin;
Os, poil retors, Romain force
prouvee,
Classe agiter au port de Methelin.

A deep column of fine Porphyry
shall be found,
Under whose base shall be important writings,
Bones, hairs twisted, Roman force
tried,
A fleet about the port of Methelin.

The Rosetta Stone, with its important writing, was discovered in 1799
and describes events that took place in 197–196 B.C. The stone was probably ruined and buried by Roman legions in the early Christian era.

33

Hercules Roy de Rome & Danne- marc,	Hercules, King of Rome, and Den- mark,
De Gaule trois Guion surnomme,	Of France three Guyon surnamed,
Trembler l'Italie & l'un de sainct Marc,	Shall cause Italy to quake and one of Venice,
Premier sur tous Monarque re- nomme.	He shall be above all a famous monarch.

We believe that the "Hercules" referred to indicates the powerful and famous Napoleon, before whom all Europe quaked.

34

La parte solus mary sera mittre.	The separated husband shall wear a mitre,
Retour conflict passera sur la tuille;	Returning, battle, he shall go over the tiles,
Par cinq cens un trahye sera tiltre,	By five hundred, one dignified shall be betrayed,
Narbon & Saulce par coutaux avons d'huille.	Narbon and Saulce shall have oil by Quintal.

Here is one of the most famous and most discussed prophecies of Nostradamus, and the most remarkable for its mention of so many actual names—Narbon (Narbonne), Louis XVI's minister of war; Saulce, oilman and mayor of Varennes; and the reference to "over the tiles" (Tuileries), which was not a palace when Nostradamus was alive, but was the location of kilns for tiles. The interpretation, then, is that the king and queen were arrested at Varennes because Saulce betrayed them to the soldiers when they came to his shop. The five hundred men were the Marseillais who attacked the palace of Tuileries and formally put the king under arrest. At that time the king was wearing the red "miter" of the Revolution.

35

Et Ferdinand blonde sera descorte,	And Ferdinand having a troop of blond men,
Quitter la fleur, suyure le Macedon,	Shall leave the flower to follow the Macedonian,
Au grand Besoing defaillira sa routte,	At his great need his road shall fail him,
Et machera contre le Myrmidon.	And he shall go against the Myrmi- don.

King Ferdinand, of Bulgaria, with a German Army at his command, shall campaign against the Greeks and Macedonians, but he shall fail to conquer them.

36

Un grand Roy prins entre les mains d'un jeune,	A great King taken in the hands of a young one,
Non loin de Pasques, confusion, coup cultre,	Not far from Easter, confusion, of a knife,
Perpet. cattif temps, que foudre en la hune,	Shall commit, pitiful time, the fire at the top of the mast,
Trois freres lors se blesseront, & meurtre.	Three brothers then shall wound one another, and murder done.

The reference here is to the execution of Louis XVI, on January 21, 1793; and also indicating the confusing state of affairs in France at that time.

37

Pont & molins en Decembre versez	Bridges and mills in December overturned,
En si hault lieu montera la Garonne;	In so high a place the Garonne shall come,
Murs, edifice, Tholose renversez,	Walls, buildings, Toulouse overturned,
Qu'on ne scaura son lieu autant matronne.	So that no one shall know its place, so much Matrone.

A tremendous overflowing of the Garonne River shall occur in December with disastrous destruction of life and property.

38

L'entree de Blaye par Rochelle & l'Anglois,	The entrance of Blaye, by Rochelle and the English,
Passera outre le grand Aemathien,	Shall go beyond the great Aemathien,
Non loing d'Agen attendra le Gaulois,	Not far from Agen shall expect the French,
Secours Narbonne deceu par entretien.	Help from Narbonne deceived by entertainment.

The English will attempt an invasion of France by way of Bordeaux (Blaye). The French will issue a call for help to the people of Southern France, but, spurred on by traitors in their midst, they shall refuse to aid their countrymen.

39

En Arbissela, Vezema & Crevari	By Arbisella, Vezema and Crevari,
De nuict conduicts par Savone attraper,	Being conducted by night to take Savonna,
Le vif Gascon, Giury & la Charry.	The quick Gascon, Giury and the Charry,
Derrier mur vieux & neuf palais gripper.	Behind old walls and new palaces to grapple.

An incident concerning the minor disturbances between the Italians and Gascons in Nostradamus' day is described.

40

Pres de Quentin dans la forest Bourlis.	Near St. Quentin in the forest of Bourlis.
Dans l'Abbaye seront Flamens tranchez,	In the Abbey the Flemish shall be slashed,
Les deux puisnais de coups my estourdis,	The two younger sons half astonished with blows,
Suitte oppressee & garde tous haches.	The followers oppressed, and the guards cut to pieces.

An incident during the war in the Flemish lowlands between Flamans and the Spaniards, this concerns a peculiar accident which caused much talk at that time.

41

Le grand Chyren soy saisir d'Avignon,	The great Henry shall seize upon Avignon,
De Rome lettres en miel plein d'amertume,	Letters from Rome shall come full of bitterness,
Lettre ambassade partir de Chanignon,	Letters and embassies shall go to Chanignon,
Carpentras pris par Duc noir rouge plume.	Carpentras taken by a black Duke with a red feather.

This prophecy was fulfilled when Avignon, the one time seat of Papal power, was seized by the French King.

42

De Barcelonne, de Gennes &
    Venise,
De la Sicille pres Monaco unis,
Contre Barbare classe prendront la
    vise,
Barbar poulse bien loing jusqu'a
    Thunis.

From Barcelona, from Genoa and
    Venice,
From Sicily near Monaco united,
Against the Barbarians the fleet
    shall take her aim,
The Barbarian shall be driven back
    as far as Tunis.

Spain and Italy united in war, shall be driven back in Africa as far as Tunis.

43

Proche a descendre l'armee cru-
    cigere,
Sera guettee par les Ismaelites,
De tous costez batus par nef
    Raviere,
Prompt assaillis de dix galeres
    d'eslites.

The crusading army being about
    the land,
Shall be watched by the Ismaelites,
Being beaten on all sides, the ship
    carried away,
Presently assaulted by ten chosen
    warships.

A crusading (Christian) army shall attempt an incursion against non-believers. They shall meet with great resistance and will be forced to withdraw.

44

Migrez, migres de Geneve tres-
    tous,
Saturne d'or en fer se changera,
Le contre Raypoz exterminera tous,
Avant l'advent le Ciel signes fera.

Leave, leave, go forth out of
    Geneva, all
Saturn of gold, shall be changed
    into iron,
The contrary of the positive ray
    shall exterminate all,
Before it happens, the Heavens
    shall show signs.

Startling! Nostradamus here foretells the advent of atomic power. He indicates clearly that this force can be used for useful or destructive purposes. But, with terrifying finality, he warns of the eventual destruction of our civilization by means of the release of atomic energy—holding out but one ray of hope, "the Heavens shall show signs," meaning that we will be given one final chance to determine our destiny.

45

Ne sera soul jamais de demander,	He shall never be weary of asking,
Grand Mendosus obtiendra son empire	Great Liar shall obtain his dominion,
Loing de la court fera contre-mander,	Far from the court he shall be countermanded,
Piedmont, Picart, Paris, Tyrhen le pire.	Piedmont, Picardy, Paris, Tyrhenia the worse.

This points to the doctrine of lies and deceit which was the cornerstone of the Nazi philosophy; and indicates the final downfall of the regime.

46

Vuydez, fuyez de Tholose les rouges,	Get you gone, fly from Toulouse, ye red ones,
Du sacrifice faire expiation,	There shall expiation be made of the sacrifice,
Le chef du mal dessous l'ombre des courges,	The chief cause of the evil under the shadow of the gourds,
Mort estrangler carne omination.	Shall be strangled, a presage to the destruction of much flesh.

In Toulouse, the red ones (cardinals) are warned of an imminent onslaught against members of the clergy.

47

Les soub signez d'indigne delivrance,	The undersigned to a worthless deliverance,
Et de la multe auront contre advis,	Shall have from the multitude a contrary advice,
Change monarque mis en perille pence,	Changing their monarch and put him in peril,
Serrez en cage se verront vis a vis.	They shall see themselves shut up in a cage.

The Islamic revolution in Iran is predicted here but the faithful end up isolated from the Arab world.

48

La grand cite d'ocean maritime,
Environnee de marets en crystal;
Dans le solstice hyemal & la prime,
Sera tentee de vent espouvental.

The great maritime city of the ocean,
Encompassed with marshes of crystal,
In the winter solstice and the spring,
Shall be tempted with a fearful wind.

The people of London are warned of the approach of a great hurricane which will cause much damage to the city.

49

Gand & Bruxles marcheront contre Anvers,
Senat de Londres mettront a mort leur Roy,
Le sel & vin luy seront a l'envers,
Pour aux avoir le regne en desarroy.

Ghent and Brussels shall march against Antwerp,
The Senate of London shall put their King to death,
The salt and wine shall not be able to do him good,
That they may have the kingdom into ruin.

This is a most remarkable prophecy, for here we have a concatenation of circumstances starting with the number of the quatrain itself, 49; and the unmistakable event referred to was the execution of King Charles 1 in the year 1649.

50

Mendosus tost viendra a son haut regne,
Mettant arriere un peuple Norlaris,
Le rouge blesme, le mesle a l'interregne,
Le jeune crainte & frayeur Barbaris.

Mendosus shall soon come to his high government,
Putting aside a little the Norlaris,
The red pale, the male at the inter-reigne
The young fear, and dreadful barbarism.

The great liar (see Quatrain 45) shall gain supremacy, being especially successful in operations among young people.

51

Contre les rouges sectes se banderont,	Against the reds, sects shall gather themselves,
Feu, eau, fer, corde, par paix se minera,	Fire, water, iron, rope, by peace it shall be destroyed,
Au point mourir ceux qui machineront,	Those that shall conspire shall be put to death,
Fors un que monde sur tout ruynera.	Except one, who above all shall ruin the world.

The latter half of the twentieth century best fits this prophecy with the anti-Communist movement in eastern Europe and Latin America. Stalin or Hitler certainly fulfill line 4.

52

La paix s'approche d'un coste & la guerre,	Peace is coming on one side, the war on the other,
Oncques ne fut la poursuite si grande,	There never was so great a pursuit,
Plaindre homme, femme, sang innocent par terre,	Man, woman, shall bemoan, innocent blood shall be spilt,
Et ce sera de France a toute bande.	It shall be in France at all sides.

Nostradamus here foresees the conflict between peace groups and militants. Also bombing of civilians, particularly during the anti-French rebellion in Algeria in the 1960s.

53

Le Neron jeune dans les trois cheminces,	The young Nero in the three chimneys,
Fera de paiges vifs pour ardoir jetter,	Shall cause pages to be thrown to be burnt alive,
Heureux qui loing sera de tels menees,	Happy shall be he, who shall be far from this doing.
Trois de son sang le feront mort guetter.	Three of his own blood shall cause him to be put to death.

A tyrannical leader (here referred to as a Nero) shall cause much destruction of life and property. Three men of his own class shall destroy him.

54

Arrivera au port de Corsibonne,
Pres de Ravenna qui pillera la dame,
En mer profonde legat de la Ulisbonne,
Sous roc cachez raviront septante ames.

There shall come into the port of Corsibonne
Near Ravenna, those that shall plunder the lady,
In the deep sea shall be the Ambassador of Lisbon,
The hidden under the rock, shall carry away seventy souls.

Corsica shall be the birthplace of one (Napoleon) who shall plunder Italy and cause great damage to the whole of Europe.

55

L'horrible guerre qu'en occident s'appreste;
L'an ensuivant viendra la pestilence,
Si fort terrible, que jeune, vieil, ne beste,
Sang, feu, Mercu, Mars, Jupiter en France.

The horrible war is in preparation in the west,
The year following shall come the plague,
So strangely terrible, that young, old, nor beast shall escape.
Blood, fire, Mercury, Mars, Jupiter in France.

In the western area, a horrible war is in preparation; following this will come a terrible plague, such as the world has never seen before.

56

Camp pres de Noudam passera Goussanville,
Et a Maiotes laissera son enseigne,
Convertira en instant plus de mille,
Cherchant les deux remettre en chaine & legne.

A camp shall by Noudam pass Goussanville,
And shall leave its flag at Maiotes,
And shall in an instant convert more than a thousand,
Seeking to put the two parties in good understanding.

Events and towns related here are of no importance now, but had local significance in Nostradamus' day.

57

Au lieu de Drux un roy reposera,
Et cherchera loy changeant d'an-
    atheme,
Pendant le ciel si tresfort tonnera,
Portee neufue Roy tuera soy-
    mesme.

In the place of Drux a king shall
    repose,
And shall seek a law changing
    anathema,
In the meanwhile the heaven shall
    thunder so strongly,
That a new gate shall kill the King
    himself.

Drux is a city in Normandy; and in this region the King shall attempt
to alter the local religious customs, without success.

58

Au coste gauche a l'endroit de
    Vitri,
Seront guettez les trois rouges de
    France,
Tous assoumez rouge, noir non
    meurdry,
Par les Bretons remis en asseurance.

On the left coast over against
    Vitry,
The three red ones of France shall
    be watched for,
All the red shall be beaten to death,
    the black not murdered,
By the Britons set up again in secu-
    rity.

The British shall re-establish a government in France; radicals shall
be eliminated from any participation in it.

59

A la Ferte prendra la Vidame,
Nicol tenu rouge qu'avoit produit
    la vie,
La grand Loyse naistra que fera
    clame,
Donnant Bougongne a Bretons par
    envie.

In the Ferte the Vidame shall take,
Nicol, reputed red, who is the
    product of life,
The great Louis shall be born, who
    shall lay claim,
Giving Burgundy to the Britons
    through envy.

The reds shall be beaten by the opposite party, with the aid of a British
leader named Louis, who will ask for payment in the form of an alliance
between France and England.

60

Conflict barbare, en la cornere
noire,
Sang espandu trembler la Dala-
matie,
Grand Ismael mettra son promon-
toire,
Ranes trembler, secours Lusitanie.

A barbarous fight in the black
corner,
Blood shall be spilt, Dalamatia
shall tremble for fear,
Great Ishmael shall set up his
promontory,
Frogs shall tremble, Portugal shall
bring succour.

Inter-sectional warfare among the Mohammedans is here predicted.

61

La pille faite a la coste marine,
Incite nova & parens amenez,
Plusieurs de Malte par le fait de
Messine,
Estroit serree seront mal guerdon-
nez.

The plunder shall be made on the
sea coast,
Incited by new people and friends
brought up,
Many of Malta, for the fact of
Messina,
Being kept close, shall be ill re-
warded.

A coalition of small nations, hitherto considered peaceful and harm-
less, shall attempt to gain control of Europe.

62

Au grand de Cheramonagora,
Seront croisez par rangs tous
attachez,
Le Pertinax Oppi, & Mandragora,
Raugon d'Octobre le tiers seront
laschez.

To the great one of Cheramonagora,
Shall be crossed by ranges, all tied
up.
The Pertinax Oppi, and Mandragora,
Raugon the third of October shall
be set loose.

There is a warning implicit in the words of this quatrain, of a world-
shaking event that will take place on October third.

63

Plainctes & pleurs, cris & grands
    hurlements,
Pres de Narbon a Bayonne & en
    Foix,
O quel horribles, calamitez, chan-
    gemens,
Avant que Mars revolu quelque-
    fois.

Complaints and tears, cries and
    great howlings,
Near Narbonne, Bayonne and in
    Foix,
O what horrid calamities and
    changes,
Before Mars has made somewhat
    his revolution.

Much disturbance in France is foreseen, with many changes taking place, leading to a completely reorganized government.

64

L'Aemathion passer monts Pyre-
    nees,
En Mars Narbon ne fera resistance,
Par mer & terre fera si grand
    menee,
Cap. n'ayant terre seure pour de-
    meurance.

The invader shall pass the Pyre-
    nean Mountains,
In March Narbonne shall make no
    resistance,
By sea and land he shall make so
    much ado,
Cap. shall not have safe ground to
    live in.

An invasion shall come to France, by way of the Spanish Frontier.

65

Dedans le coing de Luna viendra
    rendre,
Ou sera prins & mis en terre
    estrange,
Les fruicts immeurs seront a grand
    esclandre,
Grand vitupere, a l'un grande
    louange.

He shall come into the corner of
    Luna,
Where he shall be taken and put
    in a strange land,
The green fruits shall be in great
    disorder,
A great shame, to one shall be great
    praise.

The moon landing is predicted in lines 1 and 2. A remarkable forecast.

66

Paix, union sera & changement,
Estats, Offices, bas hault, & hault
  bien bas,
Dresser voyage, le fruict premier,
  torment,
Guerre cesser, civils proces, debats.

Peace, union, shall be and profound changes,
Estates, offices, the low high and
  the high very low,
A journey shall be prepared for, the
  first fruit, pains,
War shall cease, also civil processes
  and strife.

A Utopian age shall come into being in the course of time, but not
without pain.

67

Du hault des monts a l'entour de
  Dizere,
Port a la roche Valent, cent assem-
  blez,
De Chasteau-Neuf, Pierrelate, en
  Douzere,
Contre le Crest, Romains for as-
  semblez.

From the top of the mountains
  about Dizere,
Gate at the rock Valence, a hun-
  dred gathered together,
From Chateau Neuf, Pierrelate, in
  Douzere,
Against the Crest, Romans shall be
  assembled.

This prophecy, obscure and meaningless to us, was directed to the people in the provinces of Dauphine and Languedoc, in which all the towns
and rivers mentioned were situated.

68

Du mont Aymar sera noble obscur-
  cie,
Le mal viendra au joinct de Saone
  & Rhosne,
Dans bois cachez soldats jour de
  Lucia,
Que ne fut onc un si horrible
  throsne.

From Mount Aymar shall proceed
  a noble obscurity,
The evil shall come to the joining
  of the Saone and Rhone,
Soldiers shall be hid in the wood
  on St. Lucia's Day,
So that there was never such a horrible throne.

A group of men, banded together in a conspiracy to overthrow the
local government, shall attempt a march on the city of Lyons, but shall be
overcome by soldiers during a battle in the forest just outside the city.

69

Sur le mont de Bailly & la Bresse,	Upon the Mount of Bailly and the country at Bresse,
Seront cachez de Grenoble les fiers,	Shall be hidden the fierce ones or Grenoble,
Outre Lyon, Vien, eulx si grand gresle,	Beyond Lyons, Vienna, upon them shall fall such a hail,
Langoult en terre n'en restera un tiers.	That languishing on the ground, not even a third shall be left.

A fearful hail (bombardment) shall fall on parts of Italy and Austria, destroying two-thirds of the population.

70

Harnois trenchans dans les flambeaux cachez	Sharp weapons shall be hidden in burning weapons,
Dedans Lyon le jour de Sacrement,	In Lyons the day of the Sacrament,
Ceux de Vienne seront trestour hachez,	Those of Vienna shall be cut to pieces,
Par les Cantons Latins, Mascon eront.	By the Latin Cantons, after the example of Mascon.

This foretells the advent of terrible incendiary weapons; and deplores the rise of a science that may lead mankind to ultimate destruction.

71

Aux lieux sacrez, animaux veu a Trixe,	The place of sacred objects shall be seen at Trixe,
Avec celuy qui n'osera le jour,	With him that shall not dare in the day,
A Carcassonne pour disgrace propice,	In Carcassone for a favourable disgrace,
Sera pose pour plus ample sejour.	He shall be set to make a longer stay.

Holy objects in France shall be defiled, by temporary invaders.

72

Encor seront les saincts temples
  pollus,
Et expillez par Senat Tholosain,
Saturne deux trois siecles revollus,
Dans Avril, May, gens de nouveau
  levain.

Once more shall the Holy Temple
  be polluted,
And depredated by the Senate of
  Toulouse,
Saturn two, three cycles revolving,
In April, May, people of a new
  leaven.

According to this prophecy, there will be a complete revision of the
basic concepts of religion about the year 2150 (600 years after it was
written), and a new world order will arise (possibly one religion for all).

73

Dans Fois entrez Roy cerule Tur-
  ban,
Et regnera moins evolu Saturne,
Roy turban blanc, Bizance coeur
  ban,
Sol, Mars, Mercure, pres la hurne.

In Foix shall come a King with a
  blue Turban,
And shall reign before Saturn is
  revolved,
Then a King with a white turban
  shall make Turkey quake,
Sol, Mars, Mercury being near the
  top of the mast.

Foix, a city in southern France, shall be the center of military disturbances, culminating in the selection of a ruler who will bring great prosperity.

74

Dans la cite de Fertsod homicide,
Fait & fait multe beuf arant ne
  macter,
Retours encores aux honneurs
  d'Artemide,
Et a Vulcan corps morts sepulturer.

In the city of Fertsod, murder
  shall be done,
Causing a fine to be laid for killing a plow ox,
There shall be a return of the
  honors due to Artemide,
And Vulcan shall bury dead bodies.

In this quatrain, Nostradamus pays honor to a spiritual "contemporary," the writer Artemidorus (100 B.C.), who was widely known in his day
for his writings on augurs, and whose books on dream interpretation are
still extant.

75

De l'Ambraxie & du pays de Thrace,
Peuple par mer, mal & secours Gaulois,
Perpetuelle en Provence la trace,
Avec vestiges de leur coustumes. & loix.

From Ambraxia, and from the country of Thracia,
People by sea, evil and French assistance,
The trace of it shall be perpetual in Provence,
The footsteps of their customs and laws remaining.

Provence is shown here by Nostradamus, to have been settled originally by Thracians, with vestiges of the original laws and customs still remaining.

76

Avec le noir rapax & sanguinaire,
Yssu de peaultre de l'inhumain Neron,
Emmy deux fleuves main gauche militaire,
Sera meurtry par Joyne Chaulveron.

With the black and rapacious near a bloody peace,
Descended from the hide of the inhuman Nero,
Between two rivers, by the left military hand,
He shall be murdered by Joyn Caulveron.

One of a like character to Nero, black and rapacious, shall meet a violent death at the hands of revolutionaries.

77

Le regne prins le Roy conviera,
La dame prinse a mort jurez a sort,
La vie a Royne fils on desniera,
Et la pillex au fort de la consort.

The Kingdom being taken the King shall invite,
The lady taken to death,
The life shall be denied unto the Queen's son,
And the Pellex shall be at the height of her ease.

This is a prophecy of the French Revolution. The government was overthrown by revolutionaries, the King deposed, and the Queen guillotined.

78

La Dame Greque de beaute lay-
dique,
Heureuse faicte de proces innumerable,
Hors translatee au Regne His-
panique,
Captive prinse mourir mort
miserable.

The Grecian Lady of exquisite
beauty,
Made happy from innumerable
quarrels,
Being translated into the Spanish
Kingdom,
Shall be made a prisoner, and die
a miserable death.

The reference here is to Elizabeth of Valois who was married to King
Philip II of Spain. According to historical gossip she was in love with
another and never found any happiness in her royal liaison.

79

Le chef de classe, par fraude stratageme,
Fera timides sortir de leurs galleres,
Sortis meurtris chef renieux de
cresme,
Puis par l'embusche luy rendront
les saleres.

The commander of the fleet by
fraud and stratagem
Shall cause the timid ones to come
out of their galleys,
Come out murdered, chief re-
nouncer of baptism,
After that, by an ambush, they
shall give him his salary.

In 1932 Nordhoff and Hall related the famous story of the mutiny on
the Bounty, which occurred in 1789, and recalled the setting adrift of the
infamous Captain Bligh by his galley crewmen.

80

Le Duc voudra les siens exterminer;
Envoyera les plus forts, lieux
estranges,
Par tyrannie Bize & Luc ruyner,
Puis le Barbares sans vin feront
vendanges.

The Duke shall endeavor to ex-
terminate his own,
And shall send away the strongest
of them into strange places,
By tyranny Pisa and Lucca will be
ruined,
The Barbarians shall make vintage
without wine.

The ruthless plans for conquest of an Italian Duke are here described.

81

Le Roy ruse entendra ses em-
  busches,
De trois quartiers ennemis assaillir,
Un nombre estrange larmes de
  coqueluches,
Viendra Lamprin de tracteur faillir.

The King by a ruse, shall hear of
  the ambushes,
And shall assail his enemies on
  three sides,
A strange number of friars, tears,
Shall cause Lamprin to desert the
  traitor.

The King shall use strategy to defend himself, and the influence of the clergy shall cause the "Light Prince" to come to the King's aid.

82

Par le duluge & pestilence forte,
La cite grande de long temps as-
  siegee,
La sentinelle & garde de main
  morte,
Subite prinse, mais de nul outragee.

By the deluge and violent plague,
The great city having been long
  besieged,
The sentinal and watch being surprised,
Shall be taken suddenly, but hurt
  by nobody.

A violent earthquake shall crack dams and thereby inundate a great city (Los Angeles?, Teheran?). Mountains of water shall drown the city.

83

Sol vingt de Taurus si fort terre
  trembler,
Le grand theatre remply ruinera,
L'air, ciel & terre, obscurcir &
  troubler,
Lors l'infidele Dieu, & saincts
  voguera.

The sun being in the 20th of
  Taurus, the earth shall so quake,
That it shall fill and ruin the great
  theatre,
The air, the heaven and the earth
  shall be so obscured and
  troubled,
That unbelievers shall call upon
  God, and his saints.

The tenth of May is foretold as the exact day of the great Cataclysm.

84

Roy espose parfaira l'Hecatombe,
Apres avoir trouve son origine,
Torrent ouvrir de marbre & plomb
la tombe,
D'un grand Romain d'enseigne
Medusine.

The King exposed shall fulfill the
Hecatomb,
After he has found out his off-
spring,
A torrent shall open the sepulchre,
made of marble and lead,
Of a great Roman, with a Medusian
design.

A so-called revolutionary movement, based on the ideas advocated in
Ancient Rome, is here compared to the Medusa's head, in that it turns
the beholders thereof into stone, meaning that its concepts will lead to
a static and unprogressive society.

85

Passer Guienne, Languedoc & le
Rhosne,
D'Agen tenans de Marmande & la
Reole,
D'ouvrir par for parroy, Phocen
tiendra son throsne,
Conflict aupres sainct Pol de Man-
seole.

They shall pass over Gascony, Lan-
guedoc, and the Rhone,
From Agen keeping Marmande,
and the Reale,
To open the wall by faith Phocen
shall keep his throne,
A battle shall be by St. Paul of
Manseole.

Armies shall pass through all the above-mentioned French towns, dur
ing the course of a great war.

86

Du bourg Lareyne parviedrot droit
a Chartes
Et feront pres du Pont Anthony
pause,
Sept pour la paix cauteleux comme
Martres
Feront entree d'armes a Paris
clause.

From Bourge, La Reyne they shall
come straight to Chartres,
And shall make a stand near Anthony's Bridge,
Seven for peace as crafty as Martres
They shall enter in Paris besieged
with an army.

This continues the story in the preceding stanza, and foretells a march
on Paris, culminating in its taking.

87

Par la forest de Touphon essartee
Par hermitage sera pose le temple,
De Duc d'Estampes par sa ruse
 inventee,
De Montleheri prelat donra ex-
 emple.

By the forest of Touphon cut off,
At the hermitage shall the temple
 be set,
The Duke of Prints by his invented
 ruse,
Shall give an example to the prelate
 of Montleheri.

By the ruse of inflated money, the temporal governments shall overcome the authority of the Church.

88

Calais, Arras secours a Theroanne,
Paix & semblant simulera l'escoute,
Soul de d'Alobrox descendre par
 Roane,
Destornay peuple qui defera la
 routte.

Calais, Arras shall give help to the
 Theroanne,
Peace or the like, shall dissemble
 the hearing,
Soldiers of Allobrox shall descend
 by Roanne,
People persuaded, shall spoil the
 march.

An incident in a war between France and Spain, concerning the Netherlands.

89

Sept ans sera Philip, fortune pros-
 pere,
Rabaissera des Barbares l'effort,
Puis son midi perplex, revours
 affaire,
Jeune Ogmion abysmera son fort.

Seven years of prosperous fortune
 shall Philip have,
And shall beat down the attempt
 of the Barbarians,
Then in his heyday, perplexed
 with misdirections,
Young Ogmion shall pull down his
 strength.

The story here is clearly that of the career of Philip II of Spain.

90

Un grand Capitaine de la grand
   Germanie,
Se viendra rendre par simule
   secours,
A Roy des Roys, ayde de Pannonie,
Que sa revolte fera de sang grand
   cours.

A Captain of great Germany,
Shall come to yield himself by
   simulating help,
To the Kings of Kings, with the
   help of Hungary,
So that his revolt shall cause great
   bloodshed.

Hitler, offering help to Hungary, shall involve her in the general ruin
that follows.

91

L'horrible peste Perynthe & Nico-
   polle,
Le Chersonnez tiendra & Marce-
   loune,
La Thessalie vestera l'Amphipolle,
Mal incogneu, & le refus d'Anthoine.

The horrid pestilence shall be in
   Corinth and Nicopol,
The Crimeans and the Mace-
   donians also,
It shall waste Thessaly and Amphi-
   polis,
An unknown evil and the refusal
   of Anthony.

A great plague shall befall the places mentioned.

92

Le Roy voudra dans cite neufve
   entrer,
Par ennemis expugner l'on viendra,
Captif libere faulx dire & perpetrer,
Roy dehors estre, loin d'ennemis
   tiendra.

The King shall desire to enter into
   the New City,
With foes they shall come to overcome it,
The prisoner being freed, shall
   speak and act falsely,
The King being gotten out, shall
   keep far from enemies.

The New City shall be besieged by a powerful person helped by spies
within.

93

Les ennemis du fort bien esloignez,
Par chariots conduict le Bastion,
Par sur les murs de Bourges
  esgrongnez
Quand Hercules battra l'Haema-
  thion.

The enemies being a good way
  from the fort,
By chariots shall be conducted to
  the Bastion,
From the top of Bourges' walls they
  shall be cut less,
When Hercules shall beat the
  Bloody One.

Bourges, a city in France, south of Paris, shall be in the direct path of
a march on Paris, and shall be devastated by the invading army.

94

Foibles galeres seront unis ensemble,
Ennemis faux, le plus fort en rem-
  part,
Foible assaillies Vratislave tremble,
Lubecq & Mysne tiendront Bar
  bare part.

Weak ships shall be united together
False enemies, the strongest shall
  be fortified,
Weak assaults, and yet Bratislava
  quakes for fear.
Lubeck and Misne shall take the
  part of the Barbarians.

Weak nations, although not trusting each other, shall be forced to
unite. Bratislava, a Czecho-Slovakian city, Lubeck and Misne shall be in
the hands of the Germans.

95

Le nouveau faict conduira l'exercite,
Proche Apame jusqu'aupres du
  rivage,
Tendant secours de Milanoise
  eslite,
Duc yeux prive, a Milan fer de
  cage.

The New Man shall lead up the
  Army,
Near Apame, till near the bank,
Carrying aid of elite forces from
  Milan,
The Duke deprived of his eyes, and
  an iron cage at Milan.

A mob of rebellious soldiers aided by civilians captured and lynched
Mussolini and his paramour at Milan in April, 1945.

96

Dans cite entrer exercit desniee,	Being denied entrance into the city,
Duc entrera par persuasion,	The Duke shall enter by persuasion,
Aux foibles portes clam armee amenee,	To the weak gates, secretly the army being brought,
Mettront feu, mort, de sang effusion.	Shall put all to fire and sword.

Because of the clarity of the English verse, we feel that this needs no further interpretation.

97

De mer copies en trois parts divisees,	A fleet being divided into three parts,
A la seconde les vivres failleront,	The living shall fail the second part.
Desesperez cherchant Champs Elisees,	Being in despair, they shall seek the Champs Elysées,
Premiers en breches entrez victoire auront.	And entering the breach first, shall obtain victory.

Three armies shall converge at Paris; the second one will enter it first, and parade on the Champs Elysées.

98

Les affligez par faut d'un seul taint,	The afflicted by fault of one, only died,
Contremanant a partie opposite,	Carrying against the opposite part,
Aux Lygonnois mandera que contraint,	Shall send word to those of Lyons, they shall be compelled,
Seront de rendre le grand chef de Molite.	To surrender the great chief of Molite.

The reference here, we believe, is to Laval and the role he played in the betrayal of France.

99

Vent Aquilon fera partir le siege,
Par murs jetter cendres, chaulx, &
    poussiere,
Par pluye apres qui leur fera bien
    piege,
Dernier secours encontre leur fron-
    tiere.

The North Wind shall cause the
    siege to be raised
They shall throw ashes, lime and
    dust,
By a rain after they shall be a trap
    to them,
It shall be the last help against the
    frontier.

The siege of a city will be lifted and an enemy driven back by a wind
storm of such ferocity as to make it impossible for the armies to make
use of their weapons.

100

Navalle pugne nuict sera superee,
Le feu, aux naves a l'Occident
    ruine;
Rubriche neuve, la grand nef
    coloree,
Ire a vaincu, & victoire en bruine.

In a sea fight night shall be over-
    come,
By fire, to the ship of the west,
    ruin shall happen,
A new stratagem, the great ship
    coloured,
Anger to the vanquished, and vic-
    tory in a fog.

This tells of a naval battle which took place at night, in which the
firing from both sides was so constant and fierce, that it literally turned
night into day.

1

A l'ennemy, l'ennemy foy promise,
Ne se tiendra, les captifs retenus;
Prins preme mort, & le reste en
chemise,
Donnant le reste pour estre
secourus.

To the enemy, the enemy faith
promised,
Shall not be kept, the captives will
be detained,
The first taken, put to death, and
the rest stripped,
Giving the rest that they may be
rescued.

American embassy personnel were held hostage in Iran for over a year
and then, fortunately, were released.

2

Voile gallere voil de net cachera,
La grande classe viendra sortir la
moindre,
Dix naves proches le tourneront
poulser,
Grand vaincue, unies a soy joindre.

The galley and the ship shall hide
their sails,
The great fleet shall make the little
ones come out,
Ten ships approaching shall turn
and push it,
The great being vanquished, they
shall unite together.

This is a prophetic description by Nostradamus of the defeat of the
Spanish Armada, August, 1588.

3

En apres cinq troupeau ne mettra hors,	After five he shall not put out his flock,
Un fuytif pour Penelon laschera,	He will let loose a runaway for Penelon,
Faux murmurer secours venir par lors,	There shall be a false rumor, help shall then come,
Le chef, le siege lors abandonnera.	The commander shall forsake the siege.

A small group of men, defending their city against a large enemy army, sends out a scout who succeeds in getting through the enemy lines and in bringing back enough reinforcements to drive back the enemy and lift the siege.

4

Sur la minuict conducteur de l'armee.	About midnight the leader of the army,
Se sauvera subit esvanovy,	Shall save himself, vanishing suddenly,
Sept ans apres la fame non blasmee,	Seven years after his fame shall not be blamed,
A son retour ne dira oncq ouy.	And at his return he shall never say yes.

The career of General Douglas MacArthur fulfills this prophecy. In March 1942 he withdrew from Corregidor in the Philippines only to return, invade, and recapture the islands in 1944; however, seven years later he was relieved of his command. And to his quest for the presidency, he never did say yes.

5

Albi & Castres seront nouvelle ligue,	Albi and Castres shall make a new league,
Neuf Arriens, Lisbon & Portuges.	Nine Aryans, Lisbon and Portuguese,
Carcas, Tholose consurmeront leur brigue.	Carcasonne, Thoulouse, shall make an end of their confederacy,
Quand chef neuf monstre de Lauragues.	When the new chief shall come from Lauragais.

Although this verse is most obscurely worded and weighted down with many seemingly unconnected names, we gather from it the prognostication of the rise of the theory of Aryan supremacy which was one of the basic concepts of the Hitler regime.

6

Gardon a Nemans, eaux si hault desborderont,
Qu'on coidera Deucalion renaistre,
Dans le colosse la plus part fuyront,
Vesta sepulchre feu estaint apparoistre.

Gardon at Nismes, waters shall overflow so high,
That they think Deucalion be born again,
Most of them will run into the colossus,
And a sepulchre, and fire extinguished, shall appear.

The description here is of the great flood of the River Gardon, in 1557, which Nostradamus likens to that which was sent upon the world by Zeus and of which Deucalion and his wife were the sole survivors.

7

Le grand conflit qu'on apreste a Nancy,
L'Aemathien dira tout le soubmets,
L'Isle Britanne par vin, sel en soley,
Hem. mi. deux Phi. long temps ne tiendra Mets.

A great war is in preparation at Nancy,
The Aemathien shall say, submit to all, to me,
The British Isle shall be put in want for salt and wine,
The two bloody friends shall keep Metz long.

A war between France and Germany, instigated by the arrogant demands on the part of the rulers of Germany, is forecast. The British Isles will be involved much to the distress and suffering of the English people. France will be occupied for some years by the "two bloody friends," but will finally be liberated by the joint efforts of her allies.

8

Index & Poulse parfondera le front,
De Senegalia le Compte a son fils propre,
La Myrnamee par plusieurs de plain front,
Trois dans sept jour blessez more.

Index and Poulse shall break the forehead,
Of the son of the Earl of Senegal,
The Myrnamee by many at a full bout,
Three within seven days shall be wounded to death.

The reference here seems to be almost purposely obscured by apparently meaningless names; nevertheless, it seems clear to me that it points directly to the situation in North Africa during the early days of World War II, especially pertaining to the death of Admiral Darlan.

9

De Castillon figuires jour de brune,
De femme infame naistra sou-
    verain prince,
Surnom de chausses per hume luy
    posthume,
Onc Roy ne fut si pire en sa
    province.

Out of Castilon, signalized on a
    misty day,
From an infamous woman shall be
    born a sovereign Prince,
His surname shall be from
    breeches, born after his father's
    death,
Never a King was worse in his
    province.

The story told in this and the following two stanzas concerns the
illegitimate son of a woman of ill repute, born after the death of his
father, who grows up to be a powerful and tyrannical figure in the politics
of his day.

10

Tasche de murdre, enormes adul-
    tres,
Grand ennemy de tout le genre
    humain,
Que sera pire qu'ayeuls, oncles, ne
    peres.
En fer, feu, sanguin & inhumain.

Endeavor of murder, enormous
    adulteries,
A great enemy of all humanity,
That never saw worse grandfathers,
    uncles, or fathers,
In iron, water, bloody and inhu-
    mane.

Continuing the story told above, the infamous deeds of this tyrant are
further described.

11

Dessous jonchere du dangereux
    passage,
Fera passer le Posthume sa bande,
Les monts Pyrens passer hors son
    bagage
De Paripignan couvrira Duc a
    Tende.

Below Jonchere a dangerous pas-
    sage,
The Posthume shall cause his army
    to go over.
And his baggage to go over the
    Pyrenean Mountains.
A Duke shall run from Perpignan
    to Tende.

Here we are told that the tyrant becomes the leader of an army, powerful enough to conquer Spain and cause other nations to fear him.

12

Esleu en Pape, d'esleu sera mocque,
Subit soudain, esmeu prompt &
  timide,
Par trop bon doux a mourir pro-
  voque,
Crainte estainte la nuit de sa mort
  guide.

Elected for a Pope, from elected
  shall be baffled,
Upon a sudden, moved promptly
  and fearful,
By too much sweetness provoked
  to die,
His fear being out in the night,
  shall make a guide.

After the death of Pope Innocent IX, Cardinal Santa Severina was elected Pope. However, his election was declared illegal and Clement VIII was chosen in his place, for which shortly after the deposed one died of grief.

13

Soubs la pasture d'animaux rumi-
  nants,
Par eux conduicts au ventre Herbi-
  polique,
Soldats cachez, les armes bruit
  menants,
Non loing temptez de cite Anti-
  polique.

Under the pasture of cud-chewing
  animals,
Conducted by them to the Herbi-
  polique belly
Soldiers hidden, the weapons making a noise,
Shall be attempted not far from
  the Free City.

The shepherds of the Falkland Islands shall counterattack the insurgent Argentinians. All of this is predicted "not far from the Free City" of Port Stanley. Much bloodshed, although a limited operation.

14

Urnel Vaucile sans conseil de soy
  mesmes,
Hardit timide, par crainte prins
  vaincu,
Accompagne de plusieurs putains
  blesmes,
A Barcellone aux Chartreux con-
  naincu.

Urnel-Vaucile, without advice of
  his own,
Stout and fearful, by fear taken and
  overcome,
Pale and in company of many
  whores,
Shall be convicted at Barcelona by
  the Charterhouse.

This stanza is a reading of the horoscope of a contemporary of Nostradamus, Urnel Vaucile.

15

Pere Duc vieux d'ans & de soif charge,	A Father Duke aged and very thrifty,
Au jour extreme fils desniant les guiere,	In his extremity his son denying him the pail,
Dedans le puis vif mort viendra plonge,	Alive into a well, where he shall be drowned,
Senat au fil la mort longue & legere.	The Senate shall give to the son a death sentence.

An ungrateful son shall lead his father to a well and drown him; he is later put to death for the crime.

16

Heureux au Regne de France heureux de vie,	Happy in the Kingdom of France in his life,
Ignorant sang, mort fureur, & rapine,	Ignorant of blood, death, fury of taking by force,
Par non flateurs seras mis en envie,	By no flatterers shall be envied,
Roy desrobe, trop de foy en cuisine.	King robbed, too much faith in kitchens.

This quatrain deals with Louis XVIII, an excessive wine-consuming gourmet, who mounted the throne in 1814 while Napoleon was in exile on Elba. However, after Napoleon's escape from Elba and the ensuing famous 100 days, Louis fled. After Waterloo, Louis again assumed the throne and ruled from 1814–1824.

17

La Reyne Ergaste voyant sa fille blesme,	Queen Ergast seeing her daughter pale,
Par un regret dans l'estomach enclos.	By a regret contained in her breast,
Crys lamentables seront lors d'Angolesme,	Then shall lamentable cries come out of Angolesme,
Et au germain mariage forclos.	And the marriage shall be denied to the German.

Marie Antoinette's daughter, Madame Royale, was married to the Count of Angouleme in 1799.

18

Le rang Lorrain fera place a Van-
dosme,
Le haut mis bas, & le bas mis en
haut,
Le fils d'Hamon sera esleu dans
Rome,
Et les deux grands seront mis en
defaut.

The house of Lorraine shall give
place to Vendome,
The high pulled down, the low
raised up,
The sons of Haman shall be elected
in Rome,
And the two great ones shall not
appear.

The reference here is to the downfall and subsequent triumph of two
rival ruling Houses of France.

19

Jour que sera par Royne saluee,
Le jour apres le salut, la priere;
Le compte fait raison & valbuee,
Par avant humble oncques ne fut si
fiere.

The day that she shall be saluted
Queen,
The next day after the evening
prayer,
The account being settled and
paid,
She that was humble before, never
was so proud.

A woman of lowly birth shall become a Queen; and as soon as the
crown is placed upon her head she shall assume a regal and arrogant manner. This refers to the Maharani of Sikkim (the former Hope Cooke of
N.Y.) and also Queen Noor al-Hussein of Jordan (the former Elizabeth
Halaby).

20

Tous les amys qu'auront tenu
party,
Pour rude en lettres mis mort &
saccage
Biens publiez par fixe, grand
neanty,
Onc Romain peuple ne fut tant
outrage.

All the friends that shall have taken
the part,
Of the unlearned, put to death and
robbed,
Goods sold at public auction, great
emptiness,
Never Roman people were so much
outraged.

A period of oppression of liberals shall occur, accompanied by general
confiscation of their property. Worldwide conservative and reactionary
movements are underway.

21

Par le despit du Roy soustenant moindre	To spite the King, who took the part of the weaker,
Sera meurdry luy presentant les bagues,	He shall be murdered, presenting the jewels,
Le pere & fils voulant noblesse poindre,	The father and the son going to vex the nobility,
Fait comme a Perce jadis feirent les Magues.	It shall be done to them as the Magi did at Persia.

A King and his son, taking the part of the people against the nobility, shall be murdered by a method once used by the ancient Persians when they desired to dispose of their rulers.

22

Pour ne vouloir consentir au divorce,	For not consenting to the divorce,
Qui puis apres sera cogneu indigne,	Which afterwards shall be acknowledged unworthy,
Le Roy des Isles sera chasse par force,	The King of the Island shall be expelled by force,
Mis a son lieu que de Roy n'aura signe.	And another subrogated, who shall have no mark of the King.

Nostradamus here predicts the fate of Edward VIII, who abdicated the English throne in 1936 when he refused to divorce Wallis Warfield Simpson, a divorcée and an American commoner.

23

Au peuple ingrat faictes les remonstrances,	The remonstrances being made to ingrates,
Par lors l'armee se saisira d'Antibe,	At the time the army shall seize Antibes,
Dans l'arc Monech feront les dolesances,	In the vault of Monaco, they shall make their complaints,
Et a Freius l'un l'autre prendra ribe.	And at Freius both of them shall take their share.

A period of unrest and inter-city warfare in Southern France is here described.

24

Le captif prince aux Itales vaincu,
Passera Gennes par mer jusqu'a
Marseilles.
Par grand effort des forens sur-
vaincu,
Sauf coup de feu, barril liqueur
d'abielle.

The captive prince captured in
Italy,
Shall pass by sea through Genoa to
Marseilles,
By great efforts of foreign forces
overcome,
A barrel of honey shall save him
from fire.

Napoleon escaped from Elba on March 1, 1815, and landed near Marseilles at Cannes. His emblem was the bee ("barrel of honey").

25

Par Nebro ouvrir de Brisanne passage,
Bien esloignez el tago fara muestra,
Dans Pelligouxe sera commis l'outrage,
De la grand dame assise sur
l'orchestra.

By Nebro to open the passage of
Brisanne,
A great way off, el tago fara
muestra,
In Pelligouxe the wrong shall be
done,
On the great lady sitting in the
orchestra.

The only clear reference here is to the "great lady sitting in the
orchestra," which means a woman of noble birth. The interpretation of
the rest of the verse is hard to come by, but we believe there is no greater
significance than that some harm shall befall this woman.

26

Le successeur vengera son beau
frere,
Occuper regne soubs ombre de vengeance,
Occis ostacle son sang mort vitupere,
Long temps Bretagne tiendra avec
la France.

The successor shall avenge his
brother-in-law,
And rule under the pretense of revenge.
That obstacle killed, his dead
blood vituperated,
A long time shall Brittany hold
with France.

The prognosticated event and the fact that it refers to a quarrel between
Brittany and other provinces in France are clearly described in the verse
itself.

27

Charle Cinquiesme & un grand Hercules,	Charles the Fifth and a great Hercules,
Viendront le temple ouvrir de main bellique,	Shall open the temple with a warlike hand,
Un Colonne, Jule & Ascans reculez,	One Colonne Julius and Ascan shall put back,
L'Espagne, clef, aigle, n'eurent onc si grand picque.	Spain, the key, and eagle never at such great pique.

It is here predicted that Charles V of Spain and Henry II of France will split the Church with their quarrels.

28

Second & tiers qui font prime musique	Second and third that make first music,
Sera par Roy en honneur sublimee,	Shall by the King be raised to high honors.
Par grasse & maigre presque a demy eticque,	By a fat one, and a lean one, and one emaciated,
Rapport de Venus faux rendra deprimee.	A false report of Venus shall pull her down.

Here we have a detailed prognostication of events and people involved in the French Revolution. Because of the hostility displayed by the nobility and clergy, two of the most powerful groups in France, toward the Tiers État, this "third estate" constituted itself as a National Assembly and took one of the most active parts in the fomenting of the Revolution. The King (Louis XVI), during this time, was retained as "ruler" of the country. Perhaps the most remarkable part of this prophecy is the clarity of the descriptions of Mirabeau (the fat one), Danton (the lean one), and Marat (the emaciated one), three of the leading figures in the Revolution.

29

De Pol Mansol dans caverne caprine,	From St. Paul's house in a goats' cavern,
Cache & prins extraict hors·par la barbe,	Hidden and taken, drawn out by the beard,
Captif mene comme beste mastine,	Captive, like unto an accursed beast,
Par Begourdans amenee pres de Tarbe.	By Begourdane shall be brought near to Tarbe.

One shall seek sanctuary in the Cathedral of St. Paul, but he will be taken prisoner and subjected to great indignities.

30

Nepveu & sang du sainct nouveau venu,
Par le surnom soustient arc & couvert,
Seront chassez mis a mort chassez nu,
En rouge & noir convertiront leur vert.

Nephew and blood of the saint newly come,
By the surname, upholds arches and covers,
They shall be driven, put to death, and chased out nude,
They shall change their red and black to green.

The downfall of the totalitarian groups in Europe is here predicted; but there is also a warning that they will attempt to continue their operations even though they may change their "colors."

31

Le Sainct Empire viendra en Germaine,
Ismaelites trouveront lieux ouverts,
Asnes viendront aussie la Carmanie,
Les soustenans de terre tous couverts.

The Holy Empire shall come into Germany,
The Ismaelites shall find open places,
Asses shall also come out of Carmania,
Taking their part, and covering the earth.

The Germans, imbued with the spirit of barbarism, shall embark on a conquest of the world.

32

Le grand Empire chacun en devoit estre,
Un sur les autres le viendra obtenir.
Mais peu de temps sera son regne & estre,
Deux ans aux naves se pourra soustenir.

The great Empire, every one would want it,
One above the rest shall obtain it;
But his time and reign shall last little,
He may maintain himself two years in his shipping.

The struggle for the control of an empire is here described, and the prediction that the successful party will exercise its power for only two years.

33

La faction cruelle a robbe longue,	The cruel faction of the long robe,
Viendra cacher souz les pointus poignards,	Shall come and hide under the points of daggers,
Saisir Florence, le Duc & le diphlongue,	Seize upon Florence, the Duke and the long skins,
Sa descouverte par immeurs & flangnards.	The discovery of it shall be by vassals and serfs.

Temporal and spiritual conflict shall ensue in Florence, the city of culture.

34

Gaulois qu'empire par guerre occupera,	A Frenchman who shall occupy an empire by war,
Par son beau-frere mineur sera trahy;	Shall be betrayed by his brother-in-law, a pupil,
Par cheval rude voltigeant trainera,	He shall be drawn by a rude prancing horse,
De fait le frere long temps sera hay.	For which fact his brother shall be long hated.

A true picture, foreseen by Nostradamus, of Napoleon and his numerous relatives, whom he placed on the thrones of Europe. In fact, Napoleon's younger sister, Caroline, was married to Joachim Murat, King of Naples. He later became a traitor to Napoleon in 1814.

35

Puisnay royal flagrant d'ardant libide,	The royal son, heated with ardent love,
Pour se jouyr de cousine Germaine,	For to enjoy his German cousin,
Habit de femme au temple d'Artemide;	Shall in woman's clothes go to the temple of Artemis,
Allant murdry par incongeau du Marne.	Going shall be murdered by an unknown du Marne.

This concerns the son of a King who, very much in love with his German cousin, disguises himself in woman's clothing in order to keep a rendezvous with her in a Church. While going to meet her he is murdered by a person named du Marne.

36

Apres le Roy du Sud guerres
  parlant,
L'Isle Harmotique le tiendra a
  mespris;
Quelques ans bons rongeant un &
  pillant
Par tyrannie a l'Isle changeant
  pris.

After the King of the South shall
  have talked of wars,
The Harmotic Island shall despise
  him,
Some good years gnawing and
  pillaging,
And tyranny shall change the price
  of the Island.

The direct implication in this verse concerns King Philip II and the
defeat of his Spanish Armada by the English Fleet of Queen Elizabeth.
It is further predicted that England will go on to greater glories during the
reign of this Queen.

37

Grande asemblee pres du lac de
  Borget,
Se ralleront pres de Montmelian;
Passants plus outre pensifs, feront
  projet,
Chambary, Moriant, combat
  Sainct-Julian.

A great assembly of people near the
  lake of Borget,
Will go and gather themselves near
  Montmelian,
Going still further, they shall make
  a project,
Upon Chambary, Morienne, and
  shall fight at St. Julian.

Internal struggles shall cause great disturbances in the above-mentioned
towns of France.

38

Amour alegre non loin pose le
  siege,
Au Sainct Barbar seront les garni-
  sons.
Ursins, Hadrie, pour Gaulois
  feront plaige,
Pour peut rendus de l'Armee, aux
  Grisons.

Cheerful love lays siege not far,
At St. Barbar shall be the garrisons,
Ursini, Hadria shall be sureties for
  the French,
And many for fear shall go from the
  Army to the Grifons.

A general truce shall be declared between the French and Italians; but
a period of general conscription, in France, is to follow, because of the
large number of army deserters.

39

Premier fils veufve mal'heureux mariage,	The first son will make an unhappy marriage and a widow,
Sans nuls enfans deux Isles en discord,	Without any children, two Islands in discord,
Avant dixhuict incompetant aage,	Before eighteen, an incompetent age,
De l'autre pres plus bas sera l'accord.	Of the other, lower shall be the agreement.

Francis II, King of France, was married to Mary Stuart at the age of fourteen; before he was eighteen he died, leaving her a widow.

40

La jeune nay au regne Britannique,	The young man born to the Kingdom of Britain,
Qu'aura le pere mourant recommande,	Whom his father dying shall have recommended,
Iceluy mort Londre donra topique,	After his death, London shall give him a topic,
Et a son fils le Regne demande.	And shall ask the Kingdom away from his son.

This is a reiteration of a previous prophecy, namely, the abdication of Edward VIII of England, and the accession to the throne of his brother, George VI. This verse, however, enlarges on the subject and hints at the gossip which was directed at Edward VIII and his future wife.

41

En la frontiere de Caussade & Charlus,	On the borders of Caussade and Charlus,
Non gueres loing du fond de la valee,	Not far from the bottom of the valley,
De Ville Franche musique a son de luths,	Of Ville Franche shall be heard the music of lutes.
Environnez combouls & grand myrtee.	Great dancing and company of people met together.

Caussade, Charlus and Ville Franche are towns in Provence, all in the same general vicinity; and the event described is quite obviously a festival.

42

Le regne humain d'Angelique geniture,	The humane reign of an angelic offspring
Fera son regne, paix union tenir,	Shall cause his reign to be in peace and union,
Captive guerre demy de sa closture,	Shall make war, captive shutting it half up,
Long temps la paix leur fera maintenir.	He shall cause them to keep peace a great while.

A powerful sovereign, of great goodness, shall have a long reign of peace and prosperity.

43

Le trop bon temps, trop de bonte royale	The time too good, too much of royal bounty,
Faicts & deffaicts prompt, subit, negligence,	Feats and prompt defeats, quick negligence,
Leger croira faux, d'espouse loyale,	Fickle shall believe false of his loyal spouse,
Luy mis a mort par sa benevolence.	He shall be put to death for his benevolence.

By trusting those about him, even believing false rumors about his wife, a King shall be destroyed.

44

Par lors qu'un Roy sera contre les siens,	At the time that a King shall be against his own,
Natif de Bloys subjugeura Ligures,	One born at Blois shall subdue the Ligurians,
Mammel, Cordobe & les Dalmatiens,	Mammel, Cordova and the Dalmatians,
Des sept puis l'ombre a Roy estrennes & lemures.	Shadow of the seven, both a Royal present and spectre.

Many European countries shall be conquered by a great French leader, but he shall not hold them long.

45

L'ombre du regne de Navarre non
  vray,
Fera la vie de sort illegitime;
La veu promis incertain de Cam-
  bray,
Roy d'Orleans donra mur ligitime.

The shadow of the reign of Navarre
  not true,
Shall make the life of illegitimate
  chance,
The uncertain allowance from
  Cambrai,
King of Orleans shall give a lawful
  wall.

This deals with the legitimist quarrels of the various contending families
for the French throne.

46

Vie sort mort de l'or vilaine indigne,
Sera de Saxe non nouveau electeur;
De Brunsvick mandra d'amour
  signe,
Faux le rendant au peuple seduc-
  teur.

The living die of too much gold,
  an infamous villain,
Shall be of Saxony, not the new
  elector,
From Brunswick shall come a sign
  of love,
Rendering a false account, seducing
  the people.

Industrialists shall seduce the people of Germany, misleading them
with many promises, on the strength of which they shall change their
government.

47

De Bourze Ville a la Dame Gur-
  lande,
L'on mettra sus par la trahison
  faicte,
Le grand prelat de Leon par For-
  mande,
Faux pellerins & ravisseurs deffaicte.

From Bourze, City of the Lady
  Garland,
They shall by a set treason,
The great prelate of Leon by For-
  mande,
False pilgrims and ravishers de-
  stroyed.

Paris, City of the Garlands, shall be threatened by a treasonable conspiracy, engineered by a Spanish Prelate.

48

Du plus profond de l'Espagne ancienne,
Sortant du bout & des fins de l'Europe,
Trouble passant aupres du pont de Laigne,
Sera deffaicte par bande sa grand troppe.

From the deepest part of old Spain,
Going out to the extremities of Europe,
He that troubled the travelers by the bridge of Laigne,
Shall have his great troop defeated by another.

Nostradamus predicts the equipment by Spain of the Fascist Blue Division to fight alongside the Nazi Armies at the other extreme of Europe, and their defeat and annihilation at the hands of the Russians.

49

Jardin du Monde aupres de cite neufue,
Dans le chemin des montagnes cavees,
Sera saisi & plogne dans la cuve,
Beuvant par force eaux soulphre envenimees.

Garden of the World, near the New City,
In the way of the man-made mountains,
Shall be seized on and plunged into a ferment,
Being forced to drink sulphurous poisoned waters.

This startling prophecy of a catastrophic event at a pleasure resort not far from the great new city, predicts a tremendous tidal wave of poisoned waters that shall sweep in from the resort and overwhelm the man-made mountain-like skyscrapers of the city. Atlantic City in the "garden state" of New Jersey nicely fits this quatrain.

50

La Meuse au jour terre de Luxembourg,
Descouvrira Saturne & trois en Lurne,
Montagne & plaine, ville, cite & bourg,
Lorrain deluge, trahison par grand hurne.

The Meuse by day in the land of Luxembourg,
Shall discover Saturn and three in the Lurne,
Mountains and plains, town, city and country,
A Lorrain flood, treason by a great Heron.

Commerce and learning shall be endangered by a "flood" of wars, affecting all the peoples of the world.

51

Des lieux plus bas du pays de Lor-
    raine,
Seront des basses Allemagnes unis,
Par ceux du siege Picards Nor-
    mans, du Maisne,
Et aux Cantons se seront reunis.

In the place of peace of lower Lor-
    raine,
Shall be a basis of a German unity,
By reason of the siege of Picards
    and Normans from Maisne,
And in the Cantons they shall be
    reunited.

Germany shall endeavor to unify all Europe under her banners, but
shall meet with resistance from all the nations.

52

Au lieu ou Laye & Scelde se
    marient,
Seront les nopces de long temps
    mainees,
Au lieu d'Anvers ou la grappe
    charient.
Jeune vieillesse conforte intaminee.

In the place where the rivers Laye
    and Scelde unite,
Shall the nuptials be, that were
    long a doing,
In the place of Antwerp where they
    draw the grape,
The young unsullied will comfort
    old age.

An era of peace in Belgium is foreshadowed.

53

Les trois pellices de loing s'entre-
    batron,
La plus grand moindre demeurera
    a l'escoute;
Le grand Selin n'en sera plus
    patron,
Le nommera feu, pelte, blanche,
    routte.

The three harlots shall be long em-
    battled,
The greatest less shall remain
    watching
The great Selin shall be no more
    their patron,
And shall call it fire, pelt, white,
    route.

Three corrupt nations shall be defeated; only the weakest of them shall
survive even though it will suffer much privation.

54

Nee en ce monde par concubine furtive,
A deux halt mise par les tristes nouvelles.
Entre ennemis sera prinse captive,
Et amenee a Malines & Bruxelles.

Born in this world from a furtive concubine,
Set up at two heights by the sad news,
Shall be taken prisoner among the enemies,
And brought to Malines and Brussels.

This is the story of a noblewoman, born of a concubine, who, by the pretext of sad news, is brought to Brussels and there made captive by those who envied and resented her high position.

55

Les mal'heureuses nopces celebreront
En grande joye mais la fin mal'heureuse;
Mary & mere Nore desdaigneront,
Le Phybe mort, & Nore plus piteuse.

The unhappy nuptials shall be celebrated,
With great joy, but the end shall be unhappy,
Husband and wife shall disdain Nore,
The Phybe dead, and Nore most piteous.

This predicts the marriage, in 1572, of Henry IV, then King of Navarre, and Margaret of Valois. The tragedy of the Massacre of St. Bartholomew, in the same year, is also foreseen.

56

Prelat Royal son baissant trop tire,
Grand flux de sang sortis par sa bouche,
Le regne Anglique par regne respire,
Long temps mort vif en Tunis comme souche.

Royal Prelate bowing himself too much,
A great flood of blood shall come out of his mouth,
The English reign by reign restored,
A great while dead, alive in Tunis like a log.

Two separate and completely unrelated prophecies are contained in this stanza. One deals with the death of a dignitary of the Church by a hemorrhage of the throat. The other predicts the saving of the British Isles by the interference in their behalf of a distant nation.

57

Le subleve ne cognoistra son
    sceptre,
Les enfans jeunes des plus grands
    honnira,
Oncques ne fut un plus ort cruel
    estre,
Pour leurs espouses a mort noir
    bannira.

The exalted shall not know his
    sceptre,
He shall put to shame two young
    children of the greatest,
Never was one more dirty or cruel,
He shall put their spouses to the
    black death.

A great tyrant, raised to the dignity of King, shall misgovern greatly,
being especially harsh in his treatment of the poor.

58

Au temps du dueil que le Selin
    monarque,
Guerroyera le jeune Aemathien;
Gaule bransler, perecliter la barque,
Tenter Phossens au ponant entre-
    tien.

In the time of mourning, when
    the monarch Selin,
Shall make war against the young
    Aemathien,
France shall quake, the ship being
    in danger,
Phocens shall be tempted, the real
    danger in the west.

In the West the Germans shall make their strongest stand; France shall
be occupied by enemy forces.

59

Dedans Lyon vingt & cinq d'une
    haleine,
Cinq citoyens Germains, Bressans,
    Latins,
Par dessous noble conduiront
    longue traine,
Et descouvers par abbois de mas-
    tins.

In Lyons, five and twenty of one
    breadth,
Five citizens, Germans, Brescians
    and Latins,
Under noblemen shall conduct a
    long trail,
And shall be discovered by a bark-
    ing of mastiffs.

In a time of war, an underground conspiracy against France, fostered
by Germans and Italians, shall be shown to be in existence.

60

Je pleure Nisse, Monaco, Pise, Gennes,
Savone, Sienne, Capue, Modene, Malte,
Les dessus sang & glaive par estrennes,
Feu, trembler terre, eau, mal'heureusse nolte.

I bewail Nice, Monaco, Pisa, Genoa,
Savona, Sienna, Copua, Modena, Malta,
Upon them blood and sword for a new year's gift,
Fire, earthquake, water, unhappy ending.

All places mentioned are cities on the Mediterranean; great disasters to befall them are foreseen.

61

Betta, Vienne, Comorre, Sacarbance,
Voudront livrer aux Barbares Pannone,
Par pique & feu, enorme violance,
Les conjurez descouverts par matrone.

Betta, Vienna, Comorre, Sacarbance,
Shall endeavor to deliver Hungary to the Barbarians,
By pike and fire, enormous violence,
The conspirators discovered by a matron.

A conspiracy to betray and surrender Hungary to "barbarians" shall be uncovered by an elderly woman.

62

Pres de Sorbin pour assaillir Hongrie,
L'herauld de Budes les viendra advertir,
Chef Bizantin, Sallon de Sclavonie,
A loy d'Arabes les viendra convertir.

Near Sorbin, to invade Hungary,
The herald of Buda, shall give notice,
The chief Easterner, Sallon of Sclavonia,
Shall convert them to the Asiatic law.

This stanza has some bearing on the preceding one, inasmuch as it portends the eventual surrender of Hungary to a "barbarian" form of government.

63

Cydron, Raguse, la cite au Sainct
Hieron,
Reverdira le medicant secours,
Mort fils de Roy par mort de deux
heron,
L'Arabe, Hongrie, feront un mesme
cours.

Cydron, Ragusa, the city of St.
Jerome,
Shall revive again the medical help,
The King's son dead, by the death
of two herons,
Oriental Hungary shall go the same
way.

This predicts a plague that will fall on Hungary and which, because
of the lack of doctors and medical supplies, will kill off great numbers of
people, including the son of the King.

64

Pleure Milan, pleure Lucques,
Florence,
Que ton grand Duc sur le Char
montera,
Changer le siege pres de Venice
s'advance,
Lors que Colonee a Rome chan-
gera.

Weep Milan, weep Lucques, and
Florence,
When the great Duke shall go
upon the Chariot,
To change the siege near Venice he
advances,
When Colonee shall change at
Rome.

An attempt to change the residence of the Pope from Rome to some
place near Venice is predicted.

65

O vaste Rome ta ruyne s'approche,
Non de tes murs, de ton sang &
substance;
L'aspre par lettres fera si horrible
coche,
Fer poinctu mis a tous jusques au
manche.

Oh mighty Rome, thy ruin approaches,
Not of thy walls, but of thy blood
and substance,
The sharp by letters, shall make so
horrid a notch,
Sharp iron thrust in all the way
to the shaft.

Rome is doomed to destruction, not actually, but metaphorically by
verbal and literary assault.

66

Le chef de Londres par regne l'Americh,	The chief of London by rule of America,
L'Isle d'Escosse t'empiera par gelee;	The Island of Scotland shall be tempered by frost,
Roy Reb auront un si faux Antechrist,	Kings and Priests shall have one, who is a false Anti-Christ
Que les mettra trestous dans la meslee.	Who will put them altogether in discord.

British and American leaders, united in a political venture, shall set up a dictator, who shall in the end betray both leaders and common people.

67

Le tremblement si fort au mois de May,	The earthquake shall be so great in the month of May,
Saturne, Caper, Jupiter, Mercure au Boeuf;	Saturn, Caper, Jupiter, Mercury in Taurus,
Venus aussi, Cancer, Mars en Nonnay,	Venus also, Cancer, Mars in Zero,
Tombera gresle lors plus grosse qu'un oeuf.	Then shall hail fall bigger than an egg.

Confirmation of a previous prophecy, this again signifies May 10th as a fateful day, when the earth shall tremble violently and be bombarded by hitherto unknown weapons.

68

L'armee de mer devant cite tiendra,	The marines shall stand before the city,
Puis partira sans faire longue allee;	Then shall go away for a little while,
Citoyens grande proye en terre prendra,	A citizen army shall then hold the ground,
Retourner classe reprendre grande emblee.	The fleet returning and recovering a great deal.

France shall be blockaded both on land and sea, but a citizen's army will break through on all lines.

69

Le fait luysant de neuf vieux esleve,
Seront si grands par midy Aquilon,
De sa soeur propre grandes alles
    leve;
Fuyant, meurdry au buisson d'Am-
    bellon.

The bright action of new old ex-
    alted,
Shall be so great throughout the
    North and South,
By his own sister great forces shall
    be raised,
Fleeing, murdered near the bush
    of Ambellon.

Civil wars are forecast as between the North and South in the United
States in 1860, North and South Korea in 1954, North and South Vietnam
in 1970, North and South India; North and South Yemen, etc.

70

L'oeil par object fera telle excrois-
    sance,
Tant & ardente que tombera la
    neige,
Champ arrouse viendra en decrois-
    sance,
Que le primat succombera a Rhege.

The eye of the object shall make
    such an excrescence,
Because so much, and so burning
    shall fall the snow,
The field watered shall come to de-
    cay,
That the primat shall succumb at
    Reggio.

A volcanic-like eruption at Reggio in Italy shall cause widespread destruction.

71

La terre & l'air geleront se grand
    eau,
Lors qu'on viendra pour Jeudy
    venerer;
Ce qui sera jamais ne feut si beau,
Des quatre parts le viendront hon-
    orer.

The earth and air shall freeze with
    so much water,
When they shall come to worship
    Thursday,
That which shall be, never was so
    fair,
From the four parts, they shall
    come to honour him.

Nostradamus here predicts the Pilgrims' first Thanksgiving in New
England in the cold of winter and on a Thursday, no less.

72

L'an mil neuf cens nonante neuf sept mois,	In the year 1999 and seven months,
Du ciel viendra un grand Roy d'effrayeur,	From the skies shall come an alarmingly powerful king,
Resusciter le grand Roy d'Angolmois,	To raise again the great King of the Jacquerie,
Avant apres, Mars regner par bon heur.	Before and after, Mars shall reign at will.

A tremendous world revolution is foretold to take place in the year 1999, with a complete upheaval of existing social orders, preceded by worldwide wars.

Nostradamus shows his mystic knowledge of the great secret of the book of revelations and solves for us the identity of the "Beast of the Apocalypse" and the time of his arrival which John of Patmos (Rev. XIII:18) records "Here is wisdom. Let him that hath understanding count the number of the Beast: for it is the number of a man; and his number is 666." By a simple reversal of the numbers and turning 999 upside down we obtain 666.

Also in agreement with the prophetic vision of H. G. Wells and other gifted History and Science-Fiction writers, Nostradamus actually ties in the date 1999 when "from the skies shall come an invasion . . . and Mars shall reign at will." Time alone will tell whether this "War of the Worlds" is to be accepted literally or metaphorically.

"Roy d'Angolmois" is an anagram for "Roi de Mongulois" (king of the Mongolians). The threat of war will come from the east. Eastern Russia? Tibet? China? Mongolia?

74

Au revolu du grand nombre septiesme,	The year seven of the great number being past,
Apparoistra au temps ieux d'Hecatombe,	There shall be seen the sports of the ghostly sacrifice,
Non esloingne du grand age milliesme,	Not far from the great age of the millennium,
Que les entrez sortiront de leur tombe.	That the buried shall come out of their graves.

The "great number" refers to X.72 (the year 2000), and here he indicates that in the year 2007 the dead will rise up.

75

Tant attendu ne reviendra jamais,
Dedans l'Europe, en Asie apparo-
    istra,
Un de la ligue yssu du grand Her-
    mes,
Et sur tous Roy des Orients cois-
    tra.

So long expected shall never come,
Into Europe, in Asia shall appear,
One issued of the line of the great
    Hermes,
And shall be over all the Kings of
    the Orient.

A consolidation of nations of the East is forecast, under the leadership of a notable scientist.

76

Le grand Senat decernera la
    pompe,
A un qu'apres sera vaincu, chasse;
Des adherans seront a son de
    trompe,
Biens publiez, ennemy dechasse.

The great Senate will bestow a
    great honour,
To one who afterwards shall be
    vanquished and expelled,
The goods of his partners shall be,
Publicly sold, and the enemy shall
    be driven away.

A man, once held in high esteem by his countrymen, shall betray their interests and shall be exiled for his misdeeds. And in 1982 was not Senator Harrison Williams of New Jersey expelled from the Senate? And were not the Abscam conspirators driven away?

77

Trente adherans de l'ordre des Qui-
    rettes,
Bannis, leurs biens donnez ses ad-
    versaires,
Tous leurs bienfaits seront pour
    demerites,
Classe espargie, delivrez aux cor-
    saires.

Thirty adherents of the order of
    the Quirettes,
Banished, their goods shall be
    given to their adversaries,
All their good deeds shall be re-
    puted to them as crimes,
The feet scattered, they shall fall
    in the hands of the corsairs.

This continues the preceding stanza, going on to relate the similar fate that was meted out to the followers of the above-mentioned traitor.

78

Subite joye en subite tristesse,
Sera a Rome aux graces embras-
  sees,
Dueil, cris, pleurs, larm, sang, ex-
  celent liesse,
Contraires bandes surprinses &
  troulsees.

Sudden joy shall turn to sudden
  sadness,
At Rome to the embraced graces,
Mourning, cries, weeping, tears,
  blood, excellent mirth,
Contrary troops surprised and carried away.

Some newly married couples shall be surprised by a great disaster in the midst of their jollity.

79

Les vieux chemins seront tous em-
  bellis,
L'on passera a Memphis somen-
  trees,
Le grand Mercure d'Hercules fleur
  de lys,
Faisant trembler terre, mer, & contrees.

The old roads shall be made more
  beautiful,
There shall be a passage to Memphis summarily,
The great Mercury of Hercules,
  fleur de lys,
Making the earth, the sea and the
  countries to quake.

This foretells the time of increased and varied means of communication between the countries of the world.

80

Au regne grand, du grand regne
  regnant,
Par force d'armes les grands portes
  d'arian,
Fera ouvrir, le Roy & Duc joignant,
Port demoly, nef a fons, jour serain.

In the great reign, of the great reign
  reigning,
By force of arms the great brass
  gates,
He shall cause to be open, the King
  being joined with the Duke.
Port demolished, ship sunk on a
  fair day.

This relates the story of a great naval victory that shall take place when a King and a Duke join forces.

81

Mis thresor temple, citadins Hesperiques,
Dans iceluy retire en secret lieu
Le temple ouvrir les liens famil-
  iques,
Reprens, ravis, proue horrible au
  milieu.

A treasure put in a temple by Hesperian citizens,
In the same hid in a secret place,
The hungry serfs shall cause the
  temple to be open,
And take again and ravish, a fearful
  prey in the middle.

The treasure (gold) placed in a temple (Fort Knox) by Hesperian
(Western) citizens. Economic chaos and uprisings shall cause an attempt to storm Fort Knox.

82

Cries, pleurs, larmes viendront avec
  coteaux,
Semblanyt faux donront dernier assault,
L'entour parques planter profons
  plateaux,
Vifs repoussez & meurdris de prin-
  sault.

Cries, weeping, tears, shall come
  with daggers,
With a false semblance they shall
  give the last assault,
Set around they shall plant deep,
Beaten back alive, and murdered
  upon a sudden.

This relates to the previous stanza and foretells the failure of the
attack on Fort Knox.

83

De batailler ne sera donne signe,
Du parc seront contraints de sortir
  hors,
De Gand lantour sera cogneu l'enseigne,
Qui fera mettre de tous les siens a
  mors.

Of battle there shall be no sign
  given,
Out of the park they shall be compelled to come,
Round about Gand, shall be known
  to the ensign,
That shall cause all his own to be
  put to death.

A massacre of a surrendered garrison shall take place in a civil war, between two opposing armies of the same blood.

84

Le naturelle a si haut, haut non bas,
Le tard retour fera marris contens,
Le Recloing ne sera sans debats,
En emploiant & perdant tout son temps.

The natural to one so high, high not low,
The late return shall make the sad contented.
The Recloing shall not be without strife,
In employing and loosing all the time.

The birth of Princess Diana's child in 1982, heir to the British throne; Prince William shall give joy to even the staunchest antimonarchists.

85

Le vieil Tribun au point de la Tre-hemide,
Sera pressee captif ne delivrer,
Le vueil non vueil, le mal parlant timide,
Par ligitime a ses amis livrer.

The old Tribune, at the end of the Trehemide,
Shall be much entreated not to deliver the captain,
They will not will, the evil speaking timidly,
By legitimate to his friends shall deliver.

After three months of imprisonment, an old judge shall deliver the captive safely to his friends, in spite of contrary influences.

86

Comme un Gryphon viendra le Roy d'Europe,
Accompagne de ceux d'Aquilon,
De rouges & blancs conduira grande troupe
Et iront contre le Roy de Babylon.

As a Griffon shall come the King of Europe,
Accompanied by those of the North,
Of reds and whites shall conduct a great troop,
And then, shall go against the King of Babylon.

The Griffon, a mythical monster, half lion and half man, was supposed to keep watch over the gold of Russia. Nostradamus foretells a United States of Europe, under the leadership of Russia, opposing the forces of Mammon.

87

Grand roy viendra prendre port
  pres de Nice,
Le grand empire de la mort si en
  fera,
Aux Antipodes posera son genisse,
Par mer la Pille tout esvanoistra.

A great king shall land at Nice,
The great empire of death shall
  interpose with it,
In the Antipodes, he shall put his
  horse,
By sea all the pillage shall vanish.

An invasion of the southern coast of France shall take place. In the
Antipodes (Japan), they shall put their trust in conquest, but they shall
be defeated decisively by sea power and lose their ill-gotten empire.

88

Pieds & Cheval a la seconde veille,
Feront entree vastiant tout par la
  mer,
Dedans le port entrera de Marseille,
Pleurs, crys, & sang, onc nul temps
  si amer.

Foot and Horse upon the old
  watch,
Shall come in destroying all by sea,
They shall come into the harbor
  of Marseilles,
Tears, cries, and blood, never was
  so bitter a time.

An invasion of Marseilles by a great armada is indicated.

89

De brique en marbre serot les murs
  reduicts,
Sept & cinquante annees pacifique,
Joye aux humains, renove l'aqueduct,
Sante, grands fruits, joye & temps
  melifique.

The walls shall be turned from
  brick into marble,
There shall be peace for seven and
  fifty years,
Joy to mankind; the aqueduct shall
  be rebuilt,
Health, abundance of fruits, joys
  and a mellifluous time.

Nostradamus predicts a golden age for humanity after a great calamitous war among nations.

90

Cent fois mourra le tyran inhu-
  main,
Mis a son lieu scavant & debon-
  naire,
Tout le senat sera dessoubs sa main,
Fasche sera par malin temeraire.

The inhuman tyrant shall die a
  hundred times,
In his place shall be put a savant,
  a kindly disposed man,
All the senate shall be at his command,
He shall be made angry by a rash
  malicious person.

After the death of one of the world's greatest tyrants, a wise and kindly
man shall take his place, and shall fight against the evil laws laid down by
his predecessor. This fits the death of Stalin with his successor, Khrushchev,
who completely dominated the Party Congress (senate) only to be angered
and eventually deposed by Brezhnev.

91

Clerge Romain l'an mil six cens &
  neuf,
Au chef de l'an fera election,
D'un gris & noir de la Compagne
  yssu,
Qui onc ne fut si malin.

The Roman clergy in the year 1609,
In the beginning of the year shall
  make a choice,
Of gray and black, come out of the
  country,
Such a one never a worse was.

As stated before, Nostradamus dates all events from the Council of
Nicaea, A.D. 325. By adding 1609 to this date we have 1934, the year
Hitler was granted full power.

92

Devant le pere l'enfant sera tue,
Le pere apres entre cordes de jonc,
Genevois peuple sera esvertu,
Cisant le chef au milieu comme un
  tronc.

The child shall be killed before the
  father's eyes,
The father shall enter into ropes
  of rushes,
The people of Geneva shall not-
  ably stir themselves,
The chief lying in the middle like
  a log.

The League of Nations, its headquarters at Geneva, and its unhappy
career, are clearly foreshadowed by Nostradamus.

93

La barque neufue rescuera les voyages,
La & aupres transfereront l'empire,
Beaucaire, Arles, retiendront les hostages,
Pres deux colomnes trouvees de porphire.

The new ship shall make a voyage,
Into the place, and thereby transfer the empire,
Beaucaire, Arles, shall keep the hostages,
Near them shall be found two columns of porphyry.

A government shall change not only its political and economic structure, but shall move to a new city and establish new headquarters there.

94

De Nismes, d'Arles, & Vienne contemner,
N'obey tout a l'edict Hesperique;
Aux labouriez pour le grand condamner,
Six eschappez en habit seraphicque.

From Nismes, from Arles, and Vienna contempt,
They shall not obey the Spanish proclamation,
To the laboratories to condemn the great one,
Six escaped in a seraphical habit.

This predicts a rebellion of the cities mentioned against an edict issued by a tyrannical leader of the Spanish nation.

95

Dans les Espagnes viedra Roy trespuissant,
Par mer & terre subjugant au midy;
Ce mal sera, rabaissant le croisant,
Baisser les aesles a ceux du Vendredy.

A most potent King shall come into Spain,
Who by sea and land shall subjugate the south,
This evil shall beat down the horns of the crescent,
And lower the wings of those of Friday.

The "horns of the crescent" and those of Friday refer to the Arab (Moslem) allies. The clearest current threat lies with Libya and its aggressive leader, Muammar el-Qadaffi. It is predicted that the Arab confederation will be crushed.

96

Religion du nom des mers viendra,
Contre la secte fils Adaluncatif,
Secte obstinee deploree craindra,
Des deux blessez par Aleph &
Aleph.

Religion of the name of the seas shall come,
Against the Sect of Caitifs of the Moon,
The deplorably obstinate sect, shall be afraid,
Of the two wounded by A. and A.

One must delve deeply into these cryptic words in order to grasp their full meaning. The "Caitifs of the Moon" indicates the Arab nation. The struggle for power and recognition between the Shiites and the Sunnites among the Moslems is noted here. In Islam, the Shiites of Saudi Arabia vie with the Sunnites in Khomeini's Iran.

97

Triremes pleines tout aage captifs,
Temps bon a mal, le doux pour
amertume,
Proye a Barbares trop tost seront
hastifs,
Cupide de voir plaindre au vent la
plume.

Triremes full of captives of all ages,
Time good for evil, the sweet for the bitter,
Prey to the Barbarians, they shall be too hasty,
Desirous to see the feather complain in the wind.

A continuation of the preceding stanza, this relates the bitter struggles that will ensue.

98

La splendeur claire a pucelle jou-
euse
Ne luyra plus long temps sera sans
sel;
Avec marchans, ruffians, loups odi-
euse,
Tous pesle mesle monstre uni-
versal.

The clear splendour of the joyous maid,
Shall shine no more, she shall be a great time without salt,
With merchants, ruffians, wolves, odious,
All promiscuously, she shall see a universal monster.

France shall be closely associated for a while with nations of hitherto enemy status.

99

La fin le loup, le lyon, boeuf & l'asne,	At last the wolf, the lion, ox and ass,
Timide dama seront avec mastins,	The gentle doe, shall lie down with the mastiffs.
Plus ne charra a eux la douce manne,	The manna shall no more fall to them,
Plus vigilance & custode aux mastins.	There shall be no more watching and keeping of mastiffs.

This reiterates previous prognostications of a period of peace and plenty and elimination of war.

100

Le grand empire sera par Angleterre,	The great empire shall be in England,
Le Pampotam des ans plus de trois cens,	The Pempotan for more than three hundred years,
Grandes copies passer par mer & terre,	Great armies shall pass through land and sea,
Les Lusitains n'en seront pas contens.	The Lusitainians shall not be content therewith.

Nostradamus predicts great power and dominance for Great Britain for more than 300 years; also conflict with the Lusitanians (Portuguese). Does he see an English–Spanish (Argentina) conflict in the Falkland Islands?

73

Le temps present avec ques le passe,	The present time together with the past,
Sera juge par grand jovialiste,	Shall be judged by a great jovialist,
Le monde tard luy sera lasse,	The world shall at last be weary of him,
Et desloyal par le clerge juriste.	And shall be thought without faith by churchly critics.

This describes the influence of Rabelais, Voltaire, and Calvin on customs and manners during the time of Nostradamus.

CENTURY XI

[There follow fragments of Centuries XI and XII, the remainder of which have been lost. The original numbering of the verses has been retained.]

91

Meysinier, Manthis & le tiers qui viendra,
Peste & nouveau insult, enclos troubler,
Aix & les lieux fureur dedans mordra,
Puis le Phocens viendrot leur mal doubler.

Meysinier, Manthi and the third that shall come,
Plague and new insult shall trouble them,
The fury of it shall bite in Aix and places nearby,
Then the Phocens shall come and double their misery.

This prognosticates not only the coming of a plague to the city of Aix, in Provence, but also implies that they will have trouble with the inhabitants of Marseilles (Phocens).

97

Par Ville-franche, mascon en desarroy,
Dans les fagots, seront soldats cachez,
Changer de temps enprime pour le Roy,
Par de chalon & moulins tous hachez.

By the Ville Franche, Mascon shall be in disorder,
In the fagots shall soldiers be hidden.
The time shall change in prime for the King,
By dragnets and mills they shall be hewed to pieces.

Civil war will bedevil France in a struggle between the rulers and the people.

346

5

Feu, flamme, faim, furt, farouche, fumee,	Fire, flame, hunger, theft, wild smoke,
Fera faillir, froissant fort, foy faucher;	Shall cause to fail, bruising hard to move faith,
Fils de Deite! toute Provence humee,	Son of God! All Provence swallowed up,
Chasse de Regne, enrage sans crocher.	Driven from the Kingdom, raging and without spitting.

Religious wars, having to do with the struggle for supremacy between faiths, are visualized by Nostradamus.

24

Le grand secours venu de la Guenne,	The great help that came from Gascony,
S'arrestera tout aupres de Poitiers.	Shall stop suddenly at Poitiers,
Lyon rendu par Montluel & Vienne,	Lyon surrendered by Montluel and Vienna,
Et saccagez par tout gens de mestiers.	And ransacked by all kinds of tradesmen.

Help for oppressed France shall be delayed; meanwhile German industrialists shall entrench themselves in the economic life of the nation.

36

Assault farouche en Cypre se prepare,
Larme a l'oeil, de ta ruine proche;
Byzance classe, Morisque, si grand
tare,
Deux differente, le grand vast par
la roche.

A savage assault is preparing in
Cyprus,
Tears in my eye, thy ruin ap-
proaches,
The fleet of Turkey and the Moors
so great damage,
Two opposing, the great waste by
the rock.

Many battles between Moslems and Christians are envisaged by Nostradamus.

52

Deux corps un chef, champs divisez
en deux,
Et puis respondre a quatre ouys,
Petits pour grands, a pertuis mal
pour eux,
Tour d'Aigues foudre, pire pour
Eussovis.

Two bodies, one head, fields divided into two,
And then answer to four unheard
ones,
Small for great ones, open evil for
them,
The tower of Aigues struck by
lightning, worse for Euffovis.

Two nations shall amalgamate, electing one ruler; they shall then be
challenged by four other nations, and shall prove their united strength.

55

Tristes consiels, desloyaux, cauteleux,
Aduis meschant, la loy sera trahie,
Le peuple esmeu, farouche, querel-
leux;
Tant bourg que ville, toute la paix
haye.

Sad councils, unfaithful and malicious,
By ill advice the law shall be betrayed,
The people shall be moved, wild
and quarrelsome,
Both in country and city the place
shall be hated.

Here is a picture of the consequences of bad laws and government,
and the ills that befall the people thereby.

56

Roy contre Roy & le Duc contre Prince,
Haine entre iceux, dissension horrible,
Rage & fureur sera tout province,
France grande guerre & changement terrible.

King against King, and Duke against Prince,
Hatred between them, horrid dissension,
Rage and fury shall be in every province,
Great wars in France and horrid changes.

Civil war in France is repeatedly predicted by Nostradamus.

59

L'accord & pache sera tu tout rompue;
Les amitiez polues par discorde,
L'haine euvieillie, tout foy corrompue,
Et l'esperance, Marseille sans concorde.

The accord and pact shall be broken to pieces,
The friendship polluted by discord
The hatred shall be old, all faith corrupted,
And hope also, Marseilles without concord.

A continuation of the preceding stanza this goes on to give the evil consequences of such debacles.

62

Guerres, debats, a Blois guerre & tumulte,
Divers aguets, adveux inopinables,
Entrer dedans Chasteau Trompette, insulte,
Chasteau du Ha, qui en seront coulpables.

War and debates, at Blois fighting and tumult,
Several lying in wait acknowledgment unexpected,
They shall get into the Chateau Trompette, by abuse,
And into the Chateau du Ha, who shall be culpable.

These last few verses show the concern and uneasiness with which Nostradamus viewed the France of his day, and the France which he foresaw. Here again he warns of the horror of internecine warfare.

65

A tenir fort par fureur contraindra,
Tout coeur trembler, Langon advent terrible,
Le coup de pied mille pied se rendra,
Guiront, Garon, ne furent plus horribles.

He shall by fury compel them to hold out,
Every heart shall tremble, Langon shall have a terrible event
The kick shall return to thee a thousand kicks,
Gironde, and Garonne rivers are no more horrible.

The confusion within the League of Nations, and the role of France in its final dissolution, is foretold.

69

Eiovas proche, esloigner Lac Leman,
Fort grands appreste, retour confusion,
Loin des nepeuex, du feu grand Supelman,
Tous de leur suyte.

Eiovas is near, yet seemeth far from Lake Geneva,
Very great preparations, return confusion,
Far from the nephews of the late Supelman,
And all of their suite.

And in this stanza, Nostradamus looks far into the future to predict the coming of a French leader, stern and unyielding, who shall lead his people out of bondage.

71

Fleuves, rivieres de mai seront obstacles,
La vieille flame d'ire non appaisee,
Courir en France, cecy comme d'oracles,
Maisons, manoirs, palais, secte rasee.

Brooks and rivers, shall be a stopping to evil,
The old flame of anger being not yet appeased,
Shall run through France, take this as an oracle,
Houses, manors, palaces, sects shall be razed.

This final prediction by Nostradamus points to the fact that not until complete political and economic equality is realized in France, shall there be an end to the spirit of unrest.

INDEX